*you need to hear our
country —
love you,
Carter*

Playin' on the Tracks

A Memoir

Carter Robertson

ISBN-10: 1478111232
EAN-13: 9781478111238
Library of Congress Control Number: 2012911403
CreateSpace, North Charleston, South Carolina

What People Are Saying About
Playin' on the Tracks

"If you want an escape from your life into the hard living, hard choices of a beautiful gifted blond...let this book show you how to trip thru poverty, lack...heartbreak with heartless people along her path...to the beauty of God's hand choosing her to ride the Train To Heaven...!!!!!! You'll laugh, cry and be moved to a different level...of perspective."
Jessi Colter Jennings iconic Singer, Songwriter and Entertainer

"Reading Carter's book shines a new light on moments I lived and opened my eyes to the inner anxieties she hid so well (to me she was always the rock among us crazies). She truly nailed it, all the highs and lows of a time in such a beautiful person's life and paired with her live show 'Neighborhood of Secrets', you catch a glimpse of her awe-inspiring talent and the raw emotion of her life's story. I will always love and am blessed to know Mama Carter."
Richie Albright, Waylon's Drummer, Producer and Bandleader

"Carter Robertson is my musical family. It's a bond that not many people understand, and even less are lucky enough to experience. I grew up with her daughters like sisters and we all kind of waited as our lives dripped like molasses into the unique molds that awaited us. But us kids never really got to see, or understand, how it felt for our parents to let the many rivers of their lives lead them into the world that we just took for granted growing up. That's why having stories like this help us as the children, as well as the people who know and love us, understand where we came from. 'Playin' On The Tracks' is a wild, loving & good-timin' account of a young California girl's ascension from humble beginnings into the upper echelon of the Country Rock pantheon full of unexpected melodies, sweet harmonies and wild crescendos that keeps you hanging on every good-hearted word."
Shooter Jennings, Artist, Singer, Songwriter, Entertainer

"Just finished. Loved it. I mean, I really, really loved it."
Tank Laster, from Los Angeles, California

"This is one of the best-told stories I've ever read. Autobiographical material can be mind-numbingly boring sometimes, but 'Playin' on the Tracks' is a true breath of fresh air. Not only is it hilarious, it's dramatic and gripping as well. I've often said the great-

est senses of humor belong to those who have struggled the most. I sincerely hope that those of us who still read all recognize 'Playin' on the Tracks' as the gem it is."

Rance Wasson, Guitarist and band mate in the Waylors, and Waymore Blues Band

"Each of us has a story. Few of us have the ability to embrace our story (the good, the bad and the ugly), with grace, humor and redemptive honesty. Carter has such a gift and happily gives us a front row seat on her remarkable journey. It's a wild ride, but the valleys of sorrow and pain only serve to accentuate the mountain peaks of joy. This one thought is worth the price of the book: 'If you spin, marginalize, and homogenize the dark places of your life, you do an ultimate disservice to the generations to come. Redemption is the thread that holds the tapestry together and makes it truly beautiful.' Thanks Carter, for letting me reflect, laugh and cry with you."

Steve Green, award winning Recording Artist and Christian Music Hall of Fame Inductee

"All I can say to future readers is—beware:
Don't start this book if you have anything else to do because you will not be able to put it down and it may cause you to sin in the form of envy... Anyone who reads it will envy Carter's storytelling ability and engaging writing style. I felt as though I was in her den and she was telling me about her life. And what an amazing life!"

Ann Isaacs from Tennessee-Nurse

"As we read 'Playin' on the Tracks' we laughed until we had tears running down our cheeks, then the tears turned to tears of emotion and compassion. Carter can tell a fabulous story, sing a soulful song, and all with the glory of God behind her. Be prepared to be totally entertained by this talented new writer."

Reggie Young, Guitarist, Musicians Hall of Fame inductee and band mate in *The Waymore Blues Band*

Jenny Young, Cellist, Violinist and band mate in the *Waymore Blues Band*

"I was not sufficiently prepared to read Carter Robertson's memoir, 'Playin' on the Tracks' when I first began skimming Chapter One, while sitting at my desk, still drinking my first cup of morning coffee. My rather disciplined routine of 'To Do lists' and 'action items' was replaced by a narcotic-like reaction to keep reading as I was drawn into this extraordinary story, told so well.
There are many themes in this book that keeps the reader mesmerized; a childhood of conflicting family values, a young teen's innocence and talent hijacked by manipulative

trusted adults, a religious heritage that provoked more questions than answers. A talented 'star in the making', Carter's musical journey includes performing with the famous and infamous, walking a bit too closely to the 'wild side' all the while sensing God was reeling her back in.

Frankly, her strength and honesty are stunning as she recounts moments of great risk, pain, grace, contrition, and ultimately, the assurance she finally embraced . . . that Jesus is, truly, the healer of all wounds."

Justin A. Smith, Founder, President, and CEO, Justin Smith and Associates, Inc. and former Director of the Gospel Music Association (GMA)

"Very seldom does one get to experience the view from inside the circle around a superstar artist like we do in Carter Robertson's 'Playin' On The Tracks'. Recollections of her years as part of Country music's famed Outlaw movement with none other than Waylon Jennings are told with candor, grace, grounding and conviction. Her life is one fully lived, and fully documented, leaving her vulnerable for the benefit of every reader. What we see here is the transformation of a girl who 'shot for the moon' and found a sunrise on the other side."

John Zarling, VP/Promotion & Media Strategy – Big Machine Label Group

"Seeing Carter Robertson perform live is like being a kid sitting on the porch, listening to your mom tell family stories that you never get tired of hearing. Carter's amazing voice, interwoven with stories of her life, will tug at your heart, bringing joy and tears at the same time. Her music is just downright good. And now she has taken her live show and put it to pages. Do your heart a favor. Read this book. See her live."

Greg Janese, The Paradigm Agency

"I love stories, words and music, and my trinity of delights has found an awesome home in Carter's 'Neighborhood of Secrets.' What a creative tapestry of storytelling, melody and singing my dear friend weaves. Long known for her talent and much loved for her heart, her latest venture, 'Playin' on the Tracks', is simply vintage Carter."

Scotty Smith, Founding Pastor of Christ Community Church

"'Playin' on the Tracks' is a dynamic story that makes you wish you could have experienced a little of Carter's life while appreciating the parts you didn't. It is captivating in every sense of the word and leaves you wanting the next chapter..."

Megan Zarling, Managing Consultant

"Carter stitches together a quilted tapestry of stories of her life using comfortable prose and rare storytelling prowess. Each square of this quilt holds a story inclusive of the sharp contrasts of life: joys and sorrows, heroes and villains, highlights and disappointments, the celebrations of new life and the sadness of death. Having every justification to turn her back on God and 'religion,' she chose instead for her faith to grow stronger, despite the disappointments she faced from a few Pharisees along the way. I can't wait for the next installment of stories as her journey continues, because despite what she feared at one point in her past, her 'art has not lost its voice.'"

Cheryl Farrar, IT Professional, Horsewoman, and burgeoning Artist

"I've always believed in Carter's voice and her ability to tell a story...She skillfully invites the reader to enter into her family heritage and her musical legacy with wit, honesty, and true vulnerability. Her artistry as a writer and singer is worthy of our listening ears...I'm standing and applauding!"

Tess Cox, International Executive Consultant/Coach

This book is dedicated to:

My precious daughters,
Becky, Emily & Joanna
Who have expanded my heart's capacity for love beyond anything I
could have ever imagined.

To Barny,
My true love
"The only man that I choose to be with, that I choose to breathe with,
that I choose."

And
All the "little wounded soldiers with no voice…"

Memoirs are interesting. No writer has the luxury of having every day of his or her life on film to be able to refer back to. There's a fine line the narrator is called to walk. You strain and squint looking through your own history and the characters that make up your story, desperately wanting those remembrances confirmed and validated. In a desire to protect and not expose the *Innocents,* a writer often becomes overly cautious about what to share and what to leave in the closet.

The question you grapple with is how to tell the story with integrity of heart. As I'm writing this I realize I can't, with one hundred percent satisfaction, answer that question. But I can tell you that I have been wrestling with it for about ten years now and have decided the time has come to let it go.

I realize that in any given family or cultural community, recollections may differ. Some stories in this book have never been shared before and may come as a surprise to family members and friends. However, just because someone didn't know or doesn't want to know isn't a fair reason to remain mute. I've discovered over and over again that the truth *does* promote healing and freedom, while secrets enslave our hearts to the worst kind of bondage.

Countless hours have been spent researching historical moments and affirming memories with newspaper articles, legal documents, pictures, calendars and one-on-one interviews. I, along with many other writers, have come to the conclusion that emotional truth holds an equal if not greater weight at times in the telling.

This is not an exposé, but rather a quirky, and I admit, at times, a bit irreverent look at my life and the choices I have made. It's not without flaws, and in some cases I have taken poetic license. But it *is* a true story depicting real events and real people. The names and identifying details of some characters and events in this book have been changed.

Hopefully the above will satisfy the legal department.

Contents

"*I suppose belonging has everything to do with coming out of hiding, making yourself visible to the world and giving up any sense of immunity.*

The astonishing thing is that with your feet on the ground of your being, in the territory of your own life, the possibilities are much greater than you had built with these ghost-like abstracts of the person you thought you should be in order to live out your life."

David Whyte

Prologue

I grew up in a house where stories and music were gifted to us on a daily basis. It's the way our heritage was passed from one generation to the next. My mother was an ardent, and at times zealous, Pentecostal woman in a rural setting, which is quite different than being a Pentecostal from the big city like Fresno or Bakersfield. She was the oldest of six children and loved every one of them as if they were her own. But lying just below the surface of big family gatherings and small church congregational culture were secrets that were dark and remained buried for years. Those secrets explained so much of her passionate fervor for holiness that sometimes bordered on fanaticism.

My dad on the other hand didn't care that much for religion and all of its rules. He had a well-developed twisted sense of humor, and was known to enjoy walking on the heathen side of life sometimes. He came from a long line of rowdy brawlers who loved their families, but on occasion, could become dangerous.

Daddy's family along with thousands of others fled their homes in Oklahoma during the Dust Bowl and headed for California in search of the land of "milk and honey." They were told work was plenteous and the streets were paved with gold. Mama believed the "land of milk and honey" and "streets of gold" were reserved in heaven for those who lived a pure and righteous life.

Those two worlds colliding afforded me a rather rich perspective on life. I suppose you could say in some ways I was looking for the same thing. But instead of waiting for heaven or looking for it in the small towns of the great San Joaquin Valley, I chose what was behind Door Number 3: Hollywood.

This is the journey of a young girl who against all odds finds herself front and center on the infamous stages of the "Outlaw" Movement. Get comfortable because I have a story I want to tell you.

The year is 1952 and the date is December 29th. Less than ten years before, the whole world had been at war. The previous month General Dwight D. Eisenhower had been elected president of the United States of America. The yearly *wage for an average American family was $3400.00. Three out of five families owned a car, two out of three had a telephone, and one out of three had a television. The cost for a gallon of gas was between 20 and 25 cents. Doctor Jonas Salk had just developed the Polio vaccine and Mother Teresa opened the home for the dying and destitute in Calcutta.*

But in a little town called Dinuba, just a few miles outside of Fresno, California, something truly miraculous was taking place...

Part One

Neighborhood of Secrets

Go Toward the Light

Mama died when Diana was born. Her spirit kind of floated out of her body and just hovered there for a while, looking at herself and the new baby girl. She was good-sized, that baby. Ten pounds and a hundred ounces at least, and who knows how many weeks Mama had been in horrible, painful labor. There were frantic voices all around her and Dr. Erkie was working feverishly to bring her back. It was during all that confusion and commotion that she saw it. At first, it appeared to be a glimmer at the end of a long corridor, beckoning, calling her by name. She felt compelled to get up and walk toward it. The closer she got the brighter it became until "Lo and Behold," she was in Heaven, and that's where she met up with God.

I guess they talked for a time, there on the streets of gold, just catching up on life and stuff. But then he told her she had to go back and raise her children. There was certainly no way Bill could do it! Why, left up to him they'd all be dancing barefoot in the park somewhere like Gypsies while he played his harmonica. Lord, have mercy! How could she marry such a man? She knew better. She figured it was on account she was backslid and all when she met him, and this was just one of her many punishments for being desperate and foolish. She should've known there's always a price to pay for leaving your father's house.

But there she was, talking to the almighty God, suspended between life and death. She said she wanted to stay in the most powerful way, but knew better than to stand there arguing with the Creator of Heaven and Earth. The decision had been made. At least, like the Apostle Paul, she'd been given a little taste of Paradise that would help carry her through the many dark years that waited ahead. So she obediently went back and crawled into her lifeless body lying there on the table. It was a miracle you know, her coming back and all. Always kind of made me wonder about things…

Dr. Erkie told her not to have any more children. Said she might not be so lucky next time. But in a moment of reckless disregard and duty driven obedience on her part, I took up residence in my mother's womb. Now *that* was a miracle. Makes you want to put your fingers in your ears and talk about nothing 'til the pictures go away.

A short fourteen months after Mama's trip to Heaven, I was welcomed into this world with my very first spanking. A predictor of things to come...

Danna-Carter...the Early Years

For sixteen years I shared a bed with the one who killed Mama. She never acted all that guilty, but I later found out that she suffered for it. Said she felt branded and accused, and even though I did give her a black eye once (it was sort of an accident), I loved my sister with all my heart. Like most siblings, we fought. But Grandma Ennis told us, "Never let the sun go down on your wrath." Eventually one of us would give in. It went something like this:

"I'll forgive you if you forgive me."

"Same to you but more of it."

"Tap, tap no erasies."

Then we would quickly ask Jesus to forgive us of all our sins, the ones we knew about and the ones we didn't. We had to make sure we had it all covered before we went to sleep. If even one little itsy bitsy sin slipped through, and we died or Jesus came back, we'd go straight to hell.

At the sound of our "amen," we would establish the invisible line in the middle of that old bed, knowing full well the consequences of any breach. Come to think of it, there were a lot of lines we knew better than to cross. However, we didn't always use the good sense the Lord gave us, and we paid a serious price.

I was born Carolyn Ann Walker, but Diana, being just fourteen months older than me couldn't say Carolyn and named me Carter. It became a family nickname that later would be the name I chose to go by. Turnabout's fair play, and when I started talking I chose to call her Danna. Mama already dressed us like twins on Sundays so Daddy made it easier on everybody and called us "Danna-Carter" which we both responded to.

We were the youngest and did everything together, even taking time out of our busy early childhood schedules to cut our own hair. Now to some this may seem like a normal sibling misadventure, but you would be wrong to assume such a thing. Because as I grew older I discovered that "normal" is a relative term, and I'm not talking about all my disturbed, dysfunctional, long lost kinfolk either. I don't know what our older sister and brother were doing on our self-initiated "haircut day." Who knows, but they weren't taking a nap.

Our house was small, and all four kids shared one bedroom unless it was summer when my brother Norman slept on the old screened in porch. But at naptime the room was all ours. For some reason we weren't very tired that day. Children usually aren't. It's adults that need the nap. Having all that unsupervised time in our bedroom made us feel "heady" and grown up.

Now you must understand that in our small town, rural Pentecostal circle, hair was often considered a woman's glory. Mama was never too legalistic about it, but there was an undeniable element of pride when it came to our beautiful long golden locks and perfectly straight bangs. Our hair was so blond it was almost white, and at one time if we put our heads back far enough we could nearly sit on it. During the week we wore it in ponytails and braids, but on Saturday nights Mama would put it in rag curls so we could be *really glorious* for Sunday church. I don't know who originally came up with our brilliant haircut idea, but we continue to blame each other even to this very day.

Our older sister, Sharon, had a friend who lived down the street named Brenda Carnton. She came over one day to show off her new "doo." It was the late fifties and the bobbed haircut had just reached our little town. That was it. We really liked Brenda Carnton, even though her parents were alcoholics, and her daddy tended to go outside in his jockey shorts to pick up the paper. Mama made us hide our eyes, but I must confess I peeked a couple of times. That alone should have been enough for us to know that we were conceiving evil in our hearts by even considering the worldly bobbed haircut. But Daddy's rebellious heathen genes were alive and kickin' in both of us that day and in many days since.

With visions of looking like Brenda dancing in our heads Diana, aka Danna, claims I tightened her ponytail, took the blunt scissors and started cutting away *above* the rubber band. There was so much hair you could almost hear it thud when it hit the floor. Samson had nothing on us! She returned the favor, and in a matter of minutes the deed was done.

We were so smart—gifted, actually, by today's standards—that we thought we would never get caught if we just got rid of the evidence. It was Adam and Eve all over again. But where would we hide all that hair? In our closet was a small hole about an inch and a half around. The plan was complete. The rest of naptime we stuffed all our beautiful blond glory down the hole in the closet.

Knowing that our mother not only had eyes in the back of her head but a literal open and di-rect line to heaven, (a little gift left over from her previous visit) makes our shortsighted logic hard to follow. Did we really think she wouldn't notice?

Before we knew it naptime was over and it didn't take long for the consequences of our momentary insanity to catch up with us. Mama made us pick out our own switch off the Willow tree. When that green switch hits the back of your bare bottom and legs, you don't soon forget the wages of sin.

At church the following Sunday Brother Branson welcomed the two new little boys. Danna cried. I probably did too. I don't remember, but we had our new bobbed haircut.

....

Daddy in the Radio

How did Daddy get in the radio? This mornin' Danna and I were just sittin here at the kitchen table eatin' our Cream of Wheat when Cousin (the real guy who lives in the radio) said "Hi" to Hatchet! That's our daddy's other name. We been lookin' and lookin' at the radio to see if there's some kind of magic door or somethin' but we can't find it. We tried talking to it and then thought maybe he couldn't hear us so we started hollerin' at the top of our lungs! Sharon and Norman just stood there and laughed at us. I still don't see what's so funny. You gotta shrink an awful lot to fit in there. We're gonna keep watchin' though. When he comes out we might put him in our pocket.

Fear and Death

There were two things I grew up with that were certain: fear and death. They weren't exactly my friends, but we were well acquainted with one another. Grandma Walker dying was my first experience with death, but fear is something I was born with. Do you know what phrase in the Bible is repeated more often than any other? "Do not fear." If our Creator had to say that more than anything else there must be a lot of "scaredy cats" runnin' around. I know I'm one.

I was afraid of *everything*—forgetting my memory verse on Sunday mornings, giving oral reports in front of the classroom at school, the "bomb" being dropped, flat tires, bee stings, peanuts, the rapture—if it had a name I was afraid of it. On top of all of that, I was skinny, sickly, and the youngest. It made me an easy target for my older brother. I loved him with all of my heart but I had to learn the hard way that he was not always to be trusted.

When I was about four years old, he asked if I wanted to see the stars. Of course I did. He took me out in the backyard, had me lie down on a blanket, and look through the sleeve of an old jacket. When I said that I didn't see any stars, he told me to keep looking. The next thing I knew he stuck the water hose down the sleeve, turned it on full blast and tried to drown me, right there on dry land in our own back yard! I was soaked, and stayed that way until Mama unlocked the door and let us back in the house. She used to lock us out on Saturdays when she was cleaning. Don't feel *too* sorry for me though. The San Joaquin Valley is famous for extreme heat in the summer, so it was just his brotherly way of cooling me off.

I sure was a slow learner, because soon after the near drowning incident, he convinced me to put a bandana around my eyes so that I wouldn't be able to see. He was going to give me directions around the yard, you know, "Take one step to the left or two steps to the right." That way I would know what it was like to be blind. To my four-year-old mind, that seemed quite reasonable and somewhat adventurous. So upon his command of, "Ready! Set! Go!" I started running full bore, as he recklessly and without conscience, proceeded to run me into the swing set, where my bottom teeth went through the skin beneath my lower lip. The scar is still there, a visual reminder about the risk and consequences of misplaced trust.

You might think that collectively Diana and I would be much more discerning. You would be wrong. In one short afternoon, he convinced her that the worms out of Daddy's worm bed that he used for fishing bait, were really spaghetti, and she ate them. It was lunchtime after all. He continued his big brother torture by digging a hole in the ground, then convincing us that he smelled smoke and saw the Devil's horns. We were scared to death that the only thing between Hell and us was one mere shovel full of dirt. He took our older sister's "Tiny Tears" doll and dropped her out of the tree house, cracking her face, forcing her to wear a Band-Aid for the remainder of her days. He definitely had issues! He is now the pastor of a church and the father of five girls, two boys and many totally adorable grandchildren. God truly works in mysterious ways.

There were other things to be afraid of though, things not quite so benign. Things like the smell of cheap wine on my uncle's breath as he hid on our porch, fighting the demons that stalked him, or the look in my father's eyes when he would *snap*. His rage was so unpredictable, seemingly coming from out of nowhere. Life would be going along all fine and normal like, when suddenly it was as though we had all stepped through some sort of invisible door into a scary parallel universe. I learned early to never trust happiness. There was always going be the other shoe dropping in from somewhere, and most likely it was going to land on one of our heads.

I remember when I was about four or five years old we had a pet canary that Grandma Ennis had given us. We named him "Tweety Bird." He sang all the time, and we loved that bird. One day Daddy came home from work and for reasons still unknown, took the bird out of the cage in mid song and in front of his four children, pulled its head off. He then stuck it back in the cage as if that somehow *righted* whatever was wrong in his world. The whole time I was growing up, my dad would talk about that moment as though it were some amusing, family anecdote. He'd get to the end of the story and tell everybody that Diana went running through the house crying, "Mama, Mama, Daddy died Tweety Bird!" Then he'd just roar with laughter, and we'd all join in.

Now it's important for us to take a step back for a minute and remember the times. Today that offense would have animal activists and many of my friends ready to lock the culprit up and throw away the key. However back then, yanking the heads off of poultry wasn't all that unusual for families who raised the fatted hens for Sunday dinners. The difference was that "Tweety Bird" wasn't lunch, he was our pet. To us he was a member of the family. So when my parents would say in a fit of frustration, "I'm gonna wring your neck" or, "She's runnin' around like a chicken with her head cut off," we paid a little closer attention. Now, did I think that my parents would literally take my head off? No, but I was acutely aware of the reality of punishment as were most of the children I grew up with.

The magnitude of my father's disconnect didn't hit me until years later when I was telling that story to my own children. It was like I was hearing it for the first time as I watched their shocked and sad expressions. I began seeing with more clarity just how broken my dad really was all those years ago. Some men lose control because of outside influences like alcohol and drugs. My father's battles were more complicated. His rage didn't happen in some weird vacuum without a trigger. In a very private part of his own life story, he lived with a reality he could never shake. The inescapable sentence of his own hopes and dreams being strangled by the sins of his father.

One day many years later, when Diana and I were in Junior High and playing *hooky* from school on my dad's day off, we watched as he brought out an old shoe box that he kept on the top shelf of his closet. We weren't sure what was in it, but we were intrigued to say the least. After bringing it into the living room, he reached in and pulled out a letter and read quietly to himself. After a couple of minutes, he folded the letter up and set it back in the old box. Then slumped down on the floor, buried his face in his hands and wept.

In some ways, that scene scared me more than any of his rages. That was the first and last time I ever remember my dad crying. When we gathered our courage and asked why, he answered in a voice that sounded almost like a young boy. He said Grandpa had been called to be a preacher but instead had turned his back on God, and the family had been forced to live with the consequences.

I wanted to ask him if they were the same kind of consequences he inflicted when he would mock my mother for dragging us to church every time the doors were open. But I was too afraid, and the subject wouldn't be brought up until years later. Even then he chose to be cryptic and evasive, speaking in half sentences. My father was from a different era. Family secrets stayed secret and little reflective girls like myself needed to mind their own business. I wanted more than he would give me. I *needed* more to help me understand him. Eventually, I had to broker an inner truce with myself and make peace with the fact that some things about my father would remain out of reach.

We didn't understand the generational implications of my father's disconnect with his father until recently when a family member broke the code of silence. Seems ol' Monroe, my grandpa, had a pretty dark side. I could fill in the blanks for you but I'm choosing not to.

My dad carried that weight everyday of his life, and so did the rest of us. We all lived with the threat of real pain when someone would say or do the wrong thing in the right moment. There was the reality of paralyzing fear when my parents' voices would be raised and the escalation of threats and violence became prediction fulfilled.

This kind of "walking on eggshells" intimidation and random violent outbursts is something my children will never know in my home. I pray they choose wisely and never allow it in their own. At some point you must stand up and say, "With God's help, it-stops-here!"

....

Death was a little more difficult to grasp. How do you explain to a young child that a person is here today and the next day their body is in the ground covered over with dirt and odd mismatched patches of green grass? It was the *whispering* that scared me. So did the sad expressions on people's faces and extra food they were dropping off. There was talk of "funeral" and "stroke." What were those things? I wanted to go to Grandma Walker's funeral real bad. I don't remember where I went, but it wasn't to the funeral. Being four and a half meant I wasn't old enough or tall enough. If someone has to pick you up so you can see inside the coffin, you're too young.

Death became a mystery. "Honey, Grandma's with Jesus in Heaven. Someday we'll see her again. Just be happy she's not suffering anymore." Suffering…I wasn't sure what that word meant. I knew that where we went to visit her when she was alive was a dark place that had a bad smell. There were a lot of other people there just like her. Sometimes their skinny arms and bony hands would reach for me, crying out, saying things I didn't understand. They scared me, and the subconscious snapshots my young mind absorbed during those times would follow me home, haunting my dreams late at night. Daddy chose not to visit very often even though she was his mother and he loved her very much.

My memories of my grandmother are pretty fuzzy, but I sure wish I had known her. I have so many questions. I've been told Frona Walker was a wonderful woman and I'm proud to be one of her many granddaughters. But I wish I knew what she knew. Secrets are a powerful means of control even beyond the grave.

Death is never easy, but it has unfortunately become more familiar. I know how the shock of it makes you feel as though you're in some kind of protective buffer zone. Noises are muffled, and voices are lips moving without articulate sound. When you find yourself able to speak, there is a mournful yet necessary detachment of emotion that enables you to "take care of business." I guess in some sense it's the shock of coming face to face with our own mortality. What *really* happens after we die?

We used to sing an old hymn that goes like this:
When we all get to heaven
What a day of rejoicing that will be.
When we all see Jesus
We'll sing and shout the victory!

Well, I for one sure hope we don't have amnesia when we get there. For me, the most beautiful and powerful aspect of redemption will be to finally understand the "why" of suffering. To see that great cloud of witnesses that have gone before, not perfect while gravity held them here, but now free to be who they were designed to be all along.

Look me up. I'll be the one dancin', singin', and shoutin', with my mama and my daddy.

....

The Road To Woodlake

"Make us lose our tummies, Daddy! We wanna lose our tummies!" I love it when Daddy drives fast over the hills on the way to Grandma's house. There's this part of the road right before we get to Woodlake that has a bunch of little hills. When Daddy goes fast it makes you feel like you're flying, especially when we have the windows rolled down! My whole family laughs so hard, even Mama. She might be saying; "Slow down, Bill!" But her laugh says; "Don't slow down, Bill!" I wish that part of the road were longer.

Hand-Me-Downs

I'm assuming that most folks know what hand-me-downs are and have probably worn them a time or two. Now, I'm *not* talking about those of you whose mamas and daddies could afford new clothes at Sears and J.C. Penney's and who now shop at thrift stores looking for vintage clothes. No, I'm talking about waiting expectantly for the box from the Texas cousins.

I'm the youngest of four children, three of which are girls. So as you can imagine, in the case of hand-me-downs, I completely lost out. My legs were so skinny they had difficulty keeping up a new pair of socks with new elastic, much less hand-me-down socks with no elastic. I always had a blister on the back of my heel from the bare skin rubbing up and down on the inside of the stiff saddle oxfords. My little white socks only stayed up when I put a rubber band around the ankle part. I also wore hand-me-down underwear, but perhaps that's over sharing a bit. My husband has come to the conclusion that everyone in my family has at one time or another been traumatized by our underwear.

There was one particular box from the Texas cousins that held a priceless underwear treasure: the very rare and highly functional "blow-up" slip. In the late fifties/early sixties, full skirts were quite the "thing" in our small community. This slip looked like an ordinary white slip except hidden in the hem was a tube not unlike a bicycle tube. It had a stem that you could blow into like a beach ball. It was really something! It made your skirt stand out in ways that would make Zsa Zsa Gabor's chest look like Twiggy.

Well, being the baby of the family and not having a waist that could support the tired elastic, my sister Diana, with the help of safety pins, got to wear it first. I remember feeling so jealous in my droopy socks and saddle oxfords as she sashayed into church like a peacock in Mooney Grove. As we walked down the aisle and turned into our familiar row of pews, I could just hear the "oohs" and "ahs" as she sat down. Looking back, that's when the "pride goeth before a fall" thing started happening. One detail we had not accounted for with the "blow-up" slip was the sitting down part. So, much to my giggly amusement, when Diana sat down it was like sitting in an old fashioned hoop skirt except shorter. Woo! Woo!

"I see London, I see France,
I see Diana's hand-me-down underwear pants!"

Being good Pentecostals, most folks averted their gaze and asked the Lord to erase it from their memories. I, however, felt somewhat vindicated as my mother quickly reached over and put her hand on the front of the skirt, showing Diana that she needed to keep her hands in her lap at all times.

After standing and sitting repeatedly throughout the course of the first part of the service, we were at last settled in for Brother Branson's Holy Ghost sermon. I'd say we were a ways in, past the handkerchief babies and getting ready to move on to some hymnal talking, when it happened. We weren't sure what it was at first, just some very high-pitched sound that had dogs all over town tiltin' their heads and taking notice. We started looking around to see where it was coming from. Brother Branson just kept right on preaching. Upon further investigation it seemed like it might be coming from Diana, kind of like air escaping. Yes, you guessed it. The blow-up slip had sprung a leak!

Now it could have been a catastrophe, but being resourceful veterans of hand-me-downs, she found the stem and simply blew it back up again. It was all good. We learned that there were certain maintenance things you had to do with the blow-up slip, like blowing it up every thirty minutes or so. Ah, but a small price to pay for high fashion all the way from Texas.

. . . .

If we all will pull together
Together, together
If we all will pull together
How happy we'll be.
For your sake is my sake
And our sake is God's sake
If we all will pull together
How happy we'll be.

I like it when they let all us kids go up front and sing that song in big church. Diana's usually my partner, but today I had to have "that boy" be my partner and he nearly pulled my arms outta my sockets! Then when we sang "Climb' climb up sunshine mountain, heavenly breezes blow" You'd think he was a dust devil stormin' all over the platform. His daddy gave him a whippin' and I wasn't even sad. That's not true. I was kinda sad, even though he did have it comin'.

I don't like his daddy very much. He's my Sunday school teacher, and he gets mad at me if I color outside the lines.

Another Saturday Night in Dinuba

It was just another Saturday night, living on Academy Way in Dinuba, California. You could taste the air with its mix of cigarettes, beer and that weird metallic smell that fresh, dead fish give off. Daddy and his friends "Big Red," "Baldy," and a few others were all squatted around the old galvanized tub with their knives out guttin' the catfish. They were telling *stories* and laughing those laughs that sounded strangely out of control, like any minute something bad might happen. They'd been out on the lake all day and it was dark now.

He said he'd be back that afternoon to fix the latch on the back door of the screened in porch from the last time Uncle Bob broke in and scared us all half to death. But here it was, past dinner, past our bedtime, and they were all just now showing up. I could tell they'd been drinking because they walked around kind of crooked and wobbly-like.

The dim porch light, mixed with the slow steady curl of smoke coming from their mouths like a charmed snake, created a sort of *ghostly* fog. Their shirts were soaked through with nicotine sweat that gave 'em "the shakes," but they continued to light up a new one with the butt of the old one, counting on the liquor to smooth it all out.

I watched from the shadows, feeling woozy as the eggs spilled out of the middle of those mama fish like someone hit the jackpot on a nickel slot. It was a familiar scene, one I had witnessed many times over. I didn't understand everything they said or the implications of the laughs behind the stories they were telling, but I was sure it wasn't language little girls should of been listening to.

It was going to be a long night, and if I knew what was good for me I'd hightail it on back to bed. I prayed with all my heart, like only a little girl can do, that Mama and Daddy wouldn't fight later on after the *boys* left. I knew she was mad, called it a *righteous* anger. She had worked hard all day cleaning house, cooking tomorrow's Sunday dinner, taking care of all us kids, and preparing for Sunday School class, which *she* was teaching. She was tired. All she wanted to do was go to bed and sleep. Now she was going to have to stay up for "who knows how long" to make sure the fish were cleaned properly and put in the refrigerator so they wouldn't spoil.

Once again, she was at his mercy, and she didn't wear that very well. Shoot, if I were her I wouldn't have worn it at all. Oh, little girls can *talk* tough can't they? But she did wear it, with dresses that hugged her one time shapely frame that now had ballooned up to one hundred and ninety pounds! She wore her hair tight and her girdle tighter, choking out the breath of any hope or dream of freedom. She was under *his* yoke. She had put herself there, and she never let any of us forget it.

Close your eyes little one. Ain't *nothin'* you can do to change it.

Just another Saturday night, in Dinuba, California.

Daddy back home with his catch

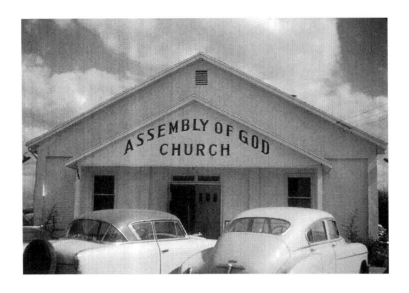

....

The Church in Cutler

You're supposed to be really quiet in church. That man that sits up front with his kids has a big long switch, and if they make even a peep he switches 'em. I try to be quiet but when I'm still my mind kinda starts floatin' around, and I make up stories and stuff. Sometimes Danna and I lay down in front of the pew. We can see Sharon's shoes and Podgie, the boy she likes. We have to be very careful not to giggle or Daddy might take us outside like he did Norman last week. He was hollerin' all the way down the aisle and out the door. "Daddy, don't beat me! Please don't beat me!" Nobody even turned to look. I think Daddy just wanted go outside for a smoke or somethin', but Norman sure got more than a little somethin'!

Sometimes I have to go to the bathroom. I try to hold it but, when ya gotta go, ya gotta go. I walk real soft and scrunch down so nobody will see me. Ya gotta walk through the nursing room before you get to the bathroom. Ewww!!! All those ladies with their babies hanging on to their titties. Ouch! I wonder what hurts worse. A whippin' from Daddy or that! I always try not to look but then they start talkin' to me and askin' me questions, and they don't even bother to put the blanket over themselves. All I wanna do is go to the bathroom! I usually pretend I'm feelin' sick so they'll let me go. Think I'll just hold it next time.

Jesus Loves Me This I Know, But...

"Jesus Loves Me This I Know, but...I'm not real sure about Willy Martin, and Mama says time's runnin' out for Gary Smothers." Gary was a teenage rebel. His family went to our little church in Cutler, which is right next to Orosi. Now some people like to pronounce it Uh-row-see, but they're wrong and probably come from Fresno, God bless 'em. We pronounced it Uh-row-suh. Yes sir, we knew all about Hell fire and brimstone. We understood the powerful persuasion of a Holy Ghost altar call, and that's how God saved Gary.

My mama was the C.A. leader. That stands for "Christ Ambassadors," the Assembly of God denomination's name for the youth group. She was a pretty powerful speaker herself. I used to like to watch her when I was little. Her voice would change dramatically, and when she was getting close to making a particularly important point, it would catch, and tears would start leaking out of her eyes. She wasn't some kind of Marjoe charlatan or anything, she just had deep concerns in her soul for the youth in Cutler.

One day I overheard her telling someone at church how worried she was about Gary Smothers. He came from such a sweet family. I don't believe he'd been baptized, and it wouldn't have made any difference anyway because he was backslid...smokin' and drinkin' and runnin' with loose girls, probably Baptists or United Pentecostals or something. Point is, if Jesus came back, he was not going to make it.

Well, that broke my heart. I always liked Gary. I didn't want him to burn in Hell where there is "weeping, wailing and gnashing of teeth".

So one Sunday night when he showed up at church, I made my way down to the front, buried my face in that old tear stained altar and prayed that God would save Gary Smothers. Now I don't ever want to hear that God doesn't answer the cries of children. I'll have you know that when Gary saw this little four-year-old girl praying that he wouldn't go to Hell, he couldn't run down to the front and get saved fast enough.

Now I know I can't take credit for saving ol' Gary, but my tender little heart was not lost on Mama. She used to tell me I was her miracle baby and that God had a mighty purpose for me on this earth. She would often recall the story of when she brought me home from the hospital as a tiny infant. I had trouble eating, and according to Mama, was allergic to everything, including her own breast milk. Come to think of it, I was probably the only child in history to be allergic to its own mother.

My little body was covered with sores and Mama had to put socks on my hands to keep me from scratching them. Seemed like whatever treatment Dr. Erkie came up with only made the situation worse. I was losing weight and cried nonstop. Everyone had exhausted all of their old homegrown family remedies and were now at a total loss as to what to do. As providence would have it, a woman evangelist was coming to our little church for a revival.

After much discussion and prayer on Mama's part I'm sure, she and Daddy decided to take me to her so she could lay hands on me and pray. With Mama's faith and Daddy's willingness to make a deal, they were hoping to secure an instant and miraculous healing. Well, as so often happens, God didn't perform on command and my parents left the church that night with the same sick little baby they had shown up with.

My mother became very discouraged. She had stepped out in her mustard seed faith claiming healing in Jesus name. It was a bold move making her hope so visible and opening herself up to ridicule if Jesus didn't come through. She didn't want me to die and if I lived she was afraid my face would be horribly scarred.

The next night, refusing to succumb to the defeat of the devil, she once again prayed with all the faith she could muster, and that's when it happened. God honored the heart and prayer of my mother, his dear friend, and started talking to her...out loud!

"Feed this child," He said.

"But Lord, what should I feed her? Everything makes her sick."

"Give her milk and regular food."

So not being one to talk back to God, she did just as he said. Within a week, my face and the rest of my body completely cleared up, and I was a normal, healthy, nine month old little baby.

Years later Daddy told me his version without Mama around. He said he told God that if he would just heal his little baby girl that he would believe in him and follow him for the rest of his life. (Which is quite a lot for a man who chain smoked Lucky Strikes and had about as many lady friends.) It made me cry. He didn't exactly live up to his end of the bargain, though. He tried for a short time, but he just couldn't get it right...enough. Mama was always so much better at it than Daddy was. Grace was not a part of our spiritual heritage and only showed up as the words to everyone's favorite hymn.

Later when Gary fell in love and got engaged, he asked me to be the flower girl. I was so excited, but Daddy was restless and we ended up moving before the wedding.

Mama always believed there was something special about me. Which is why her heart was so broken when later I grew up and walked away from everything I had been taught, and pretended to never look back.

. . . .

The Almost Flower Girl

I'm mad at Daddy! He always gets to do everything he wants to do. It's not fair! Gary's gettin' married and they want me to be the flower girl. I wanna wear that dress and those pretty shoes. I was gonna get to have flowers in my hair and carry the basket and everything! But now Daddy says he's been transferred and we gotta "saddle up" and go. Why can't we just move after the wedding?

Mama says we have to move NOW, and I don't get to be the flower girl, and my cryin' ain't gonna change a thing. She said, "What about me? I had to pack up the house in one day and I'm not cryin'!" But I know she's not happy with him. We're moving to the coast though, and I love the beach. I hope we eat fish n' chips everyday. Maybe it won't be too bad. I wonder if they got churches in Santa Maria. I know they have a school cuz Mama says I'm gonna finish Kindergarten there. I hope they have one of those play kitchens in my classroom. That's my favorite thing about school...

Bloomin' Arctic Country!

Miller Street Elementary School was just a few blocks away from our new home on Laguna Ave. The house itself was older, but it was new to us. We were now officially residents in the coastal city of Santa Maria, California. For the most part we had all made the adjustment to living on the coast in contrast to the big inland valley that my parents had considered their true home for so many years. More than once we would hear my dad mutter under his breath in response to a particularly overcast morning, "Bloomin' Arctic Country!" However, we all agreed that the trade out for the beautiful ocean and beach was well worth the chill.

I had survived the second half of kindergarten and was promoted to the first grade. The new adventure into higher education came with a few anxious moments; this was, after all, first grade! The fear diminished somewhat at snack time when the familiar small cartons of milk in the blue crates were handed out by the milk monitor along with a delicious, crispy graham cracker.

A short nap, still part of the daily routine, followed, and I along with all of the other children lay there and twitched. Our nap space was assigned in alphabetical order and since my last name began with a "W" I was placed in the far corner next to the only Negro girl in the class. Her skin was a pretty dark chocolate color, and she reminded me of the TV commercials I used to watch at Grandma Ennis's house. The little circle candies, plain and peanut, would climb a ladder and dive into a pool. "I'm milk chocolate inside, candy shell outside," they said.

Like me, the little girl would often wear the same dress more than once during the school week, and though nothing was said, we both understood. Neither one of us belonged to the Campfire's "Bluebirds" nor the Girl Scout's "Brownies" so we got along just fine.

I had no idea at that moment in other parts of the United States, people with her skin color were not allowed to sit at the same lunch counter, drink from the same water fountain, and were forced to give up their seats and sit in the back of the bus for people with my skin color. Don't get me wrong, I grew up with the "N" word, but at 6 years old my understanding and awareness of civil rights and the colored man's struggle was nil. Guess being branded a "Holy Roller" who wore hand-me-downs, with a last name that began with "W" and the color of her skin forced us both to the back of the classroom, but for much different reasons. My mother embraced the idea of integration even though it would be years before I ever heard that word.

"Red, Brown, Yellow, Black and White,

They are precious in His sight

Jesus loves the little children of the world."

That was my mother's motto, not necessarily my father's.

Our teacher Mrs. Benz wasn't exactly the warm fuzzy type. She ran a tight ship. Make no mistake, there would be no slackers on her watch, and you could take that to the bank! The following are comments made on the Spring 1960 "Teacher's Worksheet For The Child."

Social Growth:

1. Is courteous and kind—check
2. Listens attentively—*inclined to be dreamy*
3. Respects right and property of others—check
4. Shows growth in taking responsibility—check
5. Cooperates with school and obeys rules—check
6. Uses self-control—check
7. Shows self-confidence—*This, we need to work on.*
8. Seems happy and well adjusted—*Seems to lack enthusiasm. Sleep? Meals? Health? Doesn't have much stamina nor pep. She doesn't speak clearly and is difficult to understand. There is very little participation voluntarily in discussions.*

I was actually scared to death of this teacher and with good reason. One day after recess, Mrs. Benz started walking around the room setting a peanut in front of each student seated at the short rectangular tables. With *normal* little children, that would hardly merit a mention and certainly be no cause for alarm. I, however, was very allergic to peanuts. This malady was discovered after spending many Saturdays with my parents at auctions and flea markets, where tons of peanut shells were discarded on the ground and trampled by locals looking for a bargain. My eyes would swell closed and my breathing would become labored, and I wasn't even touching the peanuts. All it took was being around them.

With this firsthand experience, I watched in horror as she came closer to my table. Speaking to an adult, much less a teacher and especially this teacher, was a challenge of epic proportion for me. However, I knew I would have to find my voice or die…so I thought. As she reached out to place the peanut in front of me, and being ever so careful not to actually look her in the eye, I reminded her in a voice barely audible, of the note my mother had sent in at the beginning of the year about my allergy. She was instantly annoyed, telling me I didn't have to *eat* the peanut, I just needed to crack it open and look at the inside of the shell. PERIOD! She watched, hands on her hips as I slowly broke open the shell and began the terrifying process of peanut suicide.

Within minutes my eyes and tongue began to itch and then swell. By the time I made it home I could hardly breathe. I ended up missing a week of school because of the severity of the allergic reaction. Now a week is a long time to be "touch and go" on your deathbed when you're only six. Mama put me on the bottom bunk and tucked sheets under the mattress from above creating a kind of tent. She then got the humidifier going along with massive amounts of Vicks Vapor Rub applied to my little chest. She ironed the front of an old t-shirt making it as hot as possible and then placed it on top of the rub to help me breathe. We didn't go to doctors back then. I vividly remember fighting for air and listening to my mother pleading through the night for my deliverance, a foretaste of what was to come.

I've been told that Mama's choice was the worst possible treatment for my allergic reaction and that I'm lucky to have survived. Guess God had something else for me to do. I'm still here.

. . . .

The Girl

I don't like the way she laughs. Her, in her short shorts, black hair and Everly Brothers record albums. I don't like the way she teases my brother, tries to get him to dance and makes his face get red. She wears too much make-up, and she talks all syrupy to Daddy. His face doesn't get red. His voice sounds different when he laughs with her, and I don't like it. Mama doesn't like it either. But she's trying to save her. Says she's a lost teenage bride whose gotta live with us for a while till her husband, Chester's boy, finds a job and can come get her.

I hurt myself at school the other day. The big kids started pushin' the merry-go-round real fast, and I got scared. When I tried to get off, they laughed at me and pushed harder. They didn't stop until the recess bell rang and by then I was so dizzy I fell off and my knees got dragged around a couple of times before it stopped. Nothin' merry about that "go-round." I didn't cry though. No way was I gonna let the big kids see me cry. But when I rounded the corner of our street after school and saw Daddy leanin' up against the car, I started cryin' and runnin' all at the same time. I just wanted him to pick me up and make me feel safe. But "the girl" was there, and she started laughing at me and so did Daddy.

Boy, am I stupid, huh? I ran on into the house and washed off my knees in the bathroom. Someday if I ever have kids and somebody's mean to 'em and their knees get hurt, I'm gonna pick 'em up, hug 'em and tell 'em everything's gonna be okay. I'm not gonna laugh at 'em, and I'm not gonna let nobody else laugh at 'em neither...

I don't like that girl...and I'm not prayin' she gets saved.

Murder, One Block Over

I was only too happy to be promoted to Mrs. Hall's second grade class. With my mother and new teacher's encouragement, I discovered I was an excellent reader and actually began to feel a little more comfortable with my classmates. I still struggled with being shy and quiet, and my teacher at times would voice her concern. Mama would explain the allergies, but of course never mention the late nights at church, and all the other home factors that contributed to not getting a good night's sleep.

The reasons weren't all bad. In fact, many were self-inflicted. I had already developed a highly sophisticated sense of worry, which would show up frequently in my dreams. Sometimes I was terrified of closing my eyes, while at other times all I wanted to do was sleep.

It's somewhat surprising, given how shy I was, that "Show and Tell" became one of my favorite parts of school life. Once a week, usually on a Friday, whoever was assigned took their turn in front of the class sharing something of importance to them. Now this could be good, or this could be awkward, but always illuminating for teachers. Sharon could write a best seller of all of her side splittingly funny stories from the many young children she has taught over the years.

Once in kindergarten I shared that this very same sister, who was in sixth grade at the time, was now wearing a frog harness. Based on all the laughter of my uncles and Dad the previous night, I believed this bit of new information to be something worthy of celebration. I wasn't real sure what a frog harness was, but it sounded pretty fun and important. When school was dismissed and she came to walk me home since I was in afternoon session, my teacher complimented Sharon on her new frog harness. My sister turned ten shades of red, grabbed my hand and practically drug me down the sidewalk, promising to never walk me home from school again. I was stunned by her reaction and didn't understand her response until later, when it was explained to me that a "frog harness" was really a bra, and underwear is not something to talk about in public, especially share time at school. Lesson learned.

My favorite thing to share was Daddy's stalactite and stalagmite from Crystal Cave in Sequoia National Park. He worked there during the '40s while in the C.C.C. which is short for "California Conservation Core." They were some of his prize possessions, gleaned from the aftermath of using dynamite to make the public restrooms for the many visitors that toured the cave every year. The care of these ancient formations was a heavy responsibility and one that none of us took lightly. I would tell my classmates that, "A stalagmite grows from the floor of the cave up, saying, 'I *might* reach the ceiling, while the stalactite grows from the ceiling down, and says, 'I gotta make sure I hang on *tight* so I don't fall.'" Get it? They did, and for a day I was sort of a celebrity.

In February of my second grade year, something happened that changed my little world forever. The way it began was really quite innocent. A young boy in my class named Johnny asked me to be his girlfriend. Me, imagine that! I guess it was pretty difficult to ignore the allure of a girl who brought such interesting cave decorations for share time. He approached me one afternoon following my successful presentation.

After stammering around a bit he handed me a ring and asked if I would be his girlfriend. I waited about two seconds and said, "Uhhh, okay," and that's the reason I went home wearing a ring that day.

My brother and sisters teased me good-naturedly about it, but being my typical, over-thinking, seven year old self, I began to wonder if I now needed to plan a wedding. Perhaps it could be like Lovie's wedding when they lit candles and she walked down the aisle in the flickering light. I really liked Lovie and thought she was real pretty. Her sister's names were Gracie, Hope, Faith and Charity. Pretty cool.

Of course my new boyfriend/fiancé would have to ask Jesus into his heart first and agree to be dunked, none of that Catholic sprinkling in our family. I let my young imagination run with this picture, filling my head with all kinds of possibilities, feeling much more mature than a lowly second grader. Maybe this was God's way of making up for my not getting to be the flower girl in Gary Smother's wedding. Shoot, I might even get to wear a veil and everything. These dreams were instantly dashed once Mama got home and was apprised of the impending nuptials. So much for the candlelight wedding. Her voice started to sound kind of preachy as she set down her purse and picked up her apron.

"You are too young to even *think* about such things and besides... that's a very grownup ring you have there. How could a young boy afford such a ring? Wouldn't be surprised if he stole it. You go take that off right now and give it back to him first thing tomorrow, and I don't want to hear another word about it! Shame on you kids for egging her on like that! I can't leave this house for a minute without all kind of foolishness goin' on. Lord, why don't you just come back right now?"

She continued to murmur and pray under her breath as she prepared our dinner. I sure didn't mean to cause such a fuss but what was I supposed to say to him, "No, thank you?"

Sleep didn't come easy that night. Not so much because I was sad about the ring, I just couldn't bear the thought of hurting someone's feelings. For a few short hours I felt kind of special, and I think he did too. Now I was going to have to give this nice boy back his ring and tell him my mama said I couldn't have it. Of course there was never any question as to whether or not I would follow through, and that's just what I did, being careful to leave the stealing part out, of course.

Thankfully, he took it very well. I mean at that age you're not exactly playing the blame game or asking what you could have done differently. Our young love lasted only about twenty-four hours and honestly, that was within normal range for most second graders. The break up was amicable, and we both decided to move on. How very grown up of us.

A few weeks went by and all was forgotten until one Saturday morning when I woke up to a conversation my mother was having with my older sisters and brother. The tone of her voice cautioned me to tip toe down the hall and listen in. Mama wasn't one to hold back information, even though many times that would have been best as was the case on this day. She saw me standing in the doorway and proceeded to fill us all in.

Seems a woman was found dead in a car one street over, parked on the side of the big Catholic Cemetery. As she spoke I could see it with its towering statues and tributes to the souls that were either scratching their way out after being buried alive, or restlessly still roaming the earth. C'mon, be honest, you've heard those stories too. Most of the time they had the decency to stay within the high walls of the sacred burial ground. But they had been known on occasion, to sneak out and haunt the children living in the bungalows on Laguna Avenue.

Mama said the woman's head had been bashed in, and her purse was emptied on the floorboard in the front seat, leading investigators to believe it had been a robbery gone wrong. However, when the police went to notify her family, just two short blocks down the street from us, they found her husband outside washing blood off of the driveway as though it were just another one of his Saturday chores.

While I was trying to wrap my young mind around this gruesome picture, my mother continued in her church, prayer request voice, "Kids, you'll never guess who the man is. Remember that little boy who gave Carter the ring? It was his dad! I knew there was something wrong about all that. I think the Lord put it in my spirit to have her give it back. I wouldn't be surprised if it was his mother's. It was an awfully nice ring. There's talk the dad thought she was messin' around on him. You just never know about people. Wonder what'll happen to those poor little children now that their mama's gone and their daddy's in prison. Jesus, help them."

I stood in the doorway trying to take in the *way* too grown up conversation I had just heard. Once spoken it could never be taken back. The image so clearly articulated, would never be erased. I knew there was a lady who used to be really pretty sitting in her car one street over, dead. It was the same car she drove her children to school in and went to the grocery store and church. This was a murder, and I was a little girl who knew the little boy who would never see his mama again.

Not surprisingly, Mama knew who the victim was before the reporter did

....

Don't Wanna Know What I Know

My stomach hurts real bad sometimes. I didn't wanna go to school today but it was school vaccination day and Mama doesn't want me gettin' Polio or Small Pox. I had to go line up with all the other children in my class hoping we would get the sugar cube instead of the needle. Nope, our line got the shot and my arm is so skinny I think the needle went all the way through. Can't be sure cuz I had my eyes closed.

He wasn't there…I can't get the picture outta my mind of his daddy washing blood off the driveway while his mama was still sitting in their car with her head bashed in. Kinda scares me thinkin' it was just one street over next to the cemetery we walk by when we go to church. Messin' around…is that like what Daddy does sometimes?

I wasn't very hungry at dinner tonight. Mama thinks it's because of the shot. I wish people would stop talkin' about it. All I wanna do is go to bed and put the covers over my head. But I don't like what I see when I close my eyes. I wish I'd never given him back the ring. Maybe I should have lied and just kept it. But God would've told Mama and then I'd really be in trouble. I wish I WAS his girlfriend. I'd tell him that I was praying for him and that I'm sorry about his mama…

I don't think he's comin' back to school.

The Story

"**O**nce upon a time, a long time ago, a bunch of cowboys were sittin' round the campfire when one of them looked up and said, 'Jack, tell us a story.' So, Jack began…

Once upon a time, a long time ago, a bunch of cowboys were sittin' round the campfire when one of them looked up and said, 'Jack, tell us a story.' So, Jack began…

Once upon a time…"

"Daddy, tell us a *real* story."

He'd look at us with those crystal blue eyes, full of impish mischief and say that he *was* telling us a story. We just had to listen real good to hear it. Then he'd start in again…

"Once upon a time, a long time ago, a bunch of cowboys were sittin' round the campfire when one of them said…"

This is where we'd all join in unison,

"Jack, tell us a story!"

Some nights he'd tell us the story of the soldier during WWII, who fell in love with a beautiful French girl. He wanted to marry her, but when he went to see her, she was gone. The girl left a letter for him with her mother who gave it to him upon his arrival. Heartbroken, he left without opening it up. Later that night after several drinks to fortify him he opened the letter only to find it written in French. A couple of his buddies could converse a little in French, but none were able to read it. The soldier started to feel a sense of panic. What if she were in trouble? He became obsessed with knowing the contents of the letter.

The war raged on, and he was still unable to have it interpreted. He kept it in his jacket pocket close to his heart. He had trouble sleeping and eating, thinking he had abandoned the one he loved. One night, his unit came upon a village that had been secured earlier in the day. Knowing the desperate state of mind of the young soldier, one of his friends found an old man in the village that spoke English. He brought him to the soldier who was sitting in front of a fire trying to keep warm in the freezing night air. After explaining his sad situation, the old man asked to see the letter. With trembling hands the soldier reached into his pocket, pulled out the letter and gently kissed the seal. As he was handing the letter to the old gentleman, a breeze snatched it out of the soldier's hands and it fell into the fire.

The end.

What?!!! "Daddy, what happened? What did the letter say? Was the girl all right?"

Again those blue eyes danced.

"I dunno, guess it burned up, end of story."

As a young child, bedtime stories with Daddy would be recitations of James Whitcomb Riley's "Little Orphan Annie,"

And the Goblins will gitcha, if you don't watch out!

There was Henry Wadsworth Longfellow's "Hiawatha,"

By the shores of Gitche Gumee,
By the shining big sea water,
Stood the wigwam of Nikomis,
Daughter of the moon, Nikomis.

On especially stormy, black nights, when most children are comforted with calming pictures of warmth and protection, Daddy would tell the tale of "The Headless Horseman." I would hide behind my sisters and brother, watching them to see if I should give in to the fear of the shadows that danced on the walls like a giant drive-in theatre screen. Daddy also introduced me to Edgar Allen Poe,

Quothe the Raven, never more...

The books Mama read to us always taught a moral principle. She was great at making the characters come to life using different voices for each one. Every chapter ended with a "cliffhanger." We couldn't get enough. "Read the next one, Mama. We're not sleepy." But, she'd make us wait until bedtime the following night to find out...dun, dun, dun...how the characters survived or if they survived.

She used these same talents when she led Junior Church on Sundays. When word got out about Sister Walker's "Story Time," that place was standing room only. Even the kids that we would go pick up on the oil leases out in Betteravia sat and listened, *and* came back the next week to find out if the ol' miner survived the cave collapse. She set up her own library so the children could check out books and read them during the week at home. She had a passion for making other people's lives better, and instilling the joy of reading in children was just one more way she could make a difference.

Mama taught me dramatic timing. Whether telling a story or in her own real life drama, she was convincing and had the gift of drawing you in even when you would have preferred to just be a seven year old. She was a star in my book, and there are times when I catch my reflection in a mirror and see her. When my daughters were young, I could hear her in my voice when I taught them. Both of my parents were amazing storytellers. I miss their natural, untrained cadence. It was real, and there's no substitute for that.

Even though much of our young lives were without television or movies, we weren't exactly deprived, quite the contrary. Our imaginations were given room to expand along with vocabulary and the invitation to *think*.

Story. What a gift.

Thanks, Mom and Daddy.

Baptism by Water and Tongues

I always had a little crush on Brother Kumpe, who was our Pastor at the First Assembly of God Church in Santa Maria. Now lest you think of me as some kind of seven-year-old Lolita or something, let me clarify "crush." Pastor Kumpe looked like a movie star and not a prissy one either. Shoot, even Daddy was kind of jealous of him, and that's saying a lot because my dad was a bit of a "looker" himself.

It's reasonable to assume that his jealousy stemmed from the unwelcome exposure he experienced due to all the "spare no details" prayer requests, courtesy of my longsuffering mother. She also had a tendency to spend more time at the church than she did in her own home and frankly, who could blame her?

She held the keys to the church, and I believed at times, the Kingdom. We never missed a service even when it was cold and foggy. It was common to see Sister Walker and her four children bundled up in their coats holding their Bibles close. We were doing the "stop, look and listen" routine, as we prepared to cross dangerous Stowell Road in front of the cemetery. From there it was a short walk past the funeral parlor and then onto church property where we all knew we were safe because of God's special angels that encamped about there pretty much 24/7.

Took us ten minutes max even in the worst weather conditions. This may have been the reason the church deacon's board chose to have Brother and Sister Kumpe along with their two boys, Randy and Ernie, move in a couple houses down from ours while the new parsonage was being built. Randy would spend the night sometimes, and he and my brother Norman would shoot baskets by the hour in our driveway. Daddy was pretty much on his best behavior when Randy slept over, him being the preacher's kid and all.

Brother Kumpe was different than other preachers I'd been around. Don't get me wrong, he could definitely deliver a good hell fire and brimstone sermon, but his passion seemed to come from somewhere deep inside, not just for effect. When he talked to Diana and me before we got baptized, he never made us feel small or stupid. He listened with fatherly patience, something both of us had secretly longed for.

One Sunday Diana and I, intent on proceeding with our spiritual journey, stepped into the big baptismal at the front of the church. With the cross hanging on the wall behind us, before family and friends, we professed Jesus as our Lord and Savior. We cupped one hand over our mouth, pinching our nose shut and held our wrist with the other just as we had practiced at home. Whereupon our beloved Brother Kumpe, cradled in his strong arms, dipped us under the water, signifying the burial of our old life of sin and degradation, all seven and eight years of it. Then we rose up with the church's thin white cotton baptismal robes clinging to our appropriate clothing underneath to live a new life in Christ. We felt saved.

Shortly after our immersion, a traveling evangelist came to town for one of our many revivals. He brought a message that was heavy on the indwelling of the Holy Spirit through the evidence of speaking in tongues. Most preachers I grew up with in those early years taught that you weren't *truly* saved unless you spoke in tongues. This always puzzled me. I genuinely loved Jesus. I wanted him to love me too, but I couldn't speak in tongues. The more I heard language like the *gift* of speaking in tongues the more I felt that I wasn't good enough yet. This didn't come as any big surprise really, I mean Mama's gift was shiny and impressive, rolling off her tongue as easily as when she'd sing *On the Wings of a Snow White Dove*.

She used to sing that from time to time as the special music in church while Daddy sat in the way back, soaking up the sound of her beautiful voice. He loved the way she sang. She was so holy and gifted, made me want to be just like her. I tried everything from thanking Jesus to praising him, being still, praying harder, begging, making my mouth go slack even down to, well, it goes like this…

One night after the sermon of this particular evangelist, and under deep conviction, Diana and I went down to the altar together to receive the *gift* of tongues. We just knew that was the night we would finally finish the requirements for salvation. We had memorized all the books of the Bible and several key verses that had actually won us Midge dolls in Sunday school. We had perfect attendance and had brought several visitors, racking up a line of multi-colored stars after each of our names on the big attendance chart tacked up on the bulletin board at the front of the small Sunday school room. Now we were ready.

We'd been praying for a while, knowing that sometimes we are called to tarry and persevere, thereby convincing the Lord to gift us with unknown, heavenly languages, or possibly an African dialect if we were to someday become missionaries and go to the Congo. I never really felt the tug on Missionary Sunday however, mostly just dizziness from watching the slides of naked dark skinned men, women and children. I secretly prayed that Jesus would find something stateside for me to do considering all my allergies and stuff.

After much tarrying, people were starting to get up and leave. There was work and school the next day, and they were already going to be waking up their cranky children who were now fast asleep on the back pew. There was one particular saint however who was NOT a quitter. Sister Marvel, an older Hawaiian lady, was duty bound to make sure we spoke in tongues that night. She was highly invested and had been working hard instructing us to just let go and let God fill us.

"Stop holding back," she'd say.

She pushed on our skinny little backs and pinched our weary cheeks cheering us on, all the while reaping rubies in her crown. I was trying so hard to do all that she said but still nothing, and by now I too was getting sleepy, pretending to be praying while resting my head on the altar. Finally in exasperation she leaned down in my ear and said, "Repeat after me," Where upon she released a barrage of syllables and vowels that were easy to mimic and sounded very much like the outburst in church a couple Sunday's ago before the evangelist showed up. Brother Kumpe had called the Sister down telling her she was out of order and to sit down and be quiet.

"Hurry up, you don't want your sister to get it before you, now do you?"

Then she leaned over to Diana and repeated her sure fire instructions.

I was tempted. I really was. But I was more afraid of pretending with God than pleasing Sister Marvel. So much to her dismay and our failure to have enough faith or be good enough, we once again left the altar speaking plain old English with a little Pig Latin on the side. I decided that if Jesus didn't love me enough yet to give me the *gift* that night, then I would just have to keep trying...and try I did.

The Santa Maria church and Norman and Randy
shooting hoops on Laguna Avenue

. . . .

Dear Diary…

I sure hope Randy Kumpe doesn't get sick and die. During the communion service I saw him take more than one cup of grape juice and guzzle it like it was water or somethin', showin' off the whole time. Mama says if you eat or drink of the cup unworthily you are bringing damnation (hope I don't get in trouble for writing that word) upon yourself. Makes me scared every time the communion plate gets passed. I pray real, real, real, hard that Jesus will forgive all my sins before I eat the cracker and drink the juice.

I've been watching him like a hawk and so far so good. I don't know though. Jesus just might take care of this after Randy goes to bed. I heard Mama say that the devil shows up like a roaring lion seeking whom he may devour. Makes me glad they've moved on into the parsonage and aren't living that close to us anymore. He and Norman are still friends though.

Oh, by the way,
I sorta kinda have a secret…
I think Jimmy Wakefield likes me!

Family Man

I remember with clarity the yellow, nicotine stained, fingers of the men we called family. There was Chester, Jim-Bo, Marlin, Dick, Bob, Monroe, and my dad Bill, also known as "Hatchet." They would laugh and cough, wheezing their way through chain smoking lungs, all the while hiding secrets too dark to speak, running from demons too real to acknowledge. They thought they were invisible, under the radar, as men of that era often did. Like young children playing hide and seek in the middle of the living room floor, they believed if they didn't see us, we couldn't see them. But we *did* see them. We *felt* them. Our young lungs breathed in all the smoke of their unspoken stories without exhaling, like a cancer that lies in wait.

They were comfortable and uncomfortable, safe and scary, trustworthy and dangerous all at the same time. Confusing at it's most confusing. We were always wondering what time it was *now*. Would this be the circle that we would step into? We tried to run as fast as we could, never looking over our shoulders, feeling the breath on the back of our necks from the generations before us. Their blood was our DNA.

He had an uncanny sense of direction. He could look up in the sky and give you the time of day by where the sun was sitting. At night, he'd name the constellations, but he could also get lost quicker than anybody else I've ever known. He carried peppermint lifesavers in his pocket all neatly packed in their blue wrapper. I suppose they were to mask the scent of sins from the night before or that one last drag on his cigarette before he stepped into the church. He was always generous with the white mints and to this day the smell and taste of a peppermint lifesaver transports me back to childhood.

I can see him. I can hear his laugh and feel his big rough hands as he puts my small hand in his and marvels at the contrast between the two.

I was his "night owl" on long trips. My brother and sisters would fall asleep in the back seat, but I would sit up front between Daddy and Mama. He'd smile and tease me, as my little voice would make the sound of the blinker when he made a turn. I'd look for jackrabbits and possums, then wrinkle my nose when the familiar scent of a skunk wafted through the cracked window where Daddy would flick the ashes of his Lucky Strike. Sometimes on the trip to Grandma's house, between Santa Maria and Woodlake, he'd get sleepy. It was no wonder he fought to stay awake. He'd already put in a full day at work, and we didn't leave till after 9:00 at night. When the thermos of coffee and cigarettes failed him, he'd stick his whole head out the window choking on the thick, San Joaquin Valley air.

Mama would pray under her breath. She was perfectly capable of driving the rest of the way, but if she offered it might make him mad. So she kept quiet in her passive-aggressive way. I just sat there, between the two of them, feeling much older than my little girl self. I had a plan. If he fell asleep while driving, I'd steer until he woke up. Funny, in some ways, he never *did* wake up when it came to me, and I steered myself right into some pretty deep ditches.

He was my example of a "family man." He wasn't ever gonna make the cover of the First Assembly of God's *"EVANGEL"* magazine or nothin', but he was one *very* interesting story. At times I was terrified of him. Other times I felt sorry for him and wanted to save him. Even thought if I was a good enough little girl and prayed without ceasing for his salvation, one day he would get saved and be the daddy I knew he could be. If he'd just stop doin' *that* and start doin *this*, life might look like those first grade readers. See Spot run? See Spot sit?

He didn't get *saved* until we all left home. Thanks to Bill Bright, he finally saw the light; at least that's what Mama said. I suppose it clinched his eternity, and I'll forever be thanking God for that one, but...we're all still here, living out the consequences of one very complicated Okie. Over the years I've hated him and loved him. Thankfully, I just love him now.

My dad, the *Family Man*...

Playin' On the Tracks

...A Poetic Telling

You felt it before you heard it, that familiar deep, rumbling vibration of the train leaving the packinghouse. It was coming down those old tracks that ran parallel to the little house my grandparents built with their very own hands. We'd sit there in Grandma's living room holding on to the knick knacks so they wouldn't break while the swamp cooler did it's best to keep us cool, and the old black dog with the racist name sat in the corner and growled.

The boxcars were filled with beautiful California fruit that brought smiles to people all over the world, and I was told saved many of us from scurvy. Grandpa Ennis worked as the chief engineer at that packinghouse, while Grandma held the title of chief grader. She quit at some point in her eighties though because the powers-that-be started speeding up the belts. She said it allowed too much inferior fruit to slip by, and she felt responsible. Their greed pissed her off in a major way, and after giving them fair warning, she up and walked out in the middle of her shift. She turned her back on perfectly lovely fruit flying off the belts and landing bruised on the floor, which was scooped up and put in the baby food bin. Grandma went home and rototilled her garden. I come from strong stock!

I've heard it said that when you live long enough with something, you eventually don't even notice it any more. Like our family's cuckoo clock that cuckooed every hour, or my mother's, grandmother's Grandfather clock that faithfully clanged out the hour and half hour as long as we were faithful to wind it at regular intervals. With the clocks, I became so accustomed to their sound that I would wake up if they *stopped* ticking.

Not so with the train. That was never an ordinary experience. It was danger, curiosity and adventure all squished together, inviting us, *daring* us to take our chances and come play on the tracks. That ol' train would let its whistle howl over and over again to make sure all the cars and kids knew it was rolling' through, which was code to us for: "Do you feel *lucky*?"

I was a timid child who most of the time obeyed all the rules for fear of what would happen if I didn't. I'd seen and felt those repercussions often enough to know that to this day, you only cross the street on the green even if it *is* the middle of the night and another car won't be seen for hours. You walk on the sidewalk out of respect for your neighbor's property, and you don't taste the produce *before* you buy it because that's stealing. After all, you can't weigh the grape somebody just ate! Daddy was a grocery clerk and produce man for years and had a highly developed standard of right and wrong when it came to produce thieves.

However, timid or not, at the first hint of the train's distant rumble, all caution faded and the faint voice of warning was banished to the recesses of my young mind, devoid of the ability to anticipate mortality. Chalk it up to the willful ignorance of the young. The steady tick tock of the Grandfather clock only served to exacerbate the growing restlessness of the cousins, who randomly one by one, so as not to arouse suspicion, would sneak out to the backyard. There, once everyone was accounted for, we would dig up our collective courage to accept the dare and face the train.

My brother was usually leading the pack. I remember being scared, my heart beating so big in my little chest; I could literally see my shirt move with its pounding rhythm. I followed the pack, all the time seeing visions of squished cousins on the massive wooden railroad ties.

There was an old fence with a double hung gate that had to be conquered before you were in the clear. Each cousin had devised their own special way of wriggling through the tetanus infested rusty chicken wire to get to freedom until there was only one left standing in the safety of Grandma's backyard. I didn't *feel* safe though. I felt caught in between. I couldn't go back in the house for fear of the questions that would surely be asked about the rest of the gang, and I couldn't go forward for fear of dying. So there I stood, shaking, my asthma squeezing my lungs and making me wheeze because of the weeds that hadn't been burned off yet that stood between me and the tracks.

"C'mon Carter, you can do it!" my brother would say.

"No I can't. I can't breathe and I'm too little. We're gonna get a whippin', Norman!"

There comes a time when all scaredy cats have to make the decision. Do I stand here and watch, or do I climb through the gate? The voice in my head and the racing of my heart was telling me to remember my favorite book, besides the Bible of course, about the little engine that could. I'd been reading that book since before kindergarten and now my little seven-year-old self was reciting it under my breath.

"I *think* I can! I *think* I can!" the little engine would say.

"I *think* I can! I *think* I can!" I would echo back.

Just as I was struggling to make it up the hill in my mind, I would hear those inspiring words that would push me the rest of the way.

"What's the matter, Carter? You a…chicken? Bok, bok, bok. A little *scared* chicken!"

The others chimed in on the chorus of "Bok, bok, bok!" One of Satan's Top 10 songs on the countdown to Hell! Before I knew what I was doing, I too was scrambling through the wire that was holding me back and pushing me down. Power to the skinny, asthmatic, allergy cursed little girls of the world! I envisioned cheers, pats on the back, not thinking about what now faced me head on…the tracks.

My eyes were starting to swell and my breathing was whistlin' Dixie, but there would be no turning back. There was a maniacal, fierce look in my brother's eyes. I was in his regimen now, and there would be no further talk of retreat. I started confessing all my sins under my breath, not wanting to go to Hell when the train killed me. I wonder now what I felt compelled to ask forgiveness for.

Probably things like, "Please forgive me for looking at the men's underwear section of the Montgomery Ward catalogue," or "I'm sorry I lied about eating the liver Mama *burned* for dinner. I actually gave it to Rocky Marciano." Not the famous fighter but our Chihuahua, of whom Monroe said, and I quote: "You get the hump outta that dawg, he'd be a right smart dawg." Rocky had more serious challenges than simply being hump backed. But some things are better left unsaid. Just trust me when I tell you he had issues, but anemia would not be one of them as long as I was around. I'm sure I capped it off with "and Lord, please

forgive me of all the sins I don't remember or know about, Amen."
Now I was ready...kind of.

"Okay, here's the deal," Norman said in his best sergeant's voice,
"Everybody has to stand on the tracks. The one who stays the longest
wins."

That didn't seem too bad to me. I didn't care about winning. I'd
already won. I was standing there wasn't I? I felt downright cocky as my
skinny little ankles in my unforgiving black and white oxfords twisted
their way to the tracks. Let's get this over with, I thought.

"Where you goin' Scout?" That's what my brother called me sometimes after the brother and sister in *To Kill A Mockingbird.*

"Ya gotta wait for the train."

Surely my pea-sized female brain (compliments of my brother's in-
doctrination) had not heard him or understood him correctly.

"What do you mean?" I wheezed out.

"The train, Squirt. Ya gotta face down the train."

I looked around, hoping this was a joke and all the rest of the
troops would start laughing at any minute. I was wrong. They looked
at me like I was some kind of stupid baby or something.

"Yeah," Cousin Michael said, "we wait until the train is close, then
we go stand on the tracks and face it down. One time my foot got
caught and I just barely got out before the train ran over my shoe!"

What a liar! I knew that couldn't be true. My Aunt would've beat
him black and blue if he showed up with only one shoe and that's the
truth! But what *did* it mean? Norman had that no turning back look,
and my knees were starting to feel kind of wobbly and watery, sort of
like my skeleton was turning to liquid, and all that was left was this big
bubble of water with a head and skinny ankles sticking up out of my
shoes.

There's no way to write down the sound of a train whistle, so I'm just
going to have to trust that you've heard one before. I've always been
drawn to that plaintive wail as the trains pass through from town to
town, state to state, making zigzag lines all over the map of the United
States, carrying my Uncle Bob with 'em.

This wail was different. This sound was more than simply hearing
from a distance. It was the earth shaking low frequency of all that steel
gathering momentum on the tracks. You felt it in your feet, felt it in
your heart, heard it with your ears. It was pickin' up speed, pickin' up

hoboes, warning every foolish child, every driver in a car taking their chances on outrunning this massive, surge of weight and energy that simply could not stop on a dime, to stay clear of the tracks!

So why were my brother and my cousins denying all sanity and walking toward those steel rails? More importantly, why was I following? One by one we took our places like a sentry preparing for attack. No blinking, no questions, no fear–or maybe just fear, I don't know. All I remember was standing and waiting, my eyes staring down the back of my brother's head.

That's when I saw it. It was scarier than anything I had ever imagined. It was coming toward us at an increased rate of speed, howling as it approached, closer, closer, louder, louder. I couldn't take it anymore. I jumped off the track and ran as fast as my watery legs and asthmatic lungs would allow me. I wasn't alone either. Following behind me were all my cousins. For once *I* was the leader!

We were traveling at the speed of light through the weeds, through the chicken wire gate when I realized we were one short. Where was Norman? As I turned around I saw him standing there, on the tracks, facing down the train. It was like he had to prove to himself, or someone, that he was strong, not afraid. Who can say what dialogue was going on in his head as he stood there facing death? I wonder if he confessed his sins or the *sins against him*. Whatever was said was never shared. This was one challenge he was determined to win and win he did, decisively.

I watched as he jumped off just in time. Our shouts of triumph mixed with terror almost drowned out the wail of the whistle as the train passed miraculously without any of us plastered to the front. I was so proud of him. That was *my* brother! He beat the train! I loved him so much, like only a bratty little kid sister can.

There's a price to pay for heroism, and you may take issue with the idea of some kid facing down a train as being heroic. But it was for me and for the cousins around me. Little wounded soldiers with no voice. We felt a bit taller and a little less wounded that day as we all walked back into Grandma's house prepared for the judgment that was sure to come, and frankly, for once deserved. I mean children simply cannot go traipsin' off willy-nilly to play on railroad tracks. There was a perfectly good sand area complete with chiggers to play in and make childhood memories. I don't think I got a whippin'. I was wheezing so bad that I had to take a hit off of Cousin Ricky's inhaler so I wouldn't die from my lungs collapsing.

Now, there are all kinds of life lessons that can be mined from this story, deep spiritual applications for the truly courageous. But I'm not going there. I'm going to trust in the good old-fashioned sovereignty of God to write those on your heart and just leave it at that for now. One final thought though: next time you hear a train whistle, remember, it's never a good idea to play on the tracks when a train is coming. But if you find yourself in that position...

....

Grandpa Ennis

Diana and I have to stay in Woodlake with Grandma and Grandpa for a couple of weeks. Mama's bein' a counselor up at Camp Pinecrest with our church youth group. We're not teenagers so we didn't get to go.

I like the way orange blossoms and lemons and fresh peaches smell, even though the fuzz makes me itch somethin' awful. Grandma and Grandpa were workin' in the orchards today on the big flatbed truck. I stayed out of the way but it sure was hot. When we got back to the house, Grandpa walked Diana and me to the store and bought me my very own big bottle of Dr. Pepper. He dropped the coins in the slot and then led the neck of the bottle through that thing that looks like a maze. Then he lifted it out, hooked off the cap and handed it to me. Boy, it sure did taste good! I told him thank you, and he just smiled. I like Grandpa Ennis. He's kinda quiet but he's real strong and he likes lemon snaps. He smells like linseed oil and orange juice. I wonder why he married Grandma?

Hi, Neighbor!

The houses on our block were built so close together that had it not been for the small strip of grass between, you would have been hard pressed to know where one driveway began and the other ended. So close in fact that neighbors often became family, maybe not your favorite family-members but family all the same.

Our little house on East Laguna Avenue afforded me an education that money simply could never buy. I was a quiet "watcher," and our neighborhood was a classroom of life lessons. One such lesson was taught by the lady across the street who would send her husband off to work and then a few minutes later open the door in her robe, welcoming another man into her house with a long hug and then a kiss...on the mouth! I tattled to Mama and she shook her head and prayed for her. Daddy told me not to "Gawk out the winda" all the while getting an eyeful laughing his *special* laugh. Mama said she didn't see what was so funny and Daddy said, "You wouldn't." I left because I figured this was going somewhere I had no business going.

It was a safe enough neighborhood, inhabited by families doing the best they could to raise their children in an uncertain world. Of course, looking back, I can't help but be amazed by all the traumatic events that played out in the short four and a half years we lived there. But I never remember having a sense of it being unusual or that far from normal. Point of reference, I guess.

Our first neighbors were unforgettable for reasons that turned out to be quite tragic. They were friendly enough and even had a daughter that went to school with my oldest sister, Sharon. The dad would invite people over to their house on Sunday evenings and they would proceed to get sloppy drunk. While we were gathered around the piano at our house next door for what our church called a "Sip N' Sing," or "Sing-Spiration," they indulged in their own special version. We could hear them slurring their way through hymns making a mockery of the sacred lyrics, or maybe it was simply their way of trying to connect with a long forgotten past.

My dad had no patience for the Sunday night spectacles and chose to have as little interaction with them as possible. He considered the neighbor weak and lacking, and to Daddy, *that* was the unpardonable sin. Mama's heart was burdened and in the course of one of her conversations, found out that the man next door had grown up in the church. But sadly he had been running as fast as he could the other way for many years.

Seemed as though nothing could stop him from his backsliding. Until one day when we were at school and Daddy and Mama were at work, all that *"lacking"* showed up. His daughter arrived home in the afternoon to find him in the bathtub covered in blood. He had taken his gun and shot himself. Interestingly he didn't die. Mama told us it was a miracle and continued to pray for his spiritual healing as well as his physical healing. I just figured God didn't want him as a neighbor either. They moved shortly after that.

The next neighbors were the dreaded "Renters" and believe me they completely lived up to the stereotype. They were loud, arrogant, and obnoxious, with BB gun totin' boys who were downright mean! These people didn't just get plastered on the weekends, for them everyday was a day to be a drunken bully. As much as Mama had prayed for the previous family to get saved, she now expended every ounce of energy she had asking Jesus to just go ahead and move these folks on out!

I don't remember much about the mother but the father was, well, let's just say he knew how to make an impression. He talked real big, laughed real big, drank real big, *was* real big. I remember him getting all the neighbors out one Saturday to show off his brand new shiny, black Ford Fairlane, with a retractable hardtop. He demonstrated how with the push of a button the roof of the car disappeared into the trunk. I stood there completely mesmerized. He must be a millionaire!

Daddy wasn't impressed, and after he had walked back into the house said, "Who does he think he is anyway? Showin' off, puttin' on airs, actin' like he's better than everybody else. Well, he oughta think about bein' a little more respectful and I ain't justa Hey, Neighborin either!" When Daddy or Mama said, *"Ain't justa Hey, Neighborin' ei-*

ther," you could bet that they meant every word of it. I don't recall the circumstances surrounding their exit, I just always assumed Jesus answered Mama's prayer request to move them someplace else.

Hands down, our favorite neighbor was Grandma Trapani. When she moved in, it was like getting a whole family of love right next door. Her daughter lived on the corner and across the street with her husband and three boys. Their oldest, who was probably about 15 years my senior, left home and eventually graduated from Berkeley School of Law. He later came to play a very important, albeit short, roll in my life.

They also had the distinction of a front row seat to one of the most tragic accidents in Santa Maria history.

Fire on Stowell Road

August 16, 1963 was a Friday. At 10:40 p.m. while Sharon was baking cookies, and we were all in the living room reading, or playing a game, we heard what sounded like an explosion. Immediately our minds went to two possibilities. Either something had happened at the Gas Company down the road, or this was the beginning of the Russian invasion we had all been praying would never come. We were wrong on both accounts. As we rushed out of the house we immediately saw flames and smelled burning rubber. There was fire on Stowell Road. All the neighbors, including children, from our side of the street ran to the Meier's house on the corner, while the neighbors on the other side of the street craned their necks over their back fences to see what they shouldn't see.

A mass of twisted steel was completely engulfed in flames. The worst part was the realization that what we were looking at was the remains of a car that held people captive inside, and there was nothing anyone could do to save them. We shielded our faces and mouths trying not to inhale the smoke of fuel and death. Some neighbors said they saw two teenage boys stumbling out of another car throwing beer cans over one of the fences that backed up to Stowell Road.

The police, sheriff's deputies, and fire department stayed until 5 a.m. the next morning trying to piece together the facts of the devastating accident. It seems a father, with his daughter and niece, were on their way home from the skating rink in a small Renault. I imagined them laughing and talking, making plans for the rest of the summer weekend. They weren't aware that the car coming up fast behind them had two teenage boys flying high into a destiny that would soon become impossible to change for all of them.

As the small car slowed down to make a left turn onto College Drive, the teenage driver, in his big 55 Ford, let his impatience and impaired judgment get the better of him. Instead of slowing down, he stepped on the gas, thinking he could get around them before the Renault made its turn. They hit the car broadside going full speed. The three family members didn't stand a chance as their small car rolled and exploded in a fiery display that lit up the sky as though it were daylight.

They died that night, but in some ways so did the teenage boys involved, even though they escaped with minor injuries. They will forever live out the consequences and memories of their deadly decision to get behind the wheel of a car while drunk. Unfortunately, this would not be the only time I would be affected by someone's choice to drive under the influence.

It all felt unreal to me at the time, kind of like watching a play in our front yard. These people were just characters acting out a script. My little mind was beginning to detach from hard realities I didn't have the will or capacity to understand. I had already experienced the effects of my friend's mother being brutally murdered by his father. I had seen and lived with infidelity under our own roof, knew the reality and consequences of an adult's rage, and lived in a community that feared nuclear war. Oh, and let's not forget the Rapture. This was everyday life, and now here was one more out-of-my-control event that I needed to process.

Looking at what was left of the burned out car, I remember thinking that if some of the occupants were Catholic, they didn't have far to go with the cemetery right there and all. Of course at our church there were some serious conversations about what happens when people choose to walk on the wild side. It's just a hop, skip and a jump from the skating rink to an all out dance hall. Then what? Movies? Best to leave those temptations at the altar next to Brother Langley's red pack of Winston Cigarettes. I just hoped they were all settled into their new mansions nice and comfy.

My mother had been complaining for some time that Stowell Road was too dangerous. The speed limit was set at 65, which meant many people chose not to even look at their speedometer as they sped down the road to Highway 101, never thinking of the families and children living life a few yards from their passing car. Each time we had to cross the road on our way to church she would pray fearing this kind of thing would happen, and now it was staring her in the face.

She woke up Saturday morning with her righteous anger intact and determined to do something about it. She immediately put together a petition, and with us in tow went house-to-house gathering signatures to present to the City Council requesting a speed limit reduction from 65 to 35 miles per hour.

According to Santa Maria City Council Minutes, on Tuesday August 20th a 266 signature petition had already been submitted to reduce the 65 mile an hour speed limit. An Urgency Ordinance was set in motion and the speed limit was changed. She made a choice that day to not look the other way but instead to take action. Even though I was a just a little girl and didn't understand what it took for her to engage in this way, I knew I had a mama I could be proud of. And I was.

....

Emma's Kids

Mama cut our bangs today. She doesn't want 'em hangin' down in our eyes 'cuz it makes us look sloppy and un-kept. So we're lined up like Dominoes waitin' our turn to sit on the tall, red metal stool that makes you feel like any minute it's gonna buck you off. Mama has the shears out for Norman and scissors for us girls. She puts the sheet over our shoulders and pins it in the back. Then she takes that black rat tail comb, runs it under the faucet and carefully combs down every hair in our bangs making a straight line.

"Don't squint, Carter. When you do it moves your bangs, and then they look crooked and we have to start all over. Breathe through your nose."

She starts trimmin' away while I try my hardest not to move any part of my body or face. Most of the time it takes a few go 'rounds before she blows in my face in an effort to free all the tiny little damp hairs that are refusing to let go. Trying, trying, trying NOT to sneeze!

"There you go. All done. Hop down, now!"

I carefully slide off of that stool and wait while Mama un-pins the sheet, sweeps up, and gives me the okay to leave. My bangs are so short and straight there's no way anybody can say Emma Walker does not take care of her children!

Life On Laguna Avenue

Saturday afternoons found most of the kids of our extended neighborhood family sitting on the curb outside our house. As the day would wear on and the sun began to set, the smell of hamburger and onions being fried up told us that at any minute our mamas would be calling us in for dinner. We didn't have much time left to play, and that's exactly where we found ourselves one late afternoon in the early Fall.

"Truth or Dare, Carter?"

I could see the gleam in Diana's eyes as she asked the question. She knew I wasn't going anywhere near truth.

"Dare," I said.

"I dare you tooooooooooo…hmmmm…uhm, let's seeeeeeeeeee…"

"Diana! Come up with somethin' already. It's not that hard!"

Our brother Norman was having tolerance issues with his kid sisters. He was the undisputed heartthrob of Miller Street Elementary School's sixth grade class. He already sang better than Elvis and had a following of girls scheming to be his next girlfriend. On our vacations to Texas he'd only sing if the family paid him. Let me tell you, when he went into "Ain't Nothin' But a Hound Dog" and "Heartbreak Hotel," the boy cleaned up! Now playing with little sissy third and fourth graders was definitely beneath him and his patience was wearing thin.

"I know, I know! Do somersaults all the way around the front yard!"

"Somersaults make me dizzy, and then Mama's gonna wanna know why I'm dizzy, and then I'm gonna have to tell her that you made me, and then you know what that means. I'm just looking out for you Diana."

"Do the somersaults and quit actin' like a weakling, you little baby!" Norman was done with my whining.

So I tucked and rolled all over the yard until Mama called us in for dinner.

We had just sat down to eat our hamburger sauce, mashed potatoes and corn, when Mama asked if Diana and I had put our bike away in the backyard shed. She knew we hadn't because she'd nearly tripped over it as she was putting out the garbage. We immediately started blaming one another, claiming it was the other sister's turn. That didn't work; it never did. Within seconds, at the threat of having our backsides stinging from a well-deserved spanking, Diana and I were walking our bicycle through the side gate and into the backyard continuing the blame game as we went.

By then the sun had set and the full moon was lighting our path. The old shed with the shingles on the side was in the far back corner and served as headquarters for the "Three Kids Club" during the summer. That was an exclusive club made up of Diana, Norman and myself. We were a service-oriented organization that was heavy on the minutes and rules, which Norman made up, and light on the follow through. During the school year however, it simply housed yard equipment and our bicycle. There was a square cut out of the bottom of the door so a dog could go in and out. As we came closer, a small movement in the lower corner of the door caught our attention at the same time.

There, with the moonlight shining like a flashlight, was a man's hand attached to a GIANT body that was in position to pounce or run or turn into a werewolf, who knows? All I remember is screaming at the top of my little girl lungs while Diana's mouth was wide open but no sound was coming out. We took off like a house-a-fire, literally carrying the bike across the yard and banging on the backdoor. It wasn't locked, but we were too terrified to open it. As my mother came running to our rescue, the man jumped the fence.

Phone lines lit up like lightning. There was a prowler in the neighborhood. Last week there'd been an escape from the Atascadero State Mental Hospital, and now we were convinced he was in our midst. Lock the doors and windows. It wasn't long ago that someone had attempted to break into Yolanda and her grandma's house at the end of the street. Good thing our house was burglar proof, at least that's what Norman said.

What was this world coming to? Now crazed mental patients were hiding in our backyards just waiting to break in and do Lord knows what! On top of that, President Kennedy was telling us all to invest in bomb shelters, especially all of *us*, because we lived a short 30 minutes from Vandenberg Air Force Base. Mama would pray and mutter under her breath how Bill had abandoned all sense and moved his family to this Catholic town where everybody worshiped the President as though he were God. What this town needed was a good revival, which of course was scheduled for week after next.

Diana and I learned a couple of very important lessons that day. Never let the sun go down before putting your bike away, and screaming/praying as loud as you can and running as fast as you can just might save your life when the Boogie Man shows up, which he did, many years later.

....

Carnys

"He walks, He talks, He crawls on his belly like a reptile!"

Everybody else, and I mean everybody else, gets to go to the Carnival in the parking lot at the Purity grocery store. That's where Daddy works. They got a little Ferris wheel, carousel with horses that go round and round, the Smasher or somethin' like that and they got real gypsies that'll tell your fortune. There's gonna be cotton candy, popcorn and corndogs. Oh, I wanna go so bad! But Daddy says NO! Ain't no way his children are gonna be hangin' around a bunch a Carny's. He knows what goes on with all those ol' boys that travel and set up rides and stuff in parkin' lots and we AIN'T goin' and he don't wanna hear another word about it. He don't wanna hear no whinin' or cryin' either or he'd be only too happy to give us somethin' to cry about!

"President Kennedy's Dead and Johnson's Smiling"

Funny what sticks in a little kid's head. No matter what your age if you were alive on November 22, 1963 you remember...there's a snapshot that your mind refers back to. We received the tragic news that Friday while sitting in our classrooms smelling the fish the cafeteria ladies were cooking up so all the little Catholic children could remain Catholic. I understood that. Our church had rules too. It didn't affect me much since I always brought my lunch, which consisted of homemade bread and bologna. I rarely partook of cafeteria food, even after my mother started working there scrubbing her fingers to the bone, cleaning out those giant pots. She'd scrub so hard it made her knuckles bleed, until the head cafeteria lady told her the pots didn't need to be that shiny.

There's something especially cruel when tragedy happens in the middle of *normal.* The shock is too great and random to respond to. That day it was as though time had stopped, *really* stopped. Teachers turned pale, their bodies frozen, unable to move. They stared off as though they were trying to mentally grasp something that was inconceivable and impossible to process. We were dismissed to walk home quietly and reverently.

Santa Maria's beloved President had been murdered, and now it was just a matter of time before the bombs would start dropping and here we were, too poor for a bomb shelter. I felt real bad for Caroline and John-John. I watched the TV clip of Jackie, their mama, climbing over the back seat and then later on the plane, still in her blood soaked suit. I thought she looked pretty even then. I wanted to put my skinny little arms around them and squeeze as hard and tight as I could. Whether your family was a Democrat or not, back then there was a very genuine sense of connection for people all over the United States with this beautiful young family. I kept thinking, first my friend Johnny's mama and now their daddy.

My mother was definitely not a fan of President Kennedy, but she thought Vice President Johnson came straight from H-E-double hockey sticks! Somewhere in her conspiratorial mind she was convinced she saw a smirk on his face as he was being sworn in, and from that moment on believed that Johnson had quite possibly put out the hit on Kennedy so he could become President.

"The assassination *did* happen in his home state of Texas, you know" giving that little all-knowing shake of her head that sometimes looked like she was disagreeing with what she was agreeing with. I think there may have been a little transference going on when you consider that's where most of Daddy's people were from. Oddly enough, she wasn't the only one buying into that theory. I'd overhear her talking about young voluptuous women running around half naked in the White House and Johnson smoking, cussing, and swimming with them in the pool, all the while Lady Bird was up in her office making plans to beautify America.

I couldn't help but think of those big missiles that Vandenberg Air Force Base would show off at every downtown parade. Main Street would be lined with families eating popcorn and cheering as the floats and bands with the baton twirlers in short skirts lead the way. After the Shriners and the Rotary Club finished mowing down as many innocent bystanders as possible in their little Go-carts, the military would bring out the big guns and the missiles. I'd sit there on the curb hoping they had them strapped down real good and be praying it wouldn't hit a bump. KA-BOOM! That'd be it for the residents of Santa Maria and the rest of the West Coast.

After awhile Mama let go of some of her theories and trusted the Lord to take care of us. Shoot, for all we knew Jesus could be coming back that day and "in a moment in the twinkling of an eye," Kennedy, Johnson and the missiles would no longer be our concern. We would all be safe and sound taking leisurely strolls down the streets of gold, just one of the many perks of being the chosen and *right* denomination, while the great Tribulation warred on down here on earth. I worried about Daddy though. There was no way he was going to be a part of the rapture.

Didn't look like heaven was in his future at the moment, and that made me real sad. What was he going to do without all of us?

....

Walk Home Drill

Today we had a walk home drill at school. When the recess bell rang, Miss Searle told us to get under our desks, clasp our hands behind our heads and shield our ears with our arms. We're practicing for when the bomb gets dropped on Vandenberg Air Force Base.

I was all scrunched up with my head in my lap. At first I kept my eyes shut real tight, then I peeked them open a little bit. I never noticed the squiggly lines on the floor before. I started thinkin' about how Miss Searle doesn't like me much. She told Mama I'm not a very good reader, and Mama said she was going to go have a talk with the principal because the one thing I CAN do is read.

I had to give an oral report last week, and I was so scared to be up in front of everybody. When I was done and went back to my desk, she walked up to the front of the room and said, "Class this is an example of how NOT to give an oral report!" Then she told everybody all the bad parts and how I was too quiet and stuff. I was so embarrassed I just kept looking at the paper on my desk. Inside my head I asked Jesus if I had to like her 'cuz I don't! She's mean.

When the all-clear bell sounded, we had to get in line in an orderly fashion. That's what Miss Searle says, "An orderly fashion," and walk home. No pushing, no shoving and NO talking! Just walking! I had to wear this yellow yarn necklace with a card on it. It has my name, address, and phone number so I won't get lost when I walk home after the bomb goes off. It kinda scared me so I sang this song Mama taught me:

Safe am I, safe am I
In the hollow of his hand
Sheltered ore, sheltered ore
With his love forever more
No ill can harm me, no foe alarm me
For he keeps both day and night
Safe am I, safe am I
In the hollow of his hand

I sing it in my head sometimes when Daddy gets mad. I just put the covers over my face and move my lips. I don't want him to hear me 'cuz it might make him madder. So I'm very quiet. I'm very still and very quiet.

Sometimes Ya Just Gotta Dance

D id you know that dancing is a sin? Me neither. Well that's not completely true. It's what I'd been told all my life; I just had a hard time believing it. It's nearly impossible to stop your body from moving when your soul hears the music. I kind of stumbled over the scripture in the Old Testament that talks about King David dancing before the Lord. I sure hope he had better moves than Sister Alvin who danced most every Sunday night at some point in the service, and no offence, but it wasn't pretty.

People danced all night long at our family re-unions in the park in Oklahoma. Now *that* was fun *and* pretty. Whole families drove in from Wichita Falls, Texas to soak up the stories of days gone by as well as make up a few new ones. Daddy would play his harmonica and somebody else would call, "Allemande left and promenade all!" It was a sight to behold watching second and third cousins twirl around laughing, not afraid of the judgment of God. Mama never made a fuss about dancing on those vacations. Maybe the rules didn't apply when you were at a *Walker* family reunion. I don't recall her ever dancing there but I bet she was tempted.

I do remember one Saturday night when we were in the living room at home singing and carrying on as was so often our custom. Daddy surprised all of us by asking her to dance with him. After coaxing her out of her chair, she smiled up at him in a way I'd never seen her do before and then stepped into his arms. She surprised us at how natural and good she was. Course Daddy was awesome. He could jitterbug! I made a mental note that there was probably quite a lot I didn't know about my mother or would ever understand about their marriage.

One thing was for sure though, rules were rules, and every time square dance time rolled around at school Mama would send in the note that said dancing was against our religion. So there I was with feet that could hardly keep still taking turns with the Jehovah Witness kid working the record player.

"Jesus, I'm really trying to be sorry 'cuz I really don't want to go to hell. Please forgive me and help me not to dance anymore."

That's what I said after I got caught in the fourth grade. Actually, Diana's conscience got the better of her and she tattled on me. We had a friend, Elaine Payne, who lived across the street from us on Laguna Avenue. She was actually more my friend than Diana's even though she was closer to my sister's age. She liked horses almost as much as me, and both of us being the socially challenged little girls that we were, spent all of our recesses at school running around in the field pretending we *were* horses or cowgirls out on the range *riding* horses. Didn't exactly make us popular with our peers. I didn't care. One friend was more than enough for me. We got along just fine. Her family didn't seem to have any religious affiliation, and they ate cow tongue, so there you go.

Elaine had her very own little record player that played 45s. We started going over to her house after school and listening to music. I loved Aretha Franklin. "R-E-S-P-E-C-T, Find out what it means to me! Sock it to me! Sock it to me! Sock it to me! Sock it to me!" Whoa, before I knew what hit me I was dancin'! I couldn't stop! All thought of wrongdoing had completely vanished, and I was doing a mean version of "The Pony," the "Twist" and the "Mashed Potatoes" all at once!

There wasn't a noticeable trace of "bashful" left in me. I had found my people! I *knew* I was adopted!

Somewhere in there Diana had fled back home to purge her soul and hopefully get out of the whippin' that was sure to come. I didn't even hear the phone ring or Elaine's mother telling me I was needed back home. But in less than five minutes, I was standing before the Judgment Throne. Mama was in no mood to extend mercy. I had knowingly and willingly chosen to go against our religion, and I had not only broken her heart but the heart of God. She would do everything within her power to make sure I wasn't enticed into the world God saved her out of, or the world she had walked into when she had turned her back on God and married my dad. This spanking was going to hurt her a lot more than it hurt me. Oh really?

Life had changed quite a bit by the time I was a teenager, and I eventually *did* go to a few dances. The fast ones were great, but I never learned to slow dance. Something about being that close…doesn't feel safe. I don't know the moves or maybe somewhere inside I do. I just don't want them to hear my heart beat, see my soul, know me for the imposter I at times fear myself to be.

See, hand-me-down girls like me aren't usually asked to the dance. We stand behind the table and serve the punch. Our clothes and our self-worth are held together with fragile little safety pins. Life tells us it's best not to dream. Some things should stay deeply buried. Risking exposure means you may have to face what you've worked so hard to convince yourself about all your life. "It doesn't matter. It's ok…I *like* serving punch."

Once, years later when I was in Waylon Jennings's band, we were all in Jack Clement's studio with the lights turned low listening back to a song we'd just finished cutting. Waylon's wife Jessi Colter and his drummer Richie Albright were dancing like folks used to on Saturday nights in the Arizona cowboy bars. For a moment I felt invisible, swaying and dancing in the corner with an imaginary partner. Richie tapped me on the shoulder and asked if he could cut in. I just stood there for a moment looking at him not knowing what to do. As we started to dance I felt my face flush with embarrassment. Each time I stepped on his feet another emotional safety pin popped, and I kept apologizing for my clumsiness. Even though I knew it was just two old friends dancing, I couldn't escape the feeling of being exposed. He never knew. I kept those self-doubts all to myself. "Don't ever let 'em see you sweat," that's what I would tell myself.

I haven't forgotten that night. I know I'm always going to be kind of different, not quite the right fit, and most of the time I'm okay with that. I laugh and say that if someday I'm a gazillionaire, I'll probably still have a hole in my stockings. That's just the way it is. But boy, if you could see me dance when nobody's around! There simply are not words!

Moving Back

Can't say I was sad when Daddy put in for a transfer back to the valley. In the past five years our family had accumulated some rather disturbing and weighty remembrances. There were the frightening 1960's historical events of The Bay of Pigs, Kennedy's assassination, atomic bomb scares, wars and rumors of wars. As alarming as these catastrophic moments in time were, they were not the stumbling blocks taking the biggest toll on our family.

Santa Maria had been a place where my parents experienced grave dysfunction in their marriage, and it was exacting an emotional tax on each one of us that we would continue to pay for years to come. But maybe moving away would give my parents the opportunity to let go of old hurts and work toward something better, at least that's the way it seemed to me. Now, it was a toss up between a job opening up in Turlock or Visalia. Either way, we were moving.

Mama had been praying the transfer would land us in Visalia and not surprisingly, God obliged. He also "opened the door" to a little rental house at the end of a long dirt driveway on Bohlinger Road just off Highway 198. It was 1964, the summer before going into the fifth grade.

Many afternoons were spent nestled in the room I shared with my two sisters reading Nancy Drew and Bobsey Twin books. On particularly hot days, when I wasn't looking for a Tom Sawyer type adventure with my brother on the banks of the neighboring creek, I would get out the water hose and wet down the driveway. I loved the smell of water hitting dirt, still do.

We had a screened in porch that was used as Norman's bedroom. He had felt the call to the ministry that summer and envisioned himself a mighty preacher someday. To help him reach that goal he held revivals under the rotting roof of that little lean to, and preached the fear of God into Diana and me as we faithfully came forward every night to get saved...again.

Daddy was working at the Purity Market on Mooney Boulevard and Mama had found a job as bookkeeper for a local family owned furniture store downtown near Main Street. Sometimes we would go visit her. They had a giant chair that you could get your picture taken in. We looked so small but the grins on our faces were a clear indication of just how much fun this little outing was.

Having been given a few coins, we would head over to Newberry's or Woolworth's for a treat from the candy counter. I always wanted a bag of popcorn but since it was popped in peanut oil and I was allergic to peanuts, I would settle for chocolate stars instead. Love them to this day, even though they are nearly impossible to find.

We were all settled in at the local Assembly of God church and were fast becoming some of the busiest members there. Sharon stepped into the role of church pianist while Mama volunteered to do just about everything else. We were happy, and even our parents seemed to be getting along a lot better. I think they were both relieved to finally be back home.

Danna-Carter chillin' in the big chair

The House On Frank Road

At church one Sunday, a man came up to my dad, and introduced himself as Marvin Corley. He was a quiet man with a very kind heart. He welcomed Daddy and told him that he had heard we were looking for a home to buy. Daddy told him this was true, and the two of them set up a meeting to check out the house across from the Corley's that had gone into foreclosure. All of this was taking place without my mother's knowledge. She was busy greeting everyone during their conversation. The next day Daddy showed up at Mom's work and handed her some keys, told her he had bought a house.

"You did what?" was my mother's response.

She was so mad at him but couldn't do much because she was in public and was known as a good Christian woman. Daddy further explained that after Brother Corley had told him about the place, he had met with the realtor and signed the papers. When she got off work that night, he took her over to see our new home. She was expecting the worst and instead was blessed with a house that became our family home for more than 40 years.

It had four bedrooms, double-car garage, built in kitchen, two bathrooms, fireplace, large backyard and all for the low price of $14,500.00! We loved that house. I remember writing a letter to my friend Elaine back in Santa Maria, telling her that the living room ceiling had stars in it (blown ceiling with gold glitter-very common back then). The house in Santa Maria had three bedrooms and one bath with a single-car garage and the rental house on Bohlinger had only two bedrooms with one bath so this was definitely a huge step up! Daddy was very proud of himself and Mom gave all the glory to God.

....

Dear Diary,

Boy, am I tired, but in a good way. We moved today. I think maybe Daddy got a raise or something because this house is a mansion! I'm gonna write a letter to Elaine and tell her all about it. Norman has his own room because he's a boy and Sharon gets one because she's in high school. Of course Mom and Dad have their own room (that sounds so grown up…Mom and Dad), so Danna and I are sharing—again. I don't really care. It's pretty big and it has a shelf up high that I can put all my horses on, and you should see the closet! We're trying to decide if we want to have our beds be bunk beds or be next to each other. I'm thinking we should start out with them on the floor and then we can divide it up, my half and her half.

I like the way this house smells.
I hope we get to live here a long time…
I wonder if Jimmy Wakefield misses me.

Okies and Holy Rollers

For us, life loped along at a different speed than in other places, like Bakersfield and Fresno. They were the big sophisticated cities. We were "small town," living just a couple decades this side of Steinbeck's *Grapes of Wrath*, and that's the truth. We weren't always able to afford the luxury of a television, but I remember once that Daddy rented one because the movie with Henry Fonda in it was going to be aired, that and the fact that "Little Grandma" was coming for a visit. Whoever she visited had to have a television because of her "stories." She watched "Love of Life" every weekday without fail.

I loved "Little Grandma." She smelled clean and made a big deal about always rinsing the dishes with hot water. She was a small woman in stature from the plateaus of Colorado, but she was as strong as they come. She was my grandpa Ennis's mother. This is important to note because I wouldn't want anyone to confuse her with my grandmother's mother who died in an asylum for the criminally insane.

Daddy wanted to make sure we all watched the movie because he said that was what it was like when he and his family moved to California from Oklahoma, and we needed to be grateful for what we had. They were spit on and some were put into camps. He said the only people who took them in were the Armenian farmers who knew all about persecution because of what the Turks had done to them. People called them "Okies," but they learned to wear it like a badge of courage. Rich, deep heartland music came out of those camps, and I would give anything to hear my daddy play the train on his harmonica one more time.

They had a name for us too, and I didn't know for certain if I was supposed to be ashamed or embarrassed by it until one day when I was walking to school with a girl from my neighborhood. I believe it was a Monday morning after one of our well-advertised revivals had been going on, and she could tell I was kind of sleepy from the late night before. She came right out and asked me if I was a "Holy Roller." There was something in the way she said it, something in the tone of her voice and the tilt of her head that made me long to be anywhere but there. I'd figured the question would come someday and I dreaded it more than you can imagine. I didn't want to answer it. It was the culmination of a lot of questions, most of them my own, that forced my throat to feel tight and my heart to beat faster. I found myself mumbling and stumbling over the words, finally just blurting out "yes." She laughed at me, and when she caught her breath continued firing questions.

"So what does that mean? Do people roll around on the floor and speak in tongues and stuff?"

Well, I suppose if I were real honest the answer would be, "yeah, sometimes." Not me, but just about everybody else I went to church with. We had Jericho marches where we would all hold hands and circle the auditorium, singing and praying, "Let the walls fall down!" We had revivals where men and women (but mostly women) would be slain in the Spirit, and the hankie monitors would cover the women's knees so they wouldn't be indecent or tempting or something, I don't know. You could pretty much set your watch to Sister Alvin scaring new folks to death with her message in tongues complete with gyrations and then her own interpretation along with poor grammar. There were the occasional gay traveling evangelists, a few cheating Cads in gospel quartets, judgmental gossips and…real people who were just trying to get it *right*.

"Sticks and stones may break my bones but words will never hurt me." I must have repeated that a thousand times or more a week. If only it were true. I can heal from a physical wound, a scrape, a bruise, a sprain. It's just scar tissue that's left, and even that tends to fade with time. What doesn't fade are the words. They lie dormant and then shout at you when you least expect it; or they subtly seep through your whole being until you are convinced of their validity.

I can't tell you what I said that day as we continued walking to school. I just remember feeling different, exposed, found out, all the doubts re-enforcing my wall. She never knew, because I never spoke them out loud. I learned early when to shut up and outwardly laugh along with the mockers.

I wish I knew then what I know now. I think I would have decked her...in Christian love.

....

Mail Order Christmas

I don't think we're gettin' any presents this year. Danna and I've been watchin' out the front window for a couple weeks now and still no delivery truck. Mama and Daddy told all us kids to look through the Spiegel Catalogue and circle the toys we want for Christmas. They're not gonna get us everything we circled, it's just to help them decide on a couple for each of us. They said they sent the order in a long time ago, and the presents should arrive any day but still nothin'.

Now it's Christmas Eve, and I don't think Mama and Daddy had the heart to tell us they didn't have money for presents this year. Danna and I were kinda sad at first, but we're okay now. Daddy brought home the biggest Christmas tree I've ever seen. Had to cut the top of it off just to get it through the door! We made a popcorn string and wrapped it around the tree. Had to make a few batches because we kept eating it.

All us kids decided that since there aren't any presents, we're gonna tiptoe into each other's rooms and find stuff to wrap up and put under the tree. Can't wait for Sharon to open her bottle of Jean Naté Danna and I swiped off her dresser. We're wrappin' it as pretty as we can, even hiding the tape on the backside of the paper. Danna's better at that kinda stuff than I am.

You know what? I think this just might be my favorite Christmas so far. Gotta go. We have to try to sneak into Norman's bedroom and that's not gonna be easy. He's guardin' it like a hawk. Is that hot chocolate I smell?

Merry Christmas to us!

The Old Folks Home

Frito boats and cold root beer floats tasted especially good on a hot day in the San Joaquin Valley. They were also one of the few perks for all who volunteered part of their Saturday to go sing at the "old folks home" with Othella Smith. She was one of the sweetest ladies in the whole church. She wore her grey hair pulled tight in a kind of Pentecostal French roll. She didn't wear makeup; didn't need to 'cause she had the glory of the Lord shining through her making her pretty. Her husband, Alonzo, was one of my dad's old friends he'd worked with at the Safeway store over in Dinuba. They weren't best friends mind you because Alonzo was a church goin' man.

Every once in awhile, when Sunday night church didn't go past what was already an extended service, they'd come over to the house for a little music and singing. The two men played harmonica and would nearly pass out when they did the endless "chuga-chuga" of the train while we cheered them on. Normally Sharon would play piano, but on these nights she'd bring out the accordion, and we'd all sing to the rhythm of the pull and squeeze of that pearly box with the clicky keys and buttons. Daddy always wanted her to play Beer Barrel Polka or the Boogie Woogie. Hymns usually won out though. It was still the "Lord's Day" after all.

Daddy and Alonzo would drink coffee in the yellow Melmac cups and swap stories of days and times I knew nothing about. They were both Okies who had come out to California—the "Land of Milk and Honey"—during the Dust Bowl. They had seen things they never wanted their own children to see. They would reminisce, and we would make fun of their accents that became more pronounced as the evening wore on.

When conversation waned, and things started to wind down, Othella would ask who all was going with her to the "home" on Saturday.

"Sharon, why don't you bring the accordion and you and your sisters can sing? They just love it when you young people come out."

I didn't mind the singing part. I just hoped my brother wouldn't be invited to come as well; to him that was a clear-cut invitation to preach. Then we'd be there all day and wouldn't even get to go to the drive-in, which begs the question, why were we going?

All week long I'd dread seeing Othella pull up out front in her big white sedan after her standing Saturday hair appointment. We'd wait for her to honk the horn, which was the signal to see who could get out there first and claim their seat by the window. Most cars didn't have air conditioning, and the plastic seat covers made it impossible to stay cool. We had to be careful not to roll the windows down too far or the money spent at the beauty parlor would be a total waste, which was hard to believe seeing how much hair spray was dedicated to her doo.

On the way to the "old folks home" I'd go back and forth between dreaming of drive-in treats and chastising myself for tainting this sacrifice of service to these poor forgotten people. They were somebody's grandma and grandpa, and even though most of them couldn't remember their own name, somebody knew and *somebody* left them out there in the stench and the crowded dark rooms.

The old men weren't always covered up and they'd try to chase after us in their wheelchairs. It wasn't just the old men who were rowdy though. One time a lady got mad at her roommate who happened to be pointing her finger just a little too close. In a move that rivaled the speed of Mohammed Ali in his prime, she grabbed it and bit it off! I promise, I'm not making that up. I became very protective of my digits, and used every bit of discernment available when it came to shaking their hands. It was the county home, and they were short staffed, so it was difficult at best to meet all of the needs, one of which was safety.

Needless to say, sometimes the hollow stares of the forgotten, and the cruel insanity of a body outliving its mind was so overwhelming, that even the visit to the drive-in afterwards didn't make it worth it. I used to wonder what made Othella come back faithfully every Saturday. She had a sweet soothing voice, almost childlike, and every one of those residents loved her. She'd hug them, kiss them on top of their heads, always taking time to sit and pray with them. Church bulletins and the Evangel Magazine were placed in their old wrinkled and arthritic hands that most of their lives had stayed busy with tending children or making a living for their families that were now a mere vapor of a memory. She would just laugh off the advances of the old men in their wheelchairs who had long passed the ability to filter out right from wrong, and there was so much that was wrong.

Sharon would play "The Old Rugged Cross" and "What a Friend We Have in Jesus" on the accordion while Diana and I would join her and Othella, adding our special sister harmonies. Sometimes the stone faces would look back with slight smiles of recognition, and their mouths would sing the words of another time. They were young once…just like me.

The drive back to town was filled with a kind of relief expressing itself in laughter. We'd compare stories of what went on while we were there, being careful to never sound too disrespectful. By the time we arrived at the drive-in our hearts and our stomachs felt worthy of the treat to come.

For as many things that were there to dread until the next Saturday, there were still other moments that pressed my heart to give a little more. I never regretted being a part of Othella Smith's quiet, invisible ministry, but could never escape those images forever pressed in my memory.

. . . .

Brother Hinkey's Niece

Brother Hinkey's niece is here visiting for the summer. She's supposed to be only a couple years older than me, but I think somebody's tellin' a fib. Lately she's been staying with her grandma and grandpa a few blocks over from the church, on account of she's troubled and all. Mama wanted me to be nice to her, said she needed a good little Christian friend this summer, so I went to spend the night with her.

She reminds me of my cousin Shirley who lives in Covina and writes dirty words on the outside of her letters to Diana and me. Mama's prayin' she gets saved, but we're not holdin' out much hope. Lord knows a soul has to be willing.

But back to the new girl…she's kinda wild. Talks about things good girls don't say out loud, things that would make Mama wash your mouth out with soap, and while you'd be spittin' Lava bubbles she'd be busy tellin' Jesus all about your sins. Cleanliness is next to Godliness you know, and she's not talkin' about that little spot behind your ears either. Anyway, the girl told me she didn't want to stay at her Aunt and Uncle's house anymore.

"Why not?" I said, "They actually live in a nicer house on the good side of town."

She smiled in a way that made me nervous and then told me she left because her Uncle, Brother Hinkey, peeks through the bathroom door when she takes a shower and watches her, and he's a Deacon. Ewww!

After listenin' to her talk, and layin' there in that little stuffy house that smelled like old people, I wanted the sun to hurry up and rise in the worst way so Mama could come get me. The whole thing was givin' me the creeps. Well, the girl must've read my mind cuz right around 4 a.m. she asked if I was awake. I quickly said yes, and then she came up with a plan for us to sneak out and walk down Goshen Avenue to my house, which is about four miles or so. I was kinda scared, but I really wanted to go home.

We arrived safe and sound, but later Mama said Jesus must've sent his Guardian Angels to protect us from the farm workers who like to pick up little girls walkin' in shorts down dark roads in the wee hours. I'm grounded and can't hang out with Brother Hinkey's niece anymore, which in my opinion, is well worth the punishment.

A Slice of the Good Life

Tick...tick...tick...was it just my imagination or was time actually slowing down, seconds taking a full minute each? At this rate 3:00 p.m. was never going to get here. Fridays always felt like that, especially this Friday. Diana and I had big plans for the weekend. Our best friends Jeanne and Janie, who were twins, had invited us out to the family farm to spend the night, which all four of us knew would turn into two nights, culminating in a very lively social Sunday. Escape was only a few minutes away. 10, 9, 8, c'mon already! 4, 3, 2, 1, RRRRR-IIIIING!!! Finally, freedom! I gathered up my papers and books and headed for the door.

"Carolyn?"

Uh-Oh, here we go. What now?

"May I speak with you a moment?"

No, Mrs. Purtle, you may not speak with me for a moment. School is officially done for the week, and I have places to go. I know my rights! Of course this is NOT how I responded. Gathering as much restraint and courage as I could muster, I slowly stood up and walked toward her desk. I was dreading whatever it was she had to say to me, convinced it would have something to do with not applying myself.

Look her in the eye, look her in the eye, not over her shoulder but in the eye, otherwise she's going to think you're guilty of something. Remember, you don't *have* to be shy.

"Carolyn, I want you to know that as your teacher I appreciate the extra effort you have exhibited in recent weeks. Turning in written assignments on time and cleaning up your kitchen station after burning the cookie sheets and nearly catching the whole kitchen on fire."

Gulp.

"Your hard work and eagerness to learn have not gone unnoticed, but now we've come to an important cross-roads. I'm looking at your sewing assignment, which is a *simple* kitchen apron and wondering. Did you understand the task? Was it too difficult for you? I'm asking because *this*, (holding up my checkered masterpiece) doesn't look much like an apron."

Concentrate, steeeeady, look her in the eye and breathe...

"Well, Mrs. Purtle, I understand what you've been trying to teach me, I mean I hear it in my head, it's just when I actually start sewing it comes out looking like...well, like that. I'll do it over if you want and maybe if I just try harder, you know, apply myself?" tick, tick, tick...3:05.

"As you know, this apron assignment counts for half of your grade, one half cooking the other half sewing. Now, with the cooking you just barely scraped by, but the sewing, well, let's just get to the point: *this* is not an apron. It is my job to make sure that all young ladies graduate from Green Acres Junior High School with the skills to become a good homemaker. In all my years of teaching I have never failed anyone."

Here it comes.

"And I'm not going to let you be a blemish on my record. Do you understand what I'm saying?"

"Uhhhh, you want me to try again?"

"Oh Carolyn, if I thought for one minute that would work, you would of course be given another chance. However, I have come to the conclusion that there are exceptions to the rules. Rarely, mind you, but then again I believe you to be quite rare. The school year is rapidly coming to a close, and it has become clear to me that perhaps your gifts and talents lay in another area, any area other than cooking or sewing. It is not my desire to keep you from going on to high school, especially since you are giving one of the speeches at the eighth grade graduation ceremonies, nor do I desire to have you repeat the last quarter in summer school. So with that in mind, I am going to offer you a deal. I will finish your apron and you will promise to keep this little arrangement strictly between the two of us. So what do you say, do we have a deal?"

Tick,Tick, TICK!

"Absolutely, Mrs. Purtle. Thank you so much. Someday maybe I'll bake something wonderful for you or sew a special apron!"

"I doubt that very much but appreciate the sentiment. I hear you have musical talent. Perhaps you'll be able to make a living doing that, although show people are usually broke. Oh well, I've done my best. Now run along and don't forget our deal!"

"I won't forget Mrs. Purtle and thank you so much!"

I took off out the door as fast as my little legs would carry me. Diana was going to be madder than a hornet at me for being late. I had to be careful not to run or the hall monitor would nail me for sure. Walking at a pace faster than most runners sprint, I rounded the corner just in time to see the big white sedan sweep up to the curb in a fashion that could only be described as dramatic.

Honk!!!!!

"There you are girls. Hop in and we'll go pick up Jeanne and Janie from school. Sorry I'm a little late, some of the cows got out, and I had to help Jim put them back."

The face behind the wheel belonged to the prettiest lady I had ever known. She always wore bright red lipstick and had a smile that coaxed the sun out even on the dreariest days. She seemed almost too young to be a mom even though she was only a few years younger than my own mother. Where life and marriage had aged Mama, life and marriage agreed with the twins' mom "Frances." So much in fact that at times she seemed ageless. Don't get me wrong, she was definitely the parent, she just had a way about her that was playful, but it all still felt safe.

Not like Daddy, who would get us all riled up, laughing and carrying on, and then explode when we didn't calm down in time. Kind of made us careful about laughing sometimes, not being sure where it would lead. Lately there had been a lot of that uncertainty hovering around our house. Junior highers have enough difficulty figuring out their own baffling behavior much less the behavior of unstable adults, particularly if those adults are their parents.

A weekend at the farm was just what Diana and I desperately needed. We drank up every moment of "normal" the Ming family offered without their even knowing they were offering anything unusual.

One very vivid memory was an almost daily occurrence between Jim and Frances. The farm's kitchen was at the back of the house and had a swinging door that led to the mudroom, which led to the outside door, which stood between the milking barn and the cows, hundreds and hundreds of cows. Did I mention it was a dairy farm? P! U! Oddly enough, we eventually got used to the smell and hardly noticed it anymore. Every evening, when the milking was done and it was time for dinner, we sat at the table anxiously awaiting the arrival of the twins' dad.

He was a big man, kind of rough around the edges. He liked to smoke and drink a bit, but was madly in love with his wife, and loved the children she had given him, in his own gruff way. We could hear him as he stomped up to the back door shaking loose the manure that clung to his big heavy, rubber boots.

Any minute the next door would swing open and standing there with her eyes closed, chin lifted and her red lips puckered, would be Frances, welcoming him home with a playful greeting as all of us watched, suppressing giggles. He never let us down. With a Clark Gable-ish performance, he would crash through the doorway feigning surprise and then grab Frances, planting a giant kiss for our benefit and of course his.

Personally, I was kind of afraid of him, but I felt that way about most men. Not surprising really, just one of the many side effects or issues of transference from the disconnected relationship with my own father. But something kept telling me that if Frances wasn't afraid of him and loved him, maybe he wasn't so scary after all, at least not to the people he loved. Janie, who was *my* friend, chose to stay out of his way, which was fine with me.

Janie and I weren't exactly fearless, but we were certainly a *lot* braver than Diana and Jeanne. They saw ghosts and prowlers around every corner and the "out in the country" setting had limitless possibilities for mischief. One of our favorite past times when we spent the night and their parents were out, was to get Jeanne so scared she would pee her pants. Then we would laugh so hard she would pee them again. It didn't take much: a puzzling look, parting the curtain and then looking at each other with eyes wide open, speaking in breathless tones, saying:

"I think something's out there."

"Where?" She would answer with fear building in her voice.

Janie would squint out the window and point, "There, by the barn."

"It's probably a cow." That's what I would say. Then Janie would peek out again and say something like:

"Cows have four legs not two, and whatever it is, it's walking toward the back door and it's big! Wait! I don't remember if I locked it the last time we went out to fill the milk pitcher!"

That's all it took. Diana and Jeanne would either scramble to lock the back door or run into the bedroom and hide, while Janie and I would fall over laughing or keep the ruse going.

I felt so close to Janie. It was like we were sisters. Growing up I didn't have a lot of outside friends. It was easier that way. I didn't have to explain things. Diana was my *best* friend, so much so that we often shared the same friends as children. When the twins came into our lives it couldn't have been more perfect because we each had our own friend, but we still got to be together.

The four of us were inseparable. We went to church camp together, had crushes on the same boys, and often after church enjoyed Sunday dinner at their grandma and grandpa Grishom's house (Frances' parents) who lived next door to them on the farm. One of those meals is especially memorable. I had never had lamb before and after taking the first bite I asked what kind of roast it was. Grandma Grishom, with her dentures clacking said "Why, it's lamb dear."

I don't know why, but it sort of creeped me out. I kept wondering if perhaps we might be dining on the girls' 4-H project. I could never be sure but Jeanne and Janie did have a funny gleam in their eyes. I've never developed a taste for lamb.

Their grandfather on their dad's side was a well-known traveling evangelist who preached at our church from time to time. He was a big man, not fat, but like an ex-football player big. He'd do just about anything to make his point. I remember one time in the middle of his sermon he got down and rolled around on the platform. He said, "Gettin' saved is as easy as fallin' off a log just not as dangerous." That picture will forever be in my brain. Jeanne and Janie were mortified, but the rest of us laughed for months about it.

Like most of our peers we had special games that would get us through the long Pentecostal services. I remember we would sit in the pews and play "hymnal talking" which is taking the hymnal, looking for a title of a song, passing it to someone who would then look for another title in answer to the first, and pass it back and forth.

For example, Janie would open the hymnal to say...page 251. She would whisper in my ear or write on the bulletin that this is what my brother Norman would say to his girlfriend. The title would be "Let the Lower Lights Be Burning." I would then pass it back opened to page 268 "In the Garden" and she would pass it to me opened to page 495 with the title "Meet Me There." Put it all together and it would read; "Let the lower lights be burning in the garden, meet me there." We would try our best to stifle our giggles but not always successfully, especially if we got the whole pew involved. We were "called down" more than once from the pulpit by her grandfather, the honorable Brother Thomas Ming, and that was not pleasant.

Honestly, our church was a great place to grow up. We were there so much it felt like our second home. Most of the time it felt safe in the sense that it was familiar, and the friends I had from church didn't require an explanation of our Pentecostal beliefs. There was always an undercurrent though. The rules were clear and to choose to disobey could mean damnation. Your relationship with Christ was measurable because it was based on performance. Obey the rules, go to Heaven; disobey and go to Hell. Pretty simple. So there was a whole congregation of people outwardly obeying and judging, making up new rules that fit the times and the church culture.

One of those rules was that women were not to draw attention to themselves by wearing make-up. This was based on their interpretation of the passage in the book of 1st Peter, chapter 3, that talks about a woman's beauty not being an outer adornment of braided hair and gold jewelry but a gentle and quiet spirit. Some of the meanest women I knew had naked faces and wore their hair up tight. Times were changing, at least for the teenagers, and we wore make-up, but that particular rule was still in place for the *Godly* women in the church.

Frances came from a strong Pentecostal family as well as her husband Jim. But Jim rebelled, and Frances chose to live her love for Christ outside the confines of the church. She was an accomplished church pianist, and with some urging by my sister and the rest of us volunteered to play once for Sunday night service. We all sat in the pew and were so proud to see her on the platform, with her smile and her beautiful red lipstick. That was her first and last night playing piano for the church. She was told either the lipstick went or she did. She did.

. . . .

Under the Covers With Wolfman Jack

I had so much fun this weekend! Frances picked Diana and me up at school on Friday so we could spend the night with Jeanne and Janie. She made our favorite chocolate cake and it tasted so good with the fresh milk. Janie and I try to hide when it's time to go out and fill the pitcher but that doesn't always work. The big stainless steel lid on the milk vat is heavy so I hold it up while Janie fills the pitcher. We played all day Saturday and Jim let us take the pick-up on the back roads to the neighbor's farm. Janie didn't grind the gears once. It wasn't like it was her first time or anything. I can't wait to drive. Just a few more years and I can get my permit. We were having so much fun that Mom agreed to let us stay one more night if we all promised to be at church on time Sunday morning. Frances assured her we would be there all scrubbed up and ready to go.

Have you ever heard of Wolfman Jack? Oh my gosh, he's so groovy and he sounds exactly like a wolf-man. I'm not kidding. He howls and everything. He plays music all night long on this radio station that goes all over the world I think. Last night, after going to bed, Janie and I pretended to be asleep and then at midnight we got out her transistor radio and tuned in. I guess it was louder than we thought because Frances told us to turn it off and go to sleep. We were going to have to get up early to be at church on time. Besides, she didn't think Sister Walker would approve of me listening to anything the Wolfman might have to say or play. So we turned it off and went to sleep…well not exactly sleep. We waited for a while and then got under the covers with a flashlight and barely turned up the volume. It was so fun listening to the music. Wolfman Jack is soooooo Boss!

When Forgiveness Asks

Too Much

Life went on and so did we, but the church's shun of Frances was a deposit in my questioning account. What did lipstick have to do with knowing or loving Jesus? If Frances was offended, she never dwelt on it or invested her anger in us. She continued to live out her faith by taking in foster babies, helping her neighbors, working in her children's school, loving her husband, children and Diana and me. Her example became a very real part of my own choices for marriage and family.

The twins had two other sisters. The youngest was Jimmy Lynn who we called "Squeaky," and the oldest was Joanie and she was hot! She was dating one of the cutest guys from church, aside from my brother, and they had become quite an item. Her boyfriend's sister, who was engaged to be married, was having her bridal shower and Joanie convinced her mom to go with her. These people just might be her future in-laws someday, you never know.

The night was clear as a bell as they drove through the country with the smell of sweet fresh alfalfa scenting the air that was blowing through the vents on the dashboard. They were laughing and talking about the events of the previous couple of hours when they entered the two-way stop intersection a half-a-mile from their house. They were on Blackstone, which had the right of way and no stop sign. That stretch of road and intersection was as familiar to them as the long tree-lined driveway that led to their farm. They had traveled up and down it in every possible condition including the dense and deadly Tule fog and never thought twice.

In a split second the universe hiccupped and from out of nowhere, with no warning, a car appeared traveling at a very high rate of speed. The driver, a local sports writer who was drunk, never observed his stop sign and ran right into them, t-boning their car. In that moment, life forever changed for all of us including the man in the other car. If only Frances and Joanie had stayed a little longer at the shower, or perhaps left a few seconds earlier, they would all have escaped this destiny. But "if onlys" are just that, if only...

I don't remember the call or too many of the details; it's a foggy memory. We were told they had been transported to the hospital in Tulare with multiple serious injuries, and Frances was in critical condition.

I think our older sister Sharon drove us out to the farm to be with the girls. Jim was at the hospital when we walked through the door of what had become our preferred home. A place that just a day before was so safe and filled with beautiful memories felt foreign and un-real. I think we cried a little but not a lot. We prayed and hoped that everything would be okay. Surely God would heal Frances and Joanie. Wouldn't He? We waited and waited and then waited some more.

We heard the car pull into the long driveway, stop, ignition turn off, car door open, close and then the slow, heavy steps of their father walking to the front door. Didn't seem right, him coming through the front door. He didn't look as big as he did before. He was kind of slumped over. His voice was gruff and his eyes were red. He called the girls to come sit down which they did, quietly, all of them staring at their dad, while we sat motionless in the front bedroom, willing ourselves not to make a sound. Even our breathing sounded too loud.

We listened as he told them that their mother's injuries were severe and even though the doctors did everything they could they weren't able to save her. It was impossible to grasp what he was saying, and he must have sensed the shock of disbelief and confusion. Speaking in a voice that was unlike anything they had ever heard he said the words no one wanted to believe, their mother was dead.

Frances wasn't the only one who died that day...so did Jim. Oh, he still milked cows, walked around, breathed oxygen into his lungs and nicotine into his bloodstream, but the real Jim was dead. It was one of the most frightening and sad things I've ever witnessed in my life and have chosen not to revisit until now. I don't know how to articulate the depth of that loss. I struggle with the words, wanting to feel the weight as they sit on the page in front of me. I know there are some places I will never go...death requires too much.

For some reason we were late the day of the funeral. Daddy was driving, and we wanted him to go faster because Janie and Jeanne had asked us to sit with them in the family section. As we approached the deadly intersection, Daddy whipped around and told us to shut up or we would cause him to make a mistake in his driving and we would all end up dead like our beloved Frances! His words were fast and brutal. I could feel their steel grip on my heart. I bit the inside of my mouth and stared straight ahead, refusing to give into the urge to scream or cry. I truly opened the door to hate in that moment. But I chose to save the emotion for another time. Someday...someday I would get out of here.

We arrived just in time to see the family leaving the church and walking toward the funeral car. We had missed the service. They wanted us to ride with them to the cemetery but Mama said no.

I can't pull up any pictures in my head of that day. Maybe that's just fine. But I do remember a little about how I felt. Hate is a powerful motivator that calls itself your partner. Problem is, it refuses to play well with others or agree to be managed. That night in our bedroom at home I told Diana that I *hated* Rick Stump, then I pulled the covers up around my face and went to sleep.

In the weeks that followed, Mama told us we needed to forgive him. God was punishing him. He was sentenced to a life in a wheel chair as a paraplegic, but God had mercifully saved his soul and he had become a Christian. I don't honestly know if I ever consciously forgave him. I just chose to bury his existence and not think about him again.

We remained friends, Jeanne, Janie, Diana and I, but there was no going back. They moved into the neighboring town of Tulare, and became their own parents as Jim moved from one relationship to another. Frances had been the anchor. Frances had been the glue. Now she was gone and Jim was lost. All the unspoken things that had caused him to run from God in the first place joined up with this senseless tragedy and cemented his bitterness toward church people and God.

Mom didn't want us hanging out with them anymore because of what we all might be tempted to do; after all, I drank my first beer in that house. Who knows what else I might get in to? Meanwhile, the very same women in the church who had judged their mother so harshly for wearing lipstick now all lined up to be the righteous surrogate mother figure in their lives. Did they think we all had amnesia? There were also precious other women who did their best to love as sacrificially as the girls would allow. Our close friendship lasted for about another year, and then we grew apart in High school.

We've had long lapses of connection but have managed to maintain a thread over these many years. Diana is better at relationships than I am. She and Jeanne still talk. Janie and I were both the shy ones and went inward with our feelings. After she got married we talked back and forth, and when she gave birth to her little girl asked me to be her godmother. I accepted this honor and then never really kept a relationship with her. I failed my friend and I'm sorry. Recently we met up again. We laughed and ate lunch together over in Morro Bay with Joanie and Diana. Joanie survived her injuries and eventually became the charge nurse at the hospital in town. She has a compassion born out of her own experience that has made her an exceptional nurse.

I miss Frances. Back then I missed her more than I ever let anyone know. She represented everything that was good to me. It's easy to assign almost saintly qualities to a person after they've died, but when I say "good" it means something different. She was real, not perfect or without fault, but genuine, and she loved me. I sometimes allow myself to remember, and I wonder what she would think about all of us now?

Jim re-united with Frances a few years back. Brain cancer finished his sojourn on earth. It gives me peace to know they are together, and I suppose opens the door for forgiveness.

....

I should have forgiven you earlier. Any one of my insane choices could have put me in your shoes, but for reasons I can't explain except for the providence of God, they didn't. Your choice that night had devastating consequences for so many, not the least of which was yourself. Someday, I believe we'll understand, but now, for what it's worth...

I forgive you, Rick Stump.

Hocky

Not to be confused with Hockey
Tee, hee, hee, giggle, giggle

Okay...it's time for a disclaimer. I've thought long and hard as to whether or not I should include this next bit of family trivia. Some things are better received in a "live" situation. Like Mama and Daddy's living room. But Mom and Daddy are in Heaven, rolling their eyes as we speak, and some trucker and his wife are sitting in our old living room. My dad's "Okie" (I mean that in the best possible way) accent and my mom's understandable exasperation doesn't always transfer well to the written page. Wisdom is telling me to "Sit up and pay attention!" Wisdom, or Brother Martin, I don't know whose voice is in my head.

I just passed my two-glass limit of red wine, Lord help us, and the giggles are trumping the solid, steady, sound voice of reason. See, if this thing goes badly we can just blame it on the evil Cabernet. Now to all of my sweet, conservative, Christian friends who after reading this, have just lit up the lines of prayer chains all over the country, take a moment and breathe. If you find this offensive, I'd like to suggest that you simply skip this chapter and go to the next. *Or...you could join me in a glass of wine and giggle too?* I'll try harder a few pages further since I am still under the yoke of wanting everyone's love and approval all the time. It's a disease really. One that the much loved Presbyterian theologian Jack Miller aptly labeled as being an "Approval Suck."

As I have alluded to earlier, my dad and his brothers of Oklahoman descent assigned unique names to rather ordinary things, which is true of most families. If a woman was pregnant she was "PG," a bra was called a "Frog Harness," and for many years I believed I was the descendent of a valiant Native American called "Big Chief, Squat-n-dropit!" I think you know where I'm going with this. I'm just going to come right out and say it...my dad assigned the word "hocky" to shit.

I grew up my entire life thinking that the real name for shit was hocky. Now, we lived in a small central California town. We had football, baseball, basketball, swimming and even tennis. But we were never exposed to games on the ice. So you can imagine our horror and confusion when my sister was invited to go to L.A. with a friend and attend a *hockey* game. What? This warranted *serious* investigation. When we were told that it was a game that was played on the ice by skaters who used *hockey* sticks to chase a little *hockey* puck all around the rink... well, it was too much to take in. Why would grown men on skates, wearing lots of padding bat frozen shit back and forth trying to get it in the net and then FIGHT over it!!!!

Now, let me ease your mind, we are all much more evolved and educated now about the fine game of Hockey. However, I still giggle like a goofy little kid when I say the word and I have never developed an enthusiasm for the game...shocker!!

Lost Saving the Lost

Looking into the face of a man who was old enough to be my grandfather made me stumble a bit on my well-rehearsed *witnessing* speech. In the middle of asking him if he died today did he think he would go to heaven or hell, he interrupted me and asked how old I was. They told me this might happen but not to be intimidated. This was the Lord's work after all, and we should expect opposition. I could feel the dry lump in my throat as I tried to swallow all my presumption and responded to his inquiry in my most authoritative voice.

"Fifteen," I said, "but the Bible says not to despise my youth. Truth is truth no matter how old you may be."

"Uh-huh," was his reply as he slowly closed the door.

"Wait! Don't you wanna know how to get to heaven?"

He paused and then opened the screen just enough so that he could look me in the eyes with nothing between us.

"Fifteen ...I'll make ya a deal. Come back in twenty years, and if you still believe all this shit, *then* we'll talk." And with that he successfully closed the door before I could raise any more objections about where his eternal address may be.

It was 1969, the summer between my freshmen and sophomore year at Redwood High School. We were still attending the Assembly of God church on the north side of town, and I was feeling restless. I just couldn't see myself being trapped at home for the next few months. I wasn't driving yet, and I was too old to go swimming in the Marchbank's above ground Doughboy pool.

Life had started opening up for me, and staying home felt like a giant step backward in my forward momentum. I wanted to get out there and experience different places, different people, different *anything*, for cryin' out loud! I moped, I sighed, I prayed and then waited with the patience and attention span of a gnat, which we all know is signatory to youth. I needed a change of scenery in a desperate way, and I needed it right then!

I didn't have to wait long. The answer came while sitting in church one hot, stuffy Sunday morning listening to a group of visiting youth leaders speak about a summer program for teens. It was a mission organization that encouraged young people to volunteer for their summer to witness and bring the lost to Jesus. They would travel up and down the state of California in a bus, sleeping in local church people's homes that would put them up for the night and provide a sack lunch for the following day.

Even though there were informational gaps in the earnest presentation, their sincerity more than made up for it. They actually prided themselves in not having every day's agenda completely mapped out. After all, "We walk by faith, not by sight, can I get an Amen?" The prevailing thought was, if they were too organized and plan driven, they might quench the powerful leading of the Spirit. Like the Israelites preparing to go into the Promised Land, we needed to rely on *daily* bread and direction, a cloud by day and fire by night. It was all persuasively wrapped in spiritual verbiage, designed on some level to manipulate but for a cause with eternal implications that would forgive such tactics.

I swallowed every bit of it, hook, line and sinker. My prayers had been answered! It all sounded so exciting and mysterious, and as if that weren't enough the next part really got my attention. They would eventually end up in San Francisco, Haight-Ashbury, Golden Gate Park and Sausalito!! I could just hear Rod McKuen...

"Do you know my friend the sea? He watches everything we do..."

Oh man, I immediately felt the "call." I'll go door to door, sing on the street corners, give a testimony, WHATEVER! Just choose me! Choose me!

There was a slight catch, though. You had to raise your own support, which is a "churchy" way of saying money, and the team was leaving in a couple of days. I was flat broke. No income built up from singing at funerals and weddings, and my babysitting skills were not exactly confidence producing for parents. There was rarely extra money in the family budget for this kind of thing, and even if there had been Daddy wouldn't exactly be standing there with a check in his hand. No way!

So, I did the only thing I could, I went to Mama and pleaded my case with a conviction that rivaled Oral Roberts. I told her I felt the call of God, and it was a *powerful* call. My presentation was so persuasive that by the time I was finished I could have wiped my tears with one of her own hankies and sold it back to her for an easy profit. My mother had a weakness for the mystical possibilities of the all-powerful call, and I knew it. Not surprisingly her response was one of complete support and absolute certainty that one way or another God would provide. I would be on that bus when it left. After all, scripture says, "Where two or more are gathered in my name, I'm there and will give them anything they ask for." Loose quote, I know.

I don't remember who anteed up (not my parents) but some bene-factor in our church heard God tell them that Carolyn Walker needed to go on the summer missions trip and forked over the *support*. Within two days I was waving good-bye to family and friends, from my seat on the old church bus that was not blessed with air conditioning. I wasn't complaining though. I was making my *own* memory. Not my brother's or sister's memory but mine.

Our first stop was Lamont, California right outside Bakersfield. I think there are vineyards there now, but back then it was farm workers and rednecks. Since I played a little guitar and sang, I was afforded op-portunities the others weren't given, like hanging out in a well-lit area preparing for music and testimony time, while other members of the team made a risky sweep of the shadowy park looking for the lost.

However, at the end of the night there was no preferential treat-ment extended. I remember all of the girls sleeping in a house across the street from where we had just shared embellished testimonies of our scant few years on this planet. Our male counterparts were in the house next door. In the wee hours of the morning we woke up to loud banging and the door handle being shaken like a 6.8 on the Richter scale. Some very drunk *would be converts*, left over from the park, were trying to break in to do God knows what.

One thing was for sure; they weren't looking to get saved. The guys heard them and chased them off. It was scary, and that was just the first night. The next night I was farmed out to a family who attended the lo-cal church that we were headquartering out of in Modesto. If I thought the park from the night before was scary…well let's just say I slept fully clothed, clutching my Bible, and keeping the lamp within arms reach.

By the time I was dropped off the next morning, moldy sack lunch in hand, I had devised a mysterious illness that would show up in times of need. There was no way I was going to ingest the food packed inside that bag by hands that had not been washed in who knows how long, even if it had been prayed over. So with the acting skills reminiscent of a young Judy Garland, I convinced our zealous leader that I really couldn't eat these special provisions because of a severe upset stomach. He however, was welcome to partake. I had to be careful with this manifestation of survivor's instinct and not use it too much or I'd be "outed" for the coward I was beginning to believe I was.

Things were looking up though. We had finished our mission in the San Joaquin Valley and were finally headed for San Francisco. I was so excited as our bus gasped and rattled its way into the famous city by the sea. I was captivated by the rows of houses and the historical charm that promised stories of great novels, windows inviting me to taste and see true enlightenment for myself. A generation of flower children and hippies had found their way to this paradise by any means possible. Old VW Vans were covered with vividly painted flowers and peace signs. There was a seductive draw of abandon that was not wasted on my very green and impressionable mind, and I began to wonder…was I on the wrong bus?

As I was quietly pondering the possibilities, the old diesel engine sputtered to a stop and sighed almost human-like. The famous San Francisco hills had taken their toll, and it needed a well-deserved rest. Fortunately this happened by divine appointment at our next stop in the middle of skid row. It was the home of a very passionate street ministry. These men and women had been delivered from a life of drugs and prison, and were now exposing the dark side of the "Free Love" movement's call. They were committed to investing their lives to a community that was genuinely in desperate need of saving.

As I gathered my things and stood out on the sidewalk, a bone chilling cold covered me like the fog that this city was so well known for. I was entering something much bigger and more demanding than I was prepared to handle at fifteen. All my loopy romanticizing of this adventure quickly sobered up with the first introduction of the faces and worn out bodies around me. Some had been clean for a few years, while others a few months or even weeks. I've said before that I was born knowing fear. But this was different; this was unfamiliar fear. This was *street* fear.

Wide-eyed and completely alert, I stepped over the threshold and adjusted my vision to the dim light of the old building. I was quickly introduced to the leader of this city's ministry to runaways, drug addicts and those who had simply lost their way. He was probably in his thirties even though he looked older. I could tell he knew first hand all about the streets. I don't remember his name, but I do remember his heart. His eyes were dark and he looked tired, but even the weariness could not dim his compassion. He invited me to sing for a radio broadcast they were involved with. I felt shaky and unsteady as I agreed to follow him into a room that was set-up with a mic.

Some of the stories that came out of the mouths of the recovering free love, flower children, were compelling and at times deeply disturbing, to say the least. Many were just like me and not much older than me either. They spoke of addictions that lead to bondage and brutality, the exact opposite of what the culture right outside the door was selling. How could this happen to such normal people from normal families? I found myself singing with a depth of connection that was beyond my years. I was telling their story, and this was serious business.

Once the bus recovered enough to take up the challenge of the formidable city hills we climbed aboard, exhausted and quiet, wondering where this journey would take us next. As poor judgment and lack of planning would have it, we ended up in a part of Fillmore that was famous for being home to the Black Panthers. This was not exactly a safe place to land for a bunch of small town white kids looking to save souls they knew nothing about, in a community they had no business entering, no matter how sincere their hearts may have been.

For the next few days we slept in a large church that had outlived its original parishioners, and whose descendents and their families had long since moved to suburbs far, far away. Apart from being a place of worship on Sunday mornings for the hearty few that remained, it also served as the residence for a female missionary from Germany by the name of Hannah. That was peculiar to me. I thought missionaries only came from congregations in the United States and went to Africa or South America. I mean this was San Francisco, California U.S.A. thank you very much!

She wasn't an easy person to like, and it wasn't just because of her obvious disdain for our American hedonistic youth culture or the disconnects from her limited grasp of the English language either. She made no excuses for the fact that she considered herself to be spiritually superior, which she probably was, if such a thing exists, and we made no apologies for being young and impudent. Soon inside jokes were being passed around in loud whispers like children playing "Telephone" at a weekend sleepover. Much to my shame, at times I laughed right along with their snide observations, which served as a sort of emotional release. It felt good to laugh even if it was at someone else's expense. She made sandwiches that were dry and barely edible, but she passed them out with holy conviction, faithfully fulfilling the requirements of Servanthood.

Barely edible sandwiches were one thing, but our geographic location was something else. When driving through the neighborhood, it was crystal clear the people did not want us there. They would shout at the bus, using their favorite finger to let us know "Whitey" was not welcome. I'd never been exposed first hand to this kind of racial division. It was my father's battle, not mine.

The public schools I attended were very much multicultural, and in the height of the late 60s, we had teachers dedicated to putting an end to racism. I was proud to be a recipient of this education and was blessed with friendships that represented the beauty of diversity without even trying. Growing up in the San Joaquin Valley, it wasn't unusual to be Caucasian and the minority in certain situations. Over the years many people, from Hispanic migrant workers to Armenians to Portuguese families, had settled in this very large agricultural area. But now, I was seeing and experiencing hatred directed at me, a stranger, simply because of the color of *my* skin.

The boys would form two lines facing each other while the girls ran the gauntlet between them from the bus to the door of the church. Once inside the doors were bolted shut. This was NOT what I signed up for, and by now the Marchbank's pool was looking pretty good. Shoot, at that point, I was even willing to agree to hone my babysitting skills, go home and be a kid for the summer. Barring some miracle though, that wasn't going to happen for a while, so I knew I had better get busy and figure out a way to hunker down and get through this.

Our assignment for the next day was to walk through Haight-Ashbury and hand out tracts. We were to try to engage people in discussion about their souls. By now it was decided that no one, especially girls, were to go off on their own. After running between the guy's familiar double-file path to the bus, and arriving at our destination, we partnered up and set off to once again try and save the world. Processing the events of the day and night before had cranked up the volume for my survival meter. I closed my eyes and asked God to keep me safe and show me what He wanted me to do. I also said the "rapture" might not be such a bad idea for today's events if He was taking suggestions.

While blending in with all the other tourists on the street, I overheard a shopkeeper giving a chilling account of an event that had happened the day before. A man and his wife from the Midwest were walking down the street, just like we were, when a kid having a bad acid trip walked up and shot them in the middle of the day. He murdered them in cold blood. How's that for peace and love? People beside me started nervously looking around for any sign of whacked-out teenagers who might be tripping over the light fandango, if you know what I mean. At least, the tourists were. The residents seemed only mildly perplexed, almost like they had been lulled into acceptance of such insanity.

I made my partner pick up the pace and headed to our next destination, which was a religion fair sponsored by the B'hai faith. I think every religion and spiritual practice on the planet was represented except for Christianity. I guess that's what we were there for. Booths were everywhere, people were friendly and having fun. The sun was shining, dogs were chasing Frisbees, and friends were walking arm in arm.

My partner had felt a different leading and had wandered off to save somebody, justifying breaking the partner rule and leaving me in the all-capable care of my Guardian Angel. At that point, I didn't much care. I felt the safest I'd felt in days. There were lots of happy people around, so I started to let my guard down and enjoy my freedom.

After visiting several booths and actually asking *them* questions, I started walking toward a small grassy area on top of a hill. I was fortified with tracts from the B'hai faith as well as my own. The sky was a beautiful blue with the sound of birds singing and children laughing. I stood for a moment with my eyes closed, face toward the sun soaking in all the warmth my body could contain. I was breathing in and breathing out, my heart finally beating its relaxed steady rhythm once again.

In a moment, in a twinkling of an eye, it all changed. Something was wrong. I opened my eyes and standing there in front of me was a very large and powerful black man. All the terror of the "what if's" from the days before collided in that moment, and I was instantly paralyzed. Before I could find my voice or move in any direction I was airborne. He was speaking in low tones telling me what he was going to do to me. How could this be happening? I was there to do good work, help people, answering the call to spread the gospel, wasn't I? Or was this just punishment for a girl who was hungry for the thrill of being someplace other than Visalia, California for the summer. Inside I was screaming, "Help," but no sound was heard. I managed to finally find my voice just as we were nearing the edge of a wooded area. I yelled for help; I rebuked him in the name of Jesus, as I had heard my mother do so many times, and I screamed for God to rescue me.

Seemingly from out of nowhere, my partner appeared. She was kicking, yelling, screaming, pleading and drawing unwanted attention to the situation, at least in the attacker's eyes. He finally dropped me and nonchalantly walked away. I felt instantly cold and couldn't stop shaking thinking of what might have happened.

We hurried off to find other members of our group to stay with for the rest of the day, strength in numbers you know. As I tagged along absorbing their conversations, I became acutely aware of a change taking place inside me. I could feel it, and it wasn't just about religion either. Who was I? Who was I...*really?* How naïve could I be? There is no safe place, Carter. When are you finally going to accept that?

All successfully bolted in at the church that night, my terrifying encounter was used to inspire us to not be afraid. God had ultimately protected me, and the devil just wanted to scare us, to keep us from doing what we were supposed to be doing, which was witnessing. Well, mark one up for the devil because he had definitely scared the shit out of me!

On that note we were given the next day's assignment. In teams of two, we would be going out in this neighborhood in Fillmore and spreading the gospel. We should expect the enemy and all of his demons to be against us, but we should also expect to see great miracles. A revival was coming; a great harvesting of souls, and God was ready to do a mighty work. He was just waiting for us to obediently pick up the mantle and go out; it all depended on us.

I was done. Not only did this community of people not want us here, we were insulting them by our very presence. This had less to do with God's design than it did with man's arrogance, and I wasn't going to be a part of it anymore.

Knowing that my one voice would never be heard, I planned for my mysterious illness to once again make a timely arrival. The next morning as everyone was preparing for the day ahead, pitiful little groans could be heard from my sleeping bag. Hannah was called and after some rather stern questions, it was decided that I could serve best by staying in and being a prayer partner. Sign me up! They were going to need it.

I prayed about a lot of things that day, mostly asking for forgiveness and the protection of my new friends that had swallowed the Kool-Aid and were out there right now with misguided zeal and purpose. I wondered if they would all be coming back in one piece. As the afternoon wore on and evening approached, I started getting a genuinely sick feeling in the pit of my stomach. Where were they? They should be safely locked back in by now.

With the sun only minutes from setting they straggled in, two by two with stories mostly of protection. They weren't the same perky teenagers that left earlier looking for a Jesus Adventure. They were somber and shaken. God had protected them, that's true. However, we were still missing one very relentless and, most of the time, annoying teenage boy. Somehow he and his partner had become separated, and he was still out there.

The older leaders, along with a couple of street savvy guys, went out to find him while we held hands and prayed for their safe return. Mercifully, he was found in one piece. He had been grabbed from behind and pulled into a dark doorway. A knife had been placed at his throat, threatening to cut it if he and his group didn't leave the next day. We left the next day.

Sausalito, the end of our summer itinerary, was like cool salve on a raw wound. I was quiet, and it wasn't just me either. All the gusto and blustery visions of saving *anyone* were left in the history of the past few days. I just wanted to walk by the sea and pretend I was someone else. I gave my imagination permission to dream of another day when I would come back, free to enjoy this quaint little seaside village without the constraints of a religious culture I was secretly leaving and had been for a long time. I wasn't walking away from God…just the culture.

....

Goodbye, Summer

I got home today, and I've never been so happy to see my family, EVER! I literally kissed the living room floor. Mama says there's something different about me, and Norman says I'm a weak little girl prone to exaggerate. What does he know? He wasn't there. Think I'll keep some of these stories to myself. They wouldn't understand anyway. Every time I closed my eyes the last couple of nights I could hear "him" smell "him" feel "him."

I'm supposed to give a testimony at church on Sunday, tell all about my experiences these past several weeks. I'm not sure what to say. All I really want to do is go back and just be a kid again. It wasn't so bad playing make believe and paper dolls. I know one thing, I'm NEVER going on another mission's trip in my whole life and nobody can make me!

News flash! I LIKE happiness, I LIKE to feel safe. I don't care if I AM a sissy or a weakling. I wanna live a good, wholesome life, kinda like "Father Knows Best," "Leave It To Beaver" or maybe I'll be like the mom in "Please Don't Eat the Daisies." She has four boys and a husband who's a college professor. I WANT to live happily ever after! But I'm not putting myself in danger ever again, and I'm gonna marry somebody who will love me and keep me safe.

Wait a minute! What am I thinking? Have I lost my mind? Marriage isn't safe. Look around, goofball. I'm not gonna get married. I'm gonna be a star and have managers and agents take care of me. I'm going to sing and act on Broadway and someday write my own play. I'll be so rich nobody will ever be able to hurt me…nobody.

I think I'll to go take a bath, wash all this "summer" off of me, put on clean jammies and then go to bed. I'm not very hungry. Still don't know what I'm going to say at church tomorrow.

Mahalia Jackson

As diverse as our exposure to literature was, the same followed suit when it came to music. Daddy brought us Bob Wills, Hank Williams, Tennessee Ernie Ford and the Light Crust Dough Boys. I can still hear that old record today:

And I cried and cried and cried. Oh she cried, yes, she cried.

Or the classy favorite,

Billy goat says: "I love you, I-I-I-I, l-l-l-ove you." Nanny goat says: "I love you too. I-I-I-I, l-l-l-love you."

But thanks to the monthly record club Mama subscribed to, we were also introduced to a few others. There was Montavani, the Grand Canyon Suite and Ethel Merman in "Annie Get Your Gun."

This music showed up just when people outside the family and in our church began to discover that I could sing. My brother, sisters and I had a musical group called "The Walker Family Quartet." We not only sang at our own church, but were also invited on a regular basis to sing at banquets and small churches in the surrounding area. Sharon made our matching dresses, and our teenage brother Norman, who was working for J.C. Penney in the stock room, used his employee discount to buy our shoes. They were really cool shoes too, except to get them all three to match, I had to agree to wear a pair that was one size too small.

I could have managed this if we had been able to stay within the boundaries of our hour-long musical program. But often the time was doubled or tripled when our brother, who was a powerful speaker, would stretch the intro of a song into a full on, hell fire and brimstone sermon, while we stood at the piano and sang "oooohs." After standing until it felt like my heart was beating in my shoes and would soon explode, giving my brother a real miracle to pray for, Diana and I would quietly go sit down.

When it became clear Norman was just winding up and Sharon's hands were starting to cramp from playing *background* music, she would eventually cease playing and join us on the front pew. There was no stopping him once he got started. No amount of checking the clock on the back wall, or the older man in the second row glancing at his watch and coughing, or our fidgeting and raised eyebrows could keep him from his self-appointed mission.

As funny as it is now to look back at, a seed of confidence was beginning to grow out of this musical exposure, giving me a courage I never knew I had. The crippling shyness that had held me down for so long was losing its grip, and a whole new world was beginning to open up. I loved it all and absorbed it like a sponge.

I remember opening the monthly record delivery one day, which was all very exciting because we never knew what the musical treasure was that was waiting inside. As I pulled back the packing paper, I saw a beautiful black lady on the cover of the new album looking upward and smiling. As soon as I heard the first note, something deep resonated inside of me, and I felt a sense of belonging. This lady sang her soul and just by listening, I felt the invitation to sing mine! I finally had an artist that validated how I heard music.

I was known as the little girl with a big voice and always struggled with making that voice fit. When I sang a solo I used my chest voice instead of falsetto or upper register and preferred to adlib, rather than obeying the notes, singing the melody that was wired into my DNA instead.

With the support of family and friends, I entered a Talent Search put on by the Assemblies of God. Sharon and I performed a medley of "Nobody Knows the Trouble I've Seen" and "My Lord, What a Mornin'." As excited and proud as everyone at our church was, there were still a few well-meaning souls that had strongly encouraged me to pick a different song, in a more appropriate musical genre. It would be the first of many battles to come about music, art and embracing what I was uniquely gifted for. That night I chose to sing *from* my heart with *all* of my heart. Following in the footsteps of my new mentor, we brought the house down in Fresno, California, and brought home the first place trophy!

Mahalia Jackson knew what outside pressure felt like. She experienced the push to please others, and wrestled in ways only she and Jesus knew. I love listening to her early recordings when she just opens up and sings! There's nothing and no one like her. I can't wait to meet her one day. Side by side, black and white, we'll be singing the redemption of our souls, our stories and our hearts out for Jesus!

....

Every Head Bowed, Every Eye Closed

"I see that hand."

Really? I didn't, and I had my eyes open. The new evangelist, Martin Skinner, was giving the altar call, and that's what all Preachers say when they start the long process of wrapping it up. It's kinda like priming the pump. If you say you see someone raising his or her hand, it might make someone else feel a little braver to do the same thing.

I peeked, and I probably shouldn't have 'cause I usually get caught, but the only person raising their hand was the "special" boy who gets saved every time the doors are open.

Somethin's not right about this new Evangelist. He comes from Bakersfield and has these cards that he hands out every night asking us to dedicate our lives to Jesus in the name of his dead brother.

Daddy doesn't care for him at all and acts like he's got somethin' on the guy. He's been here nearly two weeks and there's talk of moving the show, I mean the revival, to a larger auditorium in Fresno. The church is so packed with women and Charismatic Catholics, I'm afraid we're gonna run out of hankies to lay over the ladies when they get slain in the Spirit.

I went forward last night 'cause I wanted to get slain so bad, but when he touched my forehead I didn't feel a thing except his clammy hands. When I didn't fall down he gave me a little push, which I figured was my cue to co-operate. I don't want people thinking I'm not a Christian or anything. I think I'm gonna make some changes. I don't know how yet, but I'm keepin' my eyes and ears open.

I can't help but wonder what Jesus is thinking right now. I can't say this out loud, but I don't think he's real happy about this revival...

Part two

Better a Millstone

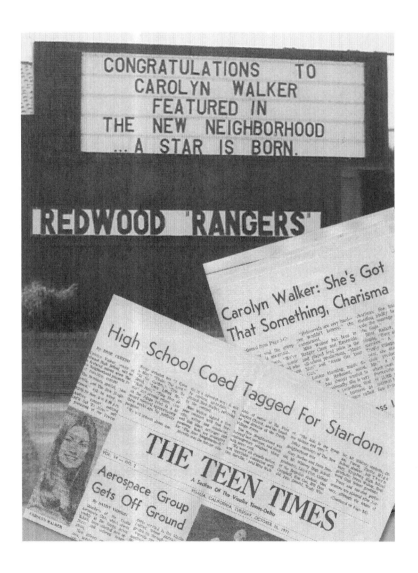

••••••••••••••••••••••

Deferred Justice

On January 4, 2012 my mother's youngest brother was found brutally murdered in the house my grandparents built. This was the house we visited on a weekly basis for most of our early years, and ate many Sunday dinners of fried chicken and Grandma's special potatoes. It's where we watched Bonanza for the first time on a color television set and played with our cousins while the aunts visited and the uncles played "Washers" outside. We were a 1950's portrait of the big happy family.

But it was also the house that trapped secrets and held them hostage for the next generation to negotiate their continued incarceration or risky and dangerous release. Looks like someone chose the latter, because now he's dead and the line of suspects is endless.

My first reaction was not one of surprise, but rage. His death didn't just magically erase the influence or consequences of his criminal acts against the helpless and innocent.

I don't know if I will ever be able to sort it all out, but today, looking back, I have a better appreciation of just how hard my mother worked to put distance between herself and the childhood that still remains a mystery on so many levels. The cumulative disconnect explains so much of my parents' rocky marriage dynamic.

I also know I'm done with being quiet.

Be Careful What You Wish For

T hanks to the encouragement of a few key teachers, my sister Sharon's invaluable investment of love and spiritual guidance, and the discovery that I could sing, I had grown into a typical 16 year-old high school student majoring in extra curricular social activities.

I worked on the staff of our newspaper, enjoyed playing the viola in the orchestra, sang in the choir as well as ensemble, and participated in regional vocal competitions. I auditioned for our school musicals and was given the lead in "The Music Man" my sophomore year and "Annie Get Your Gun" my junior year.

I was also one of five cheerleaders that made up the Varsity Cheerleading Squad. It wasn't that I was part of the *in* crowd so much, I was just friends with everybody. I had been a classmate with many of these students since fifth grade.

Once a year the great cross-town rivalry was celebrated with a week of pranks, Pep Rallies, and some serious trash talk. It was innocent enough and culminated in the big Cowhide game on Friday night, which had been in existence since Mt. Whitney High School had been built on the opposite side of town. It was an event attended by most of the community and many out of town alumni from years before. The school that won had their name branded into the cowhide and placed in a very prominent place in their hallowed halls until the next year's match-up.

My dad rarely missed one of my hometown games and *never* missed the Cowhide. Great memories. I still had trouble keeping my socks up but at least our skirts were short.

V-I-C-T-O-R-Y!! Go Redwood Rangers!!

I was now attending a different church in town at the invitation of their music minister. He had heard me perform in a local production of the Messiah and asked if I would come sing for one of their upcoming services.

This was a very prestigious church, filled with many professional people and local educators. They were known for their active and enthusiastic youth choir. It was also where my boyfriend attended on a regular basis. For the first time in my life, I was going to school with many of the same friends I was attending youth group with. And since it wasn't a Pentecostal church, movies and dances were no longer considered sin. Right from the beginning it seemed like such a great fit, and before long my sisters, mom and myself were committed and supportive members. Life was good.

The music minister, who shared a similar denominational background, became a personal friend and confidante to all three of us girls. Sharon's expertise and experience as a church pianist were quickly recognized, and she started playing for Sunday services. She also accompanied the many different musical groups that were his brainchild, and which accounted for a large part of the church's local and regional appeal. Practically every teenager in town wanted to be a part of one of this minister's groups.

Respected and loved by everyone, he had recently gone through a troubling divorce and had the shoulder and support of students as well as their parents. A mild mannered and genuinely likeable guy, he became every elderly widow's son. I remember that even on his frugal church salary he never seemed to be without *means*. He considered himself an artist of sorts and became somewhat restless with a desire to explore just how far his talent might take him. So with the backing of the church, he wrote some original material, and formed a group with me as the featured soloist.

Through the efforts of a local businessman, the minister was introduced to a self-proclaimed manager type from Hollywood and the two of them hit it off instantly. Before long they joined forces and started a management/production company. The man from Hollywood orchestrated music for television and had worked as a saxophone player in Big Bands all over the country. What part of that résumé made him a manager is unclear, but no one chose to question his credentials.

Frankie, the manager, was a bit quirky to say the least, and not exactly a card carrying Christian. He had an equally "quirky" wife with a passion for wearing hot pants to our group rehearsals that were held in the Fellowship Hall at church. Daddy had her figured out from the moment he met her, which knowing what I know now, is not at all surprising.

Once ol' *Hollywood* showed up the minister's dream became much more defined, and what was at first on a local scale, now became a grand vision. In fact, hold on to your hymnals folks, we're about to enter the "Big Time."

Seduction

ot wanting to waste any time after the ink had dried on the new production company documents, the music minister and manager, "M&M," approached me after rehearsal one day with a proposal. They were convinced that with my talent and the minister's songs, they had the unstoppable combination to make me a huge star. It was an exciting offer, one I had dreamed about for years, but I felt a little uneasy with the conversation. I was at the height of being a sixteen-year-old and was enjoying a life that I had worked hard to be a part of. It felt kind of like being coaxed out of a cocoon too early, but the idea of following the "All American Dream" was enticing and seductive to say the least.

I'd been spending quite a bit of time with the manager at our rehearsals. His comments, and the way he would talk to me and look at me didn't always feel exactly *safe*. However, the minister not only had the seal of approval from of all of my friend's parents but the church as well, so I figured it must be okay.

The manager said he had all of these Hollywood industry contacts waiting to jump on board and not just in the Christian field either. They were certain that if I signed on with their new company, within a couple of years my name would become a household word, especially if they shortened it a bit to maybe, "Carol Walker." Only problem was, I was a minor and would need my parent's legal permission. I pretty much knew Mama would be on board, but Daddy? That was going to be a little more difficult.

I remember clearly the very convincing presentation the two men gave my parents as they sat on the mismatched furniture in our living room making the *big sell*. All the while the Hamm's Beer sign on the wall just above their heads invited everyone to "Come to the land of sky blue water!" Daddy loved that sign and appreciated it as though it were fine art. It had been part of a beer display in the store where he worked. When you plugged it in, a light came on and a picture of a beautiful river with the Hamm's bear in a canoe rushed in front of you.

I had this overwhelming urge to laugh and had to force myself to focus, look at something else. I chose the picture that Daddy's sister Auntie Jack had painted of the coon dog treeing his prey. It hung right next to the beer advertisement. The whole evening seemed cartoon-like, and yet something deep and reckless continued to pull at me. I knew I was going to have to use every bit of influence I could drum up to make this thing happen.

M&M filled their heads with all kinds of fancy thoughts and painted verbal pictures of stardom, capping it off with some well placed parental guilt bordering on condescension. There was an assumption that my folks were small town hicks, no match for the smooth talking manager and his minister sidekick.

My parents were asked to not hold back or stand in the way of the gifts and talents God had so bountifully bestowed on their daughter, and they said it with evangelistic flair. All Mama and Daddy needed to do was simply *trust* them and agree to this first step of necessary legal documentation. That way they could proceed on the path that was certain to bring big success for everyone. After all, if you can't trust a minister, whom *can* you trust?

This tactic was of course completely lost on Daddy who listened and said very little. "Mr. Hollywood," being a man of the world himself, sensed that behind my dad's stare was the soul of an old Carny, "don't bullshit a bullshitter." So in an effort to connect, he told my mother that he heard she had a saxophone and asked if he might take a look at it. In an earlier conversation I had told him she played an old straight sax in the church orchestra that accompanied the choir for Christmas cantatas and Sunday morning offertories. One thing about him, he *did* play a mean horn and as quickly as you could say, "Yakety Sax" the tension in the room dissipated and we were back on track.

The goodwill didn't last long though. After they left, Daddy made it clear that he didn't like 'em or *trust* 'em. My mother on the other hand, had total faith in our minister friend and with pressure from me, I'm sorry to say, won out. The perceived victory came as sort of a surprise. There was this shadow of a feeling that I was somehow slipping through the invisible cracks of my parent's protection, but I sure wasn't going to draw anyone's attention to it.

That day my parents and I unwittingly, or maybe I should say half-wittedly, entered into an un-holy alliance that would become legal as soon as a court date could be confirmed.

Welcome to Showbiz, Baby

My seventeenth birthday came and went, and with it the end of my junior year at Redwood High School. With the demands of a developing new career, I chose not to go out for cheerleading or participate in all the senior year activities that students look forward to from the time they are in Kindergarten. In fact, with the help of my school counselor, who was the parent of one of my friends in the group and also a strong supporter of the music minister, my class schedule was set up in such a way that I would be eligible for early graduation. I was a little sad about what I would be missing out on with all of my school friends, but agreed that one must be willing to make certain sacrifices when it comes to Show Business.

The beginning of that summer couldn't have been more exciting as our whole group, which included Diana, started recording an album at The Record Plant in Hollywood where the manager's wife had connections. My sister Sharon had wisely chosen to end her musical association with the minister early on for reasons she tells best, with the biggest being that she had fallen in love with a great guy (love you, Edd!) back home. Mama and a few other parents came down for the first session to check things out and be supportive. They decided all was well and left, believing we were safe in the hands of the trusted music minister. This was a once in a lifetime opportunity for their children, and we had their full support.

Sly and the Family Stone (not exactly known for *family values*) were camped out and there was no shortage of potential "A-ha" moments in the many different magical rooms of the infamous studio. Most of us chose to stay clear and take in the stories from gabby studio personnel. It was quite an introductory education in the "behind the scenes" world of Rock n' Roll, and hedonistic indulgence. The Jackson Five had taken up residence and were recording there as well. Pretty exciting stuff for a bunch of wide-eyed, small town teens like us.

But there were also moments of never before experienced elation and heart connection. In a sense, we were "going to school" while working with all the A-list musicians in town that played on the tracks of our album. After recording my solos, I would walk into the control room to applause and accolades, one of the most addictive drugs in life. I became more convinced than ever that this was what I was destined for, no matter what price I had to pay.

My soon to be manager wasn't waiting for my parent's signature on the dotted line, and set me up with a "Dentist to the Stars" to see if he could do something about my crooked teeth. I always had to have pictures taken from the left side because the right side had a huge gap that looked like there wasn't anything there at all. I had inherited my Dad's small mouth with too many teeth. They were strong teeth, just too many of them. Daddy had all of his pulled out and wore dentures the rest of his life. They talked about pulling a bunch of mine too and then capping the rest, but the cost was prohibitive so we settled on a false tooth that I popped in with the help of Dentu-Cream. Instantly I had a full smile and for the first time didn't cringe when I looked in the mirror. It was a short gap (no pun intended) solution, but it did wonders for my self-confidence. I even asked Mama to go ahead and schedule an appointment for my senior class pictures.

I was staying with my manager and his wife off and on for the summer so I could make it to all of the appointments and meetings that were set up with various professionals. Looking back I can see a subtle type of brainwashing…too strong of a word? Maybe, but I'm not so sure about that. The tactic of showering love and attention on the mark and then isolating them from their family and friends is brainwashing 101.

They seemed very nurturing in the beginning, concerning themselves with the lack of basic health check-ups while I was growing up and acting very parental. At first I defended my parents saying they were doing the best they could, and I knew they loved me. Yes, there were some problems, but every family has those. They would smile and tell me what a good daughter I was and how lucky my parents were. In the evenings we would grill out and then later over drinks (I had just turned seventeen) they would ask me what my life was like growing up.

Living in this dream-like sense of security, surrounded by Hollywood and the promise of a big career, and with home a mere blip on my radar, I would give in to the mellowness of the alcohol, and in the moment, share more than I should. I had no defenses for this kind of attention. I basked in it like a teenager at the beach soaking up the sun on Spring Break, with no protection and no thought of the burn that was sure to follow.

Added to the seductive ambiance was the convincing apprehension of the music minister who was spending much of his time there that summer as well. He would shine his special *god light* (little "g") on many of those conversations, using spiritual jargon to slowly encourage the estrangement with my parents. His presence gave credibility to the moment, and I felt this was a safe place to abandon the "don't tell" policy, letting my walls come tumbling down.

Diana and I were together for a few of those dinners, and the two of us started thinking this new life felt pretty good. Between M&M and the manager's wife, we believed our hearts were finally being not just heard, but also protected, and it wasn't long before we eventually found ourselves embracing not only their concerns but their conclusions as well. We were hooked.

Oftentimes familiarity erases very important boundaries in relationships and eating, sleeping, and working in close quarters with my manager started proving to be no exception. He had a very *blue* sense of humor that was unleashed on everyone. He could be pretty funny, and we did a lot of laughing that summer. But there were also times when his questionable, off-color banter turned into overt advances that I would laugh off and try to deflect.

Even though he made me extremely uncomfortable, I kept telling myself this was part of the "showbiz" game. I was just a small town teenager. What did I know? Surely I had to be reading him the wrong way. Besides, what was I going to do, tell on him?

The music minister was the closest person I had to a pastor, and he laughed right along with him. I couldn't say anything to my parents or that would be the end of any hope of them going to court to sign the agreement to waive their rights to their minor child, which had now been scheduled for September. On the one hand I wanted a career and kept telling myself I could play in this new world, while at the same time in my heart I feared I was way out of my league.

The more I resisted my Manager the more intense his pursuit became, showering me with attention and promises of a career "bound for stardom, baby!" He thought he was so sneaky and would devise signals to send me messages when we were with other people. Like when riding in the seat behind him in a car, he would put his hand on the back of his head showing two fingers, which meant he was thinking about me. Being a person who always gets caught, I thought this was ridiculous, and many times his wife was sitting next to him. I wondered if he used the same tactics when he was having an affair with her before she divorced her previous husband, left her child, and followed him to Hollywood. But he liked the danger aspect. To me, it felt like Junior High all over again.

That summer my time was split between Hollywood and home where the whole community was cheering us on. I finally convinced myself that I needed to handle this on my own, and it would be best for everyone if I just kept my mouth shut. Eventually, if I played it cool enough, he would get the message and just be my manager. At that point I wasn't even telling my lifelong confidante and best friend, Diana.

When at home I would take walks in a nearby walnut orchard looking for clarity in the simple sanctuary, hoping to escape from the noise of the very loud life I was living. Seemed like everybody in my world from school to church all thought I was headed for, dare I say it, a divinely appointed career of stardom. Everything had happened so fast and was continuing at a pace that was impossible to keep up with.

The idyllic teenage life of a few months ago was now replaced with all-day vocal and choreography rehearsals. I was more than willing to put in the hours. In fact, I enjoyed the work, but I was really struggling with my manager's increasingly out of control attention.

In my heart of hearts I just wanted to be seventeen years old, doing normal seventeen-year-old things with other people my age. But instead I felt like I was walking through a minefield that at any given moment had the potential of blowing up in my face. I had also become aware of a very powerful mistress in my manager's life: pills. And while under their influence, which was pretty much all the time, he could be a very unstable person.

He had started calling our house under the ruse of business and then would try to convince me to meet him somewhere. I always took the call in the kitchen because it had a long cord and I could go around the corner into the garage and shut the door, giving me some privacy.

I remember a call coming in once while my dad was there on his day off, sitting in the living room. After talking a while, I walked back into the kitchen and saw him standing in the doorway. He gave me the third degree, telling me he *knew* what was going on. He wasn't stupid or blind, and I'd better knock that shit off right now. I acted all offended and told him I had no idea what he was talking about. He just looked me up and down and then walked away muttering under his breath.

I wish I had come clean with him and let him do whatever it was he was thinking of doing. Letting him be my hero probably would've saved me from a lot of heartache. But I honestly think I was too embarrassed to admit failure to him. As a kid, he had made fun of my dreamy aspirations, and I was determined to prove to him and everyone else that I could make it and someday be somebody in this world. His dismissal of me made me want out of Visalia more than I wanted to be rescued.

The inappropriate advances didn't completely go unnoticed by others either. At one point late that summer talk started around the church that something shady might be going on. The Pastor was strongly encouraged to investigate. M&M decided it would be best for me to go to the Senior Pastor, confess a crush on my manager and ask for forgiveness since neither one of them could risk exposure on any level. There was way too much at stake. I knew what *exposure* might mean for my manager, but wondered what that might look like for the music minister.

They made it clear that it was up to me to save the day, after all we couldn't just think about ourselves, now could we? What about the group and all of our commitments to the Community? My manager could be a very convincing guy, but you add the spiritual component of a minister to the equation and the result for me was compliance. After being coached on what to say, I did exactly what they asked. I'd been taught all my life about obedience but was never taught how to say "No!"

It wouldn't be until later that I was told the pastor had strong suspicions, if not knowledge, about the secret dark life of the music minister, and a pretty good clue about my manager as well, but I had unwittingly presented him with a way out and he let me take the heat. Wouldn't want the congregation to get a whiff of this, might mess up the church's powerful standing in the community, and then where would we be?

It was a humiliating experience, sitting there with the pastor, music minister and my manager, confessing to a crush that at least three people in the room knew was non-existent on my part. My acting skills were celebrated later that night with jokes and toasts of relief. I was applauded by the inner circle for taking one for the team, as if this proved my loyalty. But the whole time I was choking down that very strong underage Margarita, I was also pushing down the anger, which literally canceled out any buzz or relief from the alcohol. I felt ashamed and sick all at the same time.

Looking back now, there wasn't a closet big enough for either one of them to hide their warped agenda. I can't personally speak to what the pastor or *others* knew or didn't know, but it would've been pretty tough to ignore all the signs. Shoot, they were shining as bright as the collective *neons* on the Vegas Strip. It's probably more likely that most just chose to look the other way. The music minister was very talented after all, and his choirs traveled around the state while the youth numbers at church were growing by leaps and bounds. Who was I to judge? Wasn't I doing the same thing by choosing to go along?

It's amazing what the human heart is capable of justifying if the stakes are high enough. I lived the reality of that first hand and must take personal responsibility, my age aside, for what I allowed myself to get caught up in.

For every one thing I have chosen to put on paper there are probably a hundred I have decided to let die with me. It's no surprise that I vowed later to never enter a church or have any contact with Christians, other than my family, if I could possibly avoid it. I stayed away for about twelve years. To this day, even in this moment, I struggle with the credibility of pastors, teachers, and other people in authority. Hope you'll extend a little grace. I'm just a work in progress, folks.

"Being confident of this very thing, that he who began a good work in you will perform it until the day of Jesus Christ." Philippians 1:6 (KJV)

First One's Free

That summer's chain of events and my youthful, naïve decision to go it alone, eventually wore me down. If I thought things were spinning out of control on the manager/career front, the wheels had completely come off at home. For the first time ever my mother was talking about getting a divorce. Someone had counseled her that she had Biblical grounds for leaving, and she was giving it some serious thought. There were frequent conversations with Diana and me about who we would live with. Everywhere I stepped it felt like quicksand.

So, when my manager offered to give me something to make me feel better one day, I shook hands with compromise, silenced every loud warning bell going off in my head, and accepted it. For the first time in forever I felt good, mellow, agreeable. That was my introduction to downers, and I *really* liked them. I was tired of trying to be tough, tired of pretending, pleasing everybody, shoot, I was just plain tired.

Even though I would never admit it back then, in that moment, a part of me gave in and gave up. I became willfully ignorant, believing I had run out of options and even if I didn't want to go through with signing the contract, where was I supposed to go? Staring me in the face was the reality that even though my dad could be incredibly tough, when I needed him the most, he wasn't going to step up and save me, and I was right.

On September 9, 1971, without consulting an attorney, we all drove down to L.A. and stood before a judge. My parents were asked if they understood that they were giving up their legal rights to me since I was a minor, to which they answered, "Yes." The crack of the Judge's gavel made it so, and they got in their Plymouth Belvedere and drove home. I got in the car with my manager, who informed me with a big smile on his face, that he now owned me...*every part* of me.

His words sent a shiver straight to my core confirming what I already knew, what had been set in motion couldn't be stopped. I'd seen it. I'd lived it. I'd learned ways to protect myself from it, and now I had just willingly stepped over the line, and there was no turning back. What did I just do? I had pushed for this, and I was going to have to see it through.

This slick Hollywood manager started setting me up from day one long before there were even hints of a contract, and remember, I was sixteen when I first met him. I was such an easy target. I wasn't the only one either. I later discovered that he had a pattern of choosing young, talented girls who came from troubled backgrounds. The one right before me ran away from him into the arms of the Tony Alamo cult. To add insult to injury, it was becoming clear that our music minister friend was not equaling the spiritual sum that myself and everyone else back home had come up with. Hindsight's a bitch.

With all sources of escape blocked and the deal signed, my manager started handing out the pretty little pills on a regular basis. He told me he had fallen in love with me, said I needed a man to take care of me, not some teenage boy. Together we would be an unstoppable team. I'd never had any guy tell me that he loved me before.

At first, to my shame, I actually felt flattered but kind of sick to my stomach all at the same time. Why couldn't he just be my friend and leave well enough alone? I pushed him away reminding him he was a married man. What about his wife? He would smirk and say she already knew. It felt surreal, like I was in some kind of Twilight Zone episode. He would corner me after rehearsals at church saying and promising so much if I would just go away with him.

My mind felt slow and the inner rage that had always been an old friend was smothered by the effects of the drugs. Sometimes I felt like I was outside my body, watching, telling myself to run away, but my voice had no sound. On some level I told myself I wouldn't be doing anything that my dad hadn't done over and over again with his special lady friends.

As I became more compliant, my manager became more and more possessive and not just him, oddly enough, but his wife as well. I was told what to wear, what to eat, how to do my hair and make-up and who to be particularly *nice* to. I was taking pills, lying to my family and friends, and trying with all my heart to look the other way, feeling the weight of what was at stake here.

There was a whole community of people putting their hope in me, with no obvious suspicion directed at any adult.

A Star Is Born

With summer over and the calendar filled with events, I went home to finish out my senior year. But between rehearsals, shows and the morning after effects of the downers, I was rarely showing up. Rumors were running rampant in certain circles, and mothers didn't want their daughters around me any more.

I slept, and then I slept some more, at one point swallowing a few extra pills hoping to get someone's attention so they could save me from the mess I had gotten myself into. But the only people who found out were the inner circle, and they all kept telling me I was depressed because of my unstable home life.

By this time Diana was in on the secret and very worried about me, but the music minister had befriended her and made her feel special. She ate up his attention like a starving child, and in some ways I guess that's exactly what she was, always feeling as though she were in my shadow, getting only the crumbs that were left over. When little girls do not get the love and affirmation from their fathers, they will find it in some very dangerous places. Even if the situation had been different though, she was still completely without means to help me, so the insanity continued.

The ups and downs of the pills only served to make me more depressed, and I found myself chasing the high, wanting them more and more. I was afraid by how fragile I felt and knew that vulnerability sets you up for being a victim, and I hated that.

Strangely, in the middle of this abyss, something quiet and unexpected started to happen. What was intended as a means of control and manipulation began to take an interesting turn. Somewhere deep inside that old familiar anger started boiling up to the surface, and this time it refused to be dismissed.

I became edgy and distant, choosing not to answer my manager's phone calls from Hollywood, avoiding him when he came to town, almost daring him to make a scene. Everything, and I mean EVERYTHING, felt small and stupid. I hated the type of music I was being forced to sing and realized that most of his contacts were the more clubby Vegas types with the exception of a few.

Living at home, where Mama and Daddy had weathered the storm once again, and not having to see him everyday, opened the door for me to explore other relationships. I started associating with some college age friends that were outside the twisted circle, and slowly but surely began feeling stronger.

I don't think there was just one defining moment that finally gave me the courage to stand up and walk away. It was more likely a cumulative awakening. I started dating a guy who was kind of a Christian "bad boy." He thought the group's image and music was really cheesy and would make fun of the way I was coached to sing certain songs. He kept telling me to just sing how I wanted to sing and screw what they said. This guy wasn't exactly safe, relationship-wise and we were only together for a short time, but he definitely served a purpose.

One day after returning home from Reno where I was performing the lead in a very popular Christian Musical, I gathered up every bit of seventeen-year old strength I had and, by myself, gave notice that I was leaving and wanted out of the contract. It was a liberating moment, and I was banking on them letting me go for fear of being exposed. The group had a big debut show in Fresno coming up, a television special getting ready to be aired on the local station, a new record for sale and our entire church and local community was involved, giving their small town American Dream support. The school Marquee read:

"Congratulations to Carolyn Walker…A Star is born!"

The newspaper ran articles with titles like: "High School Coed Tagged For Stardom!"

To this day I struggle to articulate the turmoil I was in. I knew I was letting everyone down and felt so responsible. But I also knew I couldn't keep lying, couldn't keep medicating, even if it meant giving up everything I had fought so hard to achieve. If I didn't take back my life now, I was afraid I never would. I had gambled on a dream and lost big time. Now it was time to pay up.

My goal was to somehow keep it quiet and slowly, by doing fewer appearances, fade away. Again, I was naïve. Instead of backing off and giving me space M&M turned up the heat. There were legal threats, personal threats, and lies being circulated. I saw how all that had worked earlier. Who was going believe *me?* At this point the only people who were aware of my plans to leave were my manager, his wife and the music minister.

I hung in there, playing the part for all to see long enough to do the debut concert, television show and a few appearances here and there. With uncharacteristic resolve, I stopped swallowing the little pills and stuck to my guns, making it clear to the three of them that this association was over. I would do one final concert with the group, giving them plenty of time to find a new lead singer. If they had a problem with that, I was going to blow this whole thing wide open and go public. I was giving them an out…their call.

This time they listened. The last concert went smoothly, and I was beginning to think the nightmare just might be coming to an end. There were a few whispers from the group, but I wasn't angry with them. They didn't know about all the secrets, or perhaps they did. Maybe they had a few of their own.

As I was gathering up my things and getting ready to walk out, the music minister approached me. He had written a letter that I've kept all these years, designed to manipulate me into feeling guilty and responsible for everyone else's loss of success, and hopefully make me choose to stay. It is as follows:

A STAR IS BORN…

Friday morning, December 3, 1971

Last night I saw a beautiful performance.
It seemed so real that it moved me to tears.
But as I tossed and turned through the night I realized that it
Might not be.
She could not change overnight seventeen years that developed
a pattern – a system of insensitivity and flirtation with roles.
And now she has a new role!
The usual way

By which she had disrupted other previous relationships
          Came back to her in a painful, hurting way.
     She could not handle it.

Again she has repeated that system in a big, big way—
          Hurting not one but many who love her
                              And eventually
                    The One who loves her most.
          The story—beautifully moving, but
     Lacks heavily in drawing that necessary line between
                              idealism and responsibility
                    between self-seeking and God-given opportunity.

She always wanted to be a STAR

                              She will Always want to be;
               That part of her will never go away. But she wanted
                              it the easy way....

     The road to stardom suddenly became bumpy,

                                        phony,
                    and frustrating— so
          she chose an easier way.
On the EVE OF THE BEGINNING she gave it all up! And, now
                              She is a STAR!
          She will receive many acalades
                    for her nobly "Christian" decision.
     Some will call her ridiculously foolish—others
               Who sit comfortably in the sheltered community
                         Will love her
                    and endear her to their hearts.
BUT the people who need her <u>most</u>
                         will never know her,
          for Carolyn found it easier to withdraw into
                              the security of self-discovery
     rather than face head-on the loneliness of a world
                              without Eternal Purpose
          and it's phony facades that hide a driving search
                              for reality!

Matthew 16:24

This was from a man who was about seventeen years my senior, a trusted minister who at this very time, was engaging in a dark, undisclosed world of his own perversion. It makes me angry to think of all the pain he was allowed to inflict that went unchecked for so many years. Some simply became collateral damage in the wake of his undercover dalliances, and secretly carry the memories of shame to this day. He was a master at mental manipulation.

People are so many different shades and layers, not all bad and not all good, which makes it nearly impossible to articulate *after the fact* why a reasonable human being would fall prey to the insanity that stares back at you from a flat page. Many of us were taught to never question authority and especially a minister.

A lot had happened in the six months that followed my seventeenth birthday, and I hated myself at the thought of what I had been a part of. But even my own guilt couldn't at that time make me stay.

Desperate Measures

I went home that night; still choosing to carry the secrets, thinking it would all just someday fade away if I kept quiet. However, my stubbornness and deteriorating grasp of reality proved to be no match for my mother's prayers and prodding.

There had been no waning in the church's undying loyalty to the beloved music minister, and she was growing weary with my continued fall from grace. The salacious tidbits from the church gossips all couched in, "Give us the details so we can pray intelligently" bullshit, was taking its toll on her. No more half answers and escaping into my bedroom for another nap, it was time to tell the truth, PERIOD, and that's exactly what I did, shielding her from some of the more egregious details.

The truth doesn't always instantly set you free, but at least I wasn't alone anymore. I never had a conversation with my dad about what happened to me, and to this day I don't know what my mother told him. I can't help but wonder though what he would have done if he had known. Maybe we, or *somebody*, dodged a bullet…

Mama immediately jumped into action, seeking out the help of a previous neighbor from Santa Maria who was a Berkeley graduate practicing law in Bakersfield. A meeting was scheduled, and she and I drove the seventy miles there in silence.

Upon our arrival and after the usual pleasantries were dispensed of, our attorney friend diplomatically asked my mother to sit in the waiting room so he could speak with me privately. Even though he did his best to make me feel comfortable, it was still humiliating and scary answering the hard questions that needed to be asked. He was totally professional, taking his time and being patient, as I slowly and quietly spoke about some of the more dark parts of the truth out loud to another adult.

At one point, as I was recounting a certain incident, he put his pen down for a brief moment and just stared at the page in front of him. He was a very big guy and had watched me grow up as a little girl in Santa Maria. I believe in that moment, had my manager walked in the room, he never would have *walked* out.

When he felt he had enough evidence to pursue a certain course of action, he asked my mother to join us. I was terrified and ashamed for her to know the details. Trust is the most difficult thing to re-build, and I had lied so often to her that I wondered if she would ever be able to forgive me. As much as my mother's drama and fanaticism drove me crazy, I loved her and didn't want to disappoint her. She had suffered enough in her life, and now I was responsible for more disappointment.

I kept my head down as our attorney explained he believed the best course of action was to prepare to file statutory rape charges with the district attorney against my manager. In his evaluation of the situation, he believed we had a very strong case. However, the choice was ultimately mine.

At the time, I didn't feel strong enough to go through with it. I just wanted out so I could live a quiet little ordinary life. A preliminary letter was sent in hopes that the threat of the charges would be serious enough to force a release from my contract.

I recently found some legal correspondence informing me that the music minister had agreed to release me from the contract. I think he had a lot more to lose, and somewhere buried inside knew that what he had participated in was wrong.

My manager however, was a stubborn man and chose to call my bluff by not responding to the letter from our attorney. He was gambling that I wouldn't actually go to the DA and follow through with filing charges. He didn't believe his acts had been ones of violence but rather coercion and psychological manipulation of a minor. He hedged his bets by simply choosing to bide his time.

Things got suddenly quiet on the Hollywood front.

Enter the Imposter…

The Imposter

His pursuit of me was motivated by something sinister and secret. The boy who had laughed with me, distracted me from the hard place I was in with late night tennis games and expensive dinners, was not who he represented himself to be. On the outside he was tall, lean, well dressed and wealthy. But on the inside he was driven by an agenda only a few were aware of.

I had never stepped into his exclusive world of privilege before, the world he had citizenship in. At times, when I allowed myself to think, I wondered why me? It seemed an odd choice. I didn't fit in his social circles, and he didn't fit in mine. But when you're young there's a certain romance to relationships that are mysterious and unpredictable.

We had started spending time together late that fall. He would drive home from the prestigious college he was attending on the weekends and we'd talk, sometimes into the wee hours. However, there was always something dogging me inside that felt a little out of sync. I kept thinking we should have more of a connection, but we never did. I chalked it up to my "messed up" state of mind, once again not giving the inner warning the serious consideration that it deserved. I was in desperate need of a friend and thought he was exactly that—a friend.

We dated for a short time, but after awhile he stopped coming home as often on the weekends, and I felt a faint sense of relief. Somewhere in the back of my mind I still wrestled with an uneasiness about him but chose to let it go. Frankly, I was getting a little tired of all my drama. I was like the character in that exhausting movie, "The Perils of Pauline." I kept getting tied to the railroad tracks and then being rescued just in the nick of time. I was ready to move on.

Around this same time, I started hanging out with a group of friends from Tulare who were bound and determined to *save* me. They attended a private Christian college in Portland, Oregon and had aligned themselves with the "Jesus Freak Movement." I liked them because they didn't judge me or ask too many questions. I soon found myself defaulting to the carefree life philosophy of going wherever the Spirit leads. When they were in town we'd sit around and sing, borrowing each other's guitars and then afterwards head on over to Mearle's on Mooney Boulevard for a hamburger and fries. It was just good clean small town fun, and I welcomed it with an open heart.

In moments of reflection, I couldn't help but wonder where the next year would take me. By now my brother had married a gorgeous Catholic girl named Denise, and my older sister Sharon was engaged to the man of her dreams. Diana was still in the singing group and was counting the days before she would be moving to Los Angeles. One thing I knew for sure, I could not stay by myself with my parents. I didn't know it at the time, but a door was getting ready to open.

Jesus Freaks to the Rescue!

You can't really run from sin, but I was sure ready to try. Every time my dad looked at me I felt cheap. Every time I looked at my mom I felt guilty. So when my Jesus Freak friends suggested I go to Portland with them and attend the Christian college they went to, I jumped at the chance and so did my parents. I mean, how much trouble could Carter get into at a *Christian* college anyway, right?

One giant hurdle was to convince the people at my high school to sign off on my graduation requirements. I was already supposed to be leaving early except I hadn't been showing up much the previous semester. In fact, my P.E. teacher sent a progress report to my parents telling them I had only attended 7 days in the past quarter giving me an earned 16 points out of 68. My grade was a solid "F." This was going to take a miracle.

The first day back to school in January, I found myself sitting outside the door of our school counselor. My parents were inside, and I was awaiting my fate. I was praying, but I wasn't sure Jesus loved me all that much anymore. I couldn't even begin to imagine how embarrassed my dad was. One of the unpardonable sins to him was puttin' your shit in the street.

When the door opened, I was given a note with some transcripts and told not to read them. I went to every teacher, handed them the note and then waited while my friends and fellow students, many of which I had known since elementary school, stared at me in silence. Reluctantly, each teacher chose to give me a passing grade. There was a sadness in their eyes, and only one acted judgmental. I walked through the corridors hoping the bell wouldn't ring, hoping I wouldn't have to face the faces that knew the rumors, some right, most wrong.

I was officially granted the status of an early graduate and invited back to participate in the graduation ceremonies. I only sent out my senior announcements to a couple of friends and did not wear the cap and gown or experience my own high school graduation, a loss I regret to this day. What had happened to me was an emotional theft that continued to play out for many years to come.

But I couldn't think about all that. This was going to be a fresh start. I even agreed to be re-baptized in the cold Pacific Ocean in Southern California before heading to Portland.

I remember all of my new friends holding hands on the beach, praying for and expecting some incredible miracle as I came up out of the water. Instead I stood there crying, shivering, not being able to differentiate between the salt of my tears and the cold salt water of the ocean...nothing spectacular, once again, just me. I felt as though I had somehow let them all down. My tears came from a deep place none of them could understand at that point in their lives. I wanted it all to be so different but the whisper in my head was that the Jesus Freak Movement was just another word for Pentecostal "Holy Roller."

My roommates were amazing though and so genuinely kind to me. I fell in love with Portland almost immediately. The rain made the air feel and smell so clean. We'd go to Rosa's for the nine layer cakes or the Oyster Bar for clam chowder. Most of the time I had little or no money, and on those occasions when I wasn't mooching off of my friends, would sit and eat crackers and drink water. I wore "Billy Jack" jeans and sometimes, even in the cold, would go barefoot.

We fasted and prayed for revival waiting for the next mystical manifestation to keep us going. This was a spiritual culture that I was familiar with and could easily slip into. I knew I wouldn't last there, but it didn't matter. For now, I was someplace safe and since most of these people didn't know me, my past wasn't a part of this present world.

You Can Run But You Can't Hide

Acouple of months into school, as I was starting to ease into my new routine, I received a call from home. A telegram had arrived from my manager saying:

"DEAR CAROLYN REFERENCE IS MADE TO THE EXCLUSIVE RECORDING AGREEMENT BETWEEN YOU AND US DATED AUGUST 31, 1971 DUE TO YOUR INTENTIONAL AND WILLFUL FAILURE TO PERFORM YOUR OBLIGATION THERE UNDER WE ARE HEREBY NOTIFYING YOU THAT WE ARE SUSPENDING THE TERM OF THE AGREEMENT UNTIL SUCH TIME AS YOU ARE READY WILLING AND ABLE TO PERFORM ALL OF YOUR OBLIGATIONS THERE UNDER..."

Suspending the agreement...I guess you could call this decent news for the short term, at least they weren't hauling me off to court any time soon. But in the long run, it felt as though I would never be free from the bondage of a contract and a past that I was working night and day to erase.

Lately I had been exploring the possibilities of becoming a Junior High teacher. Yes, this shows just how out of touch with reality I really was. Mama kept telling me it was all in God's hands, and if He wanted to open a door there was no power in hell or on earth that could close it. We both had all the "God speak" down and were embarrassingly lavish in our use of it. But the telegram was a very loud wake up call. No amount of immersing myself in the underground charismatic movement was going to save me from what I would eventually have to face head on.

I had recently made friends with a guy who didn't exactly fit in the church or the Christian school scene. I know…I'm a magnet. His parents, who were pastors of a church in the Midwest, had sent him to the school hoping new friends and a different location would straighten him out. He was running, and I was too. He made no attempt to hide his rebellion while I made every attempt to hide mine. He immediately saw through me.

From time to time he'd invite me to go up on Mt. Tabor and watch the sunrise while he smoked pot. It wasn't a romantic relationship although he wanted it to be. We were just friends. I was way too broken for anything else, but I enjoyed the ease of our conversations and was able to let my guard down a bit when I was with him. I was wound pretty tight. He didn't know it, but for me he was a Godsend.

One night about a month after my parents had received the telegram, and while visiting friends at their apartment, the phone rang. I was surprised when they said the call was for me, but assumed it was one of my roommates. I still don't know how he got the number, but it was my manager. He had found me.

He wasted no time in asking me to come back to my contract, telling me our separation had been good for him, and that he'd had a spiritual awakening. He asked for my forgiveness and felt if we could just start over with a clean slate, together we could really do some great things. In my absence he had continued to promote my talent to Atlantic Records along with some of his television contacts, and now they wanted to meet me.

He also wanted me to know that Diana, who was still part of the group, had experienced a serious nervous breakdown after I left, and that she missed me terribly. That was the first time she and I had ever been separated. Sometimes I think I went back more for her than anything else. I love my sister and would do anything for her. I told him I would think about it. I hung up the phone and cried for about a week.

Where Do You Go When You Can't Go Home?

Now I wish I could say that I had become stronger during my time away, but running doesn't often lend itself to personal growth. It becomes more about survival. When college let out for the summer, I tried to go back home, but six months wasn't enough to erase the big "A" on my now eighteen-year-old forehead. I didn't fit in anywhere, not at church, not with family, or with school friends, not anywhere. Also, soon after arriving home I received a letter from my "friend," remember him? It seems that without my knowledge, during our dating period, he had taken our weekend experiences and shared them in one of his classes. I became his group's case study.

Every secret, every vulnerable part of myself that I had shared became open for dissection. My socio-economic state was reviewed and catalogued. My relationship with my father, my relationship with my mother, my numerous doubts and insecurities, the neighborhood I grew up in, down to my difficulty with math and science, was ALL up for debate and discussion. He explained that out of his love and concern for me, he wanted to share the results of the study.

His group concluded that I would never be a success because I was too afraid to pursue my dream. I had the talent but I didn't have the drive, education, or stomach for the process. They were right about that last part. It was predicted that I would marry, have children, and never really *actualize* any part of my dream. Because of my poor upbringing, I would always choose safety over challenge.

However, he had heard that I might be considering going back to the group, and if I did, perhaps my life could be different, and I would prove them all wrong. He played his hand perfectly, almost as though it had been rehearsed over and over.

So in September, I found myself packing up my stuff and moving to Hollywood to live with Diana and rejoin the rest of the group still being promoted and managed by the same production company. I told M&M that I wanted to try to put the past behind us and start over, build something new.

I had long talks with the music minister, and he asked for my forgiveness. He felt he had allowed himself to get caught up in something that went terribly wrong. He seemed genuinely tortured by it all. I felt compassion and even a sense of protection for him, knowing how it feels to wake up and realize the mess you're in. What I *didn't* know for certain until later, was that my suspicions were right about some of the more reprehensible parts of his story, and continued long after I was out of his life.

I could defend my actions and say I didn't know, but in all honesty I think I was becoming just like everyone else in the narrative. We were *willfully* ignorant people choosing to look the other way and hoping upon hope that the truth, the whole truth and nothing but the truth was not as bad as what our guts were telling us.

I made some devastating choices during that time, choices that hurt people. We all did. I felt backed into a corner, and I was hanging on to anything that would either numb my senses or help me survive. Sadly, one of those choices was to once again allow myself to be reintroduced to the lovely pills…not exactly the crowd you want to run with. Obviously, the Spiritual awakening lasted about as long as it took to get me back.

Soon after I had returned, my manager in one of his more drug-induced sloppy moments, decided to have one of those "clean the slate" conversations. He was a consummate gossip and loved exposing the murkier sides of people. He was laughing when he confirmed that my earlier instincts had been right. Seems before I had left the previous year, their production company had become over-extended and needed money. Guess who was heavily invested? My wealthy collegiate confidante, the "Imposter." He wanted a return on his money, and was willing to be a player in the game of betrayal to get it.

My manager went on to tell me that they had entered into a secret alliance, agreeing that he would pursue a relationship with me, serving as their informant while trying to help woo me back to my contract.

He looked right at me and laughed saying, "Now, here you are. Looks like it worked." I swallowed this latest revelation along with another pill, letting it go deep to that angry tomb that used to be my soul. Someday it would serve me well, till then I needed to laugh with him like I had learned to do so many years ago as a child. "Looks like it," I said.

The great physicist, Albert Einstein once said that the definition of insanity is doing the same thing over and over again, expecting a different result. If that's true, guess you could say I was down right certifiable.

....

Not So Legal Addiction

I must be crazy, comin' back here. But where else am I gonna go? I've been look-
ing for a job and found one at Fox Photo on Wilshire Blvd. Yesterday was my
first and last day there. I was totally freaked out because they wanted me to run
the cash register and everyone knows I'm stupid when it comes to math.

I was behind the counter when my manager walks in and starts telling them
I have to quit because I'm opening for Vic Damone in Vegas next week. What?
I almost laughed out loud, but hey, anything to get me out of there. Still don't
know how I'm gonna pay the rent.

This summer felt so weird at home. Too many memories that people can't
let go of. Shit, who can blame 'em? If I had any brains I would've stayed in
Portland. But at least Danna and I are together again.

Lately my amazing manager has been setting her up with a doctor in Beverly
Hills who has a very willing script pad. She's been instructed to tell him she's
having trouble sleeping because of the stress of the biz, and is fearful there could
be another breakdown on the horizon, and she sure doesn't want that to hap-
pen. Does the trick every time. He hands her a couple prescriptions and then she
leaves. Last time they set me up he handed me the scripts and told me to tell my
Manager to come in and get them himself.

He always waits for us at the curb in the red Matador Station Wagon.
Classy. Then we go to the pharmacy on Hollywood Boulevard to have them
filled. They're getting wise to him though, so he's found a couple new places.
Gotta give him points for being a resourceful son of a bitch. We hand over the
bottles of pretty little pills and he puts them in his brief case. After all, he's the
one driving this mess; we're just the passengers, right? He's starting to act crazier
than usual. What an addict!

Okay boys and girls, let this be a lesson to you, your mama is right. Don't
accept rides from strangers, and there's nothin' stranger than a Hollywood
manager.

I gotta get out of here. I don't know when or how but I GOTTA get out of
here. God help me. Right now I pretty much hate who I've become.

Holidays in Hollywood

Evil doesn't usually happen over night; it's patient, willing to wait. I was just one more statistic proving that Hollywood can be a lonely and dangerous place when you're eighteen and poor in spirit, even if you don't exactly know what that means. I was the Prodigal daughter, casting her pearls before swine and refusing to acknowledge it until I was in too deep to get myself out.

I remember waking up one Thanksgiving morning, my head fuzzy from the pills the night before. Little blue, red, pink and grey ones, a plethora of color. This was unlike any other Thanksgiving I had ever known. There were no comforting sounds of Mama's loud banging of pots and pans as she hustled to prepare the traditional annual turkey feast, complete with homemade buns and pumpkin pie. Christian radio wasn't preachin' to me from its lofty perch on top of the refrigerator, and Daddy wasn't on his second pot of coffee. Or maybe he was. I don't know because I had officially run away this time and wasn't talking to them anymore.

I rolled over to look at the clock. I'd need to kick it in high gear if I was going to make it to work on time. I cleaned up, grabbed a cup of coffee and bummed a ride to the Cinerama Dome on Sunset Boulevard for my 10 o'clock shift. I had just landed the job a month or so before with the help of my manager's wife, a real class act. She coached me on how to cross my long teenage legs *just* right and lean forward *just* enough to get the job, which didn't go unnoticed by a particularly sleazy assistant manager.

Now, here I was making the mighty coveted minimum wage, behind the counter at Hollywood's hometown, premiere, movie theatre. Yes folks, it was the *glamorous* life. The movie was "Deliverance" with Burt Reynolds, Ned Beatty and Jon Voight.

After selling as much popcorn, candy and soda as possible, it was my job to go into the theatre and make sure people weren't smoking or doing *other* things…I think you get the picture, and if I may make a suggestion, don't linger too long.

So, here I was, the small town, backslid, baby of the family with Pentecostal blood still flowing through my veins, walking up and down the aisles of this *heathen* movie house with this *heathen* movie playing, pointing my flashlight, "This little Light of Mine, I'm gonna let it Shine!" at *heathens* and saying in my nicest voice, "Put it out and knock it off! Pleeeeze!"

How strange for a girl who had been raised to believe that if Jesus came back while she was in a theatre, it would prompt her immediate arrival in hell. The first movie I ever went to was the wicked and lust filled, "Sound of Music!" I was about fourteen years old and it was playing in the nearby town of Tulare. I loved it, but kept asking Jesus to forgive me every few minutes, kind of like auto save on a computer.

After a rather unpleasant encounter with a famous crooner, who will remain anonymous, I hung up my apron, changed out of my uniform because we weren't allowed to take them home, and while dodging the aforementioned assistant manager who had a habit of sneaking into the girls dressing room, walked out the door to go meet up with Diana. Yes, she was doing the mirror of my job at the famous Pantages Theatre on Hollywood Boulevard a block over. Her movie was "Lady Sings the Blues" with Diana Ross. What a great film.

Smoking was allowed in the balcony of the Pantages and Diana, who had taken up the nasty habit, would time her breaks just right so she could pick up where she left off the day before. She eventually got to see the whole movie that way. I wonder how many breaks it took and how much time it took off her life as she lit up those long Virginia Slims? You've come a long way, baby! Reminds me of that old Merle Travis song my dad and uncles used to sing:

Smoke, smoke, smoke that cigarette,
Puff, puff, puff until you smoke yourself to death
Tell Saint Peter at the golden gate
You hates to make him wait
But you just gotta have another cigarette.

There we were, the one who killed Mama and the one who broke her heart. Two lost little girls, on the streets of Hollywood, Thanksgiving Day, 1972.

The Unlikely White Knight

Can't say I was sad to say goodbye to 1972. Goodbye and good riddance! There were times when even I didn't recognize my own reflection staring back at me in the mirror. I was never carded when ordering a drink during those years. I looked thirty, and a hard thirty at that. Let that be a lesson for you: downers and alcohol are not exactly a healthy regimen for maintaining youthful beauty.

Our cutting edge management team, with their unremarkable expertise had hooked us up with an infamous Faith Healer. We were hired to be the backup group for a Liberace type artist/pianist who opened her Crusades and television shows with his unrelenting arpeggios. We wore *appropriate* long dresses and little to no make-up was allowed for the TV shows while the "Stars" caked it on. There were more contradictions and sleight of hand than a traveling carnival show.

Daddy always told me to stay away from "Carnys." I just didn't expect to find them behind the platform with their inner circles and secret handshakes with sin; made me want to medicate even more. Whole sections of people were falling over in auditoriums night after night simply because the Faith Healer, floating across the stage in her filmy gown, with raised arm and finger pointing heavenward, would say in her most mystical tone of voice, "I belieeeeve."

To this day I can't explain it. Don't want to, don't need to. I'm letting Jesus take care of all that. One thing I do know, God will use whomever he chooses and however he chooses to get his message out. Shoot, he once used an ass in the Old Testament. Numbers 22:21-33. Check it out!

This dubious association continued, and soon we were taking the show on a West Coast tour. We would be playing a mix of larger venues when we were with the Faith Healer, and smaller venues when it was just the pianist "extraordinaire" and ourselves. The music minister half of M&M had taken a staff position at a church in Southern California, which meant we were going to need a keyboard player for our group.

There was one musician who had been highly recommended and had turned us down a couple months before. Two weeks out from the first tour date, we were still without a keyboard player. There was a very real sense of urgency bordering on desperation when the decision was made to give him one more call. We were hoping, that like most musicians, he might be a little hungry after the holidays. As luck or providence would have it, he was in need of a short-term gig and agreed to come to our rehearsal for an audition the next day.

We rehearsed in my manager's office on Cahuenga, a half a block from Hollywood Boulevard. It was a prime spot for all the Tony Alamo scouts looking to proselytize hungry young runaway stars in the making, some of whom I had already met, up close and personal. When you stepped into that old building, you were met with a musty office smell mixed with toner that kept the over-worked Ozalid machine cranking out my manager's tired musical arrangements. He worked as a ghostwriter for a much-envied peer who was bringing home the big bucks. Ain't Hollywood somethin'?

We had just finished rehearsing one of our songs when we heard the keyboard player's footsteps on the stairs. He was ascending through decades of triumphs and defeats of the previous occupants that now clung to the walls of the dimly lit stairwell like dusty trophies from a long forgotten era. He stood in the doorway for a second making sure he was in the right place. I'll never forget it. It's like a mental snapshot I take out from time to time just to look at.

His hair was dark and past his shoulders. He had on pilot's glasses and was wearing jeans, boots, and a worn out Levi jacket over an old shirt. He was a polyester-free kinda guy. I was immediately drawn to his Rock n' Roll appearance. Definitely didn't fit our hair sprayed, Christian Vegas image, and I liked that...a *lot*. He was skinny and quiet in a slightly cynical sort of way. With one sweep of the room I could tell he pretty much had the situation sized up. Not exactly his cup of tea, but he needed the money.

My manager, talking a mile a minute, quickly introduced himself and then the rest of us. There was something about this guy that I immediately connected with. He was handed a piece of music as he sat down at the piano, and from the first few measures everyone in the room understood why he had been so highly recommended. He was sight-reading and his performance was confident and flawless.

While putting another piece of music in front of him, my manager went on to explain that I was the featured soloist and a "Star" in the making. It wouldn't be long before my name was a household word. I thought, "Oh Pl-eeeeze! Can I just disappear right now?"

As he listened to the spiel I detected a slight smile on his face, and then without responding or wasting any time, he began the intro. I sang with all the passion my Valium could give me, and again, he was perfection. When he played it was like a beautiful dance, no over-thinking, just doing. He was asked to step out of the room for a minute so we could talk. My manager's wife, who by this time was in full flirt mode, led the way.

Back in the rehearsal room, our conversation focused on his undeniable talent. Despite the quiet edge and his ragged appearance, we were all in agreement. This guy could play. Only one question remained, was he hungry and broke enough to wear the back-up band uniform of black polyester pants and a cream-colored turtleneck sweater? Much to his credit and being the total professional he was, he wasn't rude or arrogant in his acceptance. He knew the drill and understood what went with the territory for gigs like this.

The next few days were spent in intense rehearsal, preparing for the upcoming tour. I didn't mind though, because it gave me an opportunity to get to know the "new guy." The more time I spent with him, the more I liked him. There were moments during that week in the middle of a conversation, when I would suddenly feel oddly exposed. It was as though he could actually see *me* hidden somewhere underneath all the thick make-up and phony façade and was challenging me to come out and play. I hadn't really been attracted to anybody in a long time but I certainly was now. He thought I was funny and interesting and yet still chose to keep his distance, not exactly making himself comfortably approachable.

It wasn't long before the whole group welcomed him as if he were an old friend. He kept his own counsel when it came to my manager and his wife, and wisely chose to keep his distance from them. They didn't quite know what to make of him at first, but eventually came to appreciate and accept his aloofness. Honestly, I don't think he was losing sleep over what anybody thought. He was there to do the tour, get his money and move on.

I couldn't explain how it happened, but this guy was in my head, big time. I'd read about these kinds of attractions and seen it played out in movies but had never experienced it before. I wasn't looking for this. My life was messed up enough. I didn't need one more crazy-ass relationship to push me over the edge, but here I was and no amount of denial was working.

After spending long days together in rehearsal, I found myself lying awake at night staring at the ceiling, recounting our conversations from earlier in the day. I wondered if he was thinking about me too. Did he have a girlfriend, and if he did how serious were they? There were guys in my life that might be considered boyfriends, in a recreational kind of way, but no real heart connection. I counted the days before we would leave on tour, anxious to hit the road because the road has a way of drawing people closer together. By the time we left, I was head over heels and there was no turning back.

Every morning there was this unspoken excitement of what the day might bring. I made it a point to try to be in whatever car he was riding in. Even if I had wanted to be sly about my intentions, it was obvious to everybody I was making a play. Diana told me that what I was *making* was an absolute fool of myself and to dial it back a bit. But I was too young and inexperienced to know how to do that, nor did I want to.

I don't know if I wore him down or what was going on in his head, but it wasn't long before he made it apparent that he was interested... in something. I wasn't sure what that *something* might look like, and I didn't care. I was all in.

After making our way through Northern California, we found ourselves in Seattle, Washington. The concert hall was nice and in spite of some earlier poor showings when it was just the pianist, his hairspray, and us, there was a decent crowd expected out to applaud the favorite, glitzy protégé. On these kinds of nights, our group would open the concert and then back him up throughout the evening.

At sound check that afternoon, the keyboard player found me, much to my delight, and handed me a nice pullover sweater he was hoping to change into after the concert. Only problem was it had a hole in it and he wondered if I might be able to sew it up for him. Damn! Why didn't I apply myself more in Home Economics? It crossed my mind that Mrs. Purtle had possibly jinxed me back in eighth grade by finishing up my apron. Now I was going to need a miracle. Where's a faith healer when you need one?

In my most grown up, sultry voice I told him I would be happy to work on the sweater and anything else he might need. He thanked me and told me his girlfriend was going to be there that night and...Whoa! Wait a minute, back up there, Cowboy. Did he just say *girlfriend?*

Sure enough! Now don't that just beat all? Seems I had a decision to make. Was I going to be one more guy's friend with privileges, or was I going to find some self respect and walk away?

The answer came in the form of a smile, never giving a hint of disappointment. I took the sweater and quickly went to find Diana. She got an "A" in Mrs. Purtle's class and maybe she could help a "Sis-tuh" out?! Her response was not what I wanted to hear.

"First of all," she said, "the whole world knows that you can't sew Carter, and second of all, what part of 'I have a girlfriend' do you not understand? Oh yea, and by the way, this is a sweater. You don't *sew* it, you have to know how to *darn* it. So no, I can't help you with this. Just tell him you don't sew and best wishes to him and his girlfriend! Duh!!"

Shoot! This was going to be more difficult than I thought but I was determined not to give up that easy. I asked myself how deep his relationship could possibly be with her? I mean, she was in Seattle and he lived in L.A. Contrary to popular belief and cheesy greeting cards, absence doesn't always make the heart grow fonder. Okay, so I was a Home-Ec flunk out, who didn't sew or cook, and didn't really stay awake at night worrying about it. I had other gifts and talents. But then again, what if his girlfriend was a gorgeous confident woman who fed the homeless, led a Bible study and was his mother's #1 choice for a daughter-in-law? No way I was going to be able to compete with that. At this point I wasn't exactly what most mamas had in mind for their boys.

After allowing this mental volley to go on for a while in my head, I decided to hand him back the sweater and make a joke out of my lack of domestic qualities. Could be interesting to see where a little raw honesty might lead. Maybe I could get some clarity on these mixed signals he was sending. Men like to go around telling the world that women are impossible to read. Well, I suppose we are a bit complicated at times, but we don't exactly have the market cornered, boys!

I found him and returned his sweater. Then, holding my head up high, I told him it wasn't my thing and maybe his *girlfriend* could help him with that. After the show, that's exactly what she did.

The sun rose the next morning and set the next night, and not much was said about the girlfriend. However, much to my approval, further down the road "Sweater Boy" began to be very intentional and clear about his interest in me. I guess the Seattle connection wasn't as strong as I had feared, or maybe our undeniable attraction was based on something a little more powerful than either one of us could articulate at that time.

As the tour continued we chose to abandon the safety of our defensive walls and dive into the adventure of getting to know one another. Let the fun begin!

....

First Day of the Rest of My Life

I don't think I have ever been this happy! We got home yesterday and Barny (that's the new guy) asked me if I wanted to come see his place. Are you kidding? I tried not to seem over-anxious but all I wanted to DO was see his place, be with him without everybody else around. My manager, frankly, has been making some not so subtle efforts to keep us apart the last few weeks on the road. Didn't work. Barny doesn't know about us; probably thinks he's just being over-protective, and I'm going to keep it that way for now. I mean, what would he do if he knew? I don't want to think about it.

I felt like such a free spirit when I jumped into his old 1964 Econoline Van. It has these curtains for the side windows made out of material that looks like a flag. If Daddy knew he'd give me a whippin' for sure! He thinks anything other than the stars and stripes waving from an appropriate flagpole is nothing short of treason!

The further I got from everybody the more like me I felt. You should see his place. It's this very private little one room cottage that used to be an old farm equipment shed. He told me that when he found it the door was hanging off its hinges, and there was a bathtub stuck in a closet with a drainpipe. Can you imagine? The guys that lived there before had left it a mess, but the rent was cheap and he knew that with a little effort it could be fixed up.

After signing the rental agreement his dad drove down from Sacramento to help him move out of a house he had been sharing with some guys he was in a band with. The two of them turned the closet with the tub into a nice shower that has these very cool wooden saloon doors that swing in and out.

The bathroom wall has this crazy black and white newspaper looking print with a bunch of naked ladies from the 1800's on it. One wall is a kitchen and in the main part of the room is a twin bed, upright piano, stereo equipment and a big bay window that looks out into a little garden area. He put the old bathtub out there and it's filled with Geraniums.

One of the other very cool things is, it's in Sherman Oaks, and since it's an old shed it's on about ½ an acre with tons of trees. There's a whole bunch of musicians that live around there, and they kind of look out for each other.

I didn't want to leave, and he didn't want me to either. I loved waking up this morning in his arms. We're both pretty skinny so the twin bed was just fine. I got up to go put on my makeup and he said he kinda likes the way I look without it. It was weird; all of a sudden I felt shy and had trouble looking him in the eyes. But he just kept smiling at me and telling me I was beautiful. I wonder if I'll ever believe that.

He made me coffee and a real breakfast. I laughed when I looked inside his refrigerator. The freezer compartment had packages of beef and chicken all neatly stacked on the left, with frozen vegetables on the right. The refrigerator part was spotless and only had a few things in there since he'd been gone for a while. I asked him where the cold pizza, chocolate stars and animal cookies were? He just laughed and came over and kissed me again.

He brought me back to my apartment a little while ago. He has to work tonight but is going to come over and pick me up later. I'm bringing a toothbrush this time.

I think I'm falling in love with this guy…
Please God, don't let me screw this up.

Leaving Slow

Within a month of leaving the tour, Barny had succumbed to his weaker side and asked me to move in with him. The almost daily drive from Sherman Oaks to L.A. was becoming expensive with escalating gas prices at the pump. I had come to see that he was an intensely private person, so my moving in required no small sacrifice on his part. Guess what I brought to his world was worth the trade out, and God knows I needed a place to stay.

Life with Barny was good. He encouraged me to renew my relationship with my parents, not knowing the background of how it had been so damaged through the years by my associations with M&M. I remember taking him home to meet the family. I was nervous to introduce Daddy to my "long haired Hippie" boyfriend, and chose a public place hoping to avoid any unnecessary awkwardness.

The grocery store where he worked seemed a neutral enough place, and to my relief Daddy didn't make a scene. When he came home later that afternoon, he asked Barny if he could play "San Antonio Rose." Mama stood in the doorway holding her breath and praying with all her might that Barny could accommodate this challenge, I mean request. I wasn't worried. I had told him my dad would probably ask him to play this song and a few others, so he practiced up and was ready to shine. Much to my dad's surprise, he followed it up with a mean version of the "Boogie Woogie."

"Dadgum!" Daddy exclaimed slapping him on the back, "This boy can tickle them ivories, can't he?"

From that moment on Barny could never do any wrong in my father or mother's eyes, and neither one of them judged me for livin' in sin. In fact, Daddy told me he was relieved. It wasn't just because Barny was an incredible musician and had won my dad over, or the fact that he was a Bakersfield boy and oh yea, had been raised Assembly of God, go figure. It was because they had their daughter back, and that was something they felt they could never repay him for. It had been a rough few years, but we were a family again and stronger for it. Nothing feels better than restoration and redemption, and there was plenty more to come.

Within a few months after the "Faith Healer" tour, the old group began to fall apart. We were only doing an occasional church concert here and there, but nothing that could sustain us financially. So by the time that summer arrived people started saying their goodbyes and going their separate ways.

My manager would come up with the occasional rabbit in a hat opportunity for me, and we'd chase it down the dark hole, but with little or no results. During this time he made it a point to reach out to Barny, partially because he wanted to keep tabs on me. But the better side of him saw the talent and believed that he could serve as a sort of mentor to him. Although Barny had his reservations, he proved to be a worthy student and was grateful for what he was learning about orchestrating and copy work. He was also booked on a few sessions from time to time and introduced to other players who later became friends.

But the red flags were still waving, and one night after having dinner with my manager and his wife, Ol' Hollywood started bragging about how over the years he had tied up a bunch of young people in seven-year contracts where he had the option. He had mixed his Harvey Wallbangers with a couple of his favorite pills and was now only too willing to brag about his seedy accomplishments, never taking into consideration that one of his victims was sitting in the backseat.

In a "shoot from the hip" moment, Barny told him that was total bullshit! He and his friends had been down that road before with a well known "Christian" organization that sent teenagers out in teams to sing all over the world. Most had a good time, but some of the more talented kids were signed to bogus contracts and promised the moon. What they got was a ride on an old bus, crappy gigs and little to no money while the fat cat back home kept all the tour "support."

He had been gone from that world for quite awhile, but this statement reminded him of just how pissed he still was and he wasn't going to sit there and say nothing. It was an awkwardly tense moment. My manager and his wife both looked at each other and kept their mouths shut, wasting no time in dropping us off.

Once inside the house, Barny had a few questions for me. The time had come and I was nervous as I gave him the Reader's Digest version, still choosing to deflect as much of the truth about my life the past couple of years as possible. He didn't push, but it became a game changer. He was seeing me in a different light, and the pieces were starting to come together. He wasn't going to be anybody's pawn, and without making a big deal out of it he chose to see less and less of them. I wanted desperately to be able to walk away from the contract, but it was tight and my manager wasn't going to let me go without a fight.

I held on to every moment I had with Barny. We filled our lives with the music we loved, and together began the long walk out of the Charlatan side of the world of Christian music culture, leaving it for the vultures and buzzards who prey upon the young and innocent. I still didn't know where we were going in this relationship but at least wherever that was, we were going there together, and that was more than fine with me.

· ·

Singin' For Food

Oh, My, Gosh! Barny's grandmother is a piece of work. She goes by "Nana Alice" and lives over in Burbank with her daughter, Barny's Aunt LeVerne, who is his mother's sister. I've never been around anyone like them. Nana sized me up real quick, letting me know without exactly saying it, that "Cliff" (that's his real name and she doesn't like to call him by his nickname, Barny) was a favorite and I had better watch my step. "Yes, Ma'am!"

Now that she knows me a little better, she actually likes me and honestly, I think she's one of the most intriguing people I've met in a long time. She has the most color-ful stories of old Hollywood. I found out that she's been married about five times that she admits to, and worked as a waitress in an after hours club during the glamour years of Hollywood. When we go over to their house for Barny to fix things for them, I sit in the front bedroom with her as she goes through all of her old photographs. She was absolutely drop-dead gorgeous!

Man, is she tough, though. She doesn't cut anybody any slack. I keep think-ing, if this is the way she treats the grandson she's partial to, what's she like with everybody else? Quite a life...she married young out of the hills of Kentucky and had three children by the time she was seventeen. Wasn't blessed with the all pow-erful maternal instinct gene and chose to leave her children with her husband when the youngest was a toddler so she could live the big life in Hollywood. Her story would make an incredible movie. I'm winning her over though. I make her laugh, and she loves the fact that we're in "Show Business."

I think she kind of has a soft spot for me because I'm young. The way she watches me and talks to me, I think she senses I have a story myself and that's something she understands.

She and Aunt LeVerne are part of the "Eastern Star" organization and recently they've been hiring us to do music at some of their functions. It's really difficult not to laugh as you watch them go through all of their marches and pro-tocol. This particular chapter is mostly made up of older Jewish people and when it comes to the food line, Nana uses her cane and parts the waters. She tells ev-eryone we're the entertainment for the night and then pushes us to the front of the line making no apologies. I love these people! They're a real hoot! We don't make any money, but it's a free meal and we feel like we're the ones being entertained.

A Case of Mistaken Identity

One morning Barny and I woke up and had our first fight. He had low blood sugar and I was exhausted from fighting ghosts in my sleep all night. There was hardly any food in the fridge, and we were both hungry. We hopped in the Van and headed to the supermarket a couple blocks over on Ventura Boulevard. Neither one of us thought much about it, but we looked pretty ragged. Well, after walking up and down the aisles a few times with Barny asking me what I wanted and me answering him with, "I don't know, what do you want?" We both became a bit edgy and walked out of the store without buying anything.

Later that night, after finishing up some leftovers Nana Alice had dropped by from an Eastern Star event, we heard a knock at the door. Since it was dark, Barny looked out the window over the stove to be sure. It was difficult to see but he could make out two men dressed in suits and a couple of uniformed guys with shotguns. He asked who they were and they said they were Los Angeles police officers and to open the door immediately, which he did.

"Are you Clifford Robertson?" they asked to which he answered "yes."

He was told to step outside for a moment, and then they proceeded to handcuff him. I stood there in shock as they informed him he was being arrested for armed robbery and read him his Miranda rights. It was one of the most terrifying and helpless moments of my life. He asked if he could go back in the house and put on a shirt and shoes, which they allowed, then quickly hustled him out the door and into a waiting cruiser outside.

It all happened so fast there was hardly time to object. I tried to explain that they must have made a mistake, but I was pushed aside and told to stay out of the way. I begged them to tell me where they were taking him, but my pleas fell on deaf ears. One of the plainclothes detectives stayed along with two other uniformed officers.

I stood there helplessly watching as they completely ransacked the little house, dumping our hamper, drawers, going through papers and even the refrigerator. I tried not to cry and did my best to remain calm, biting the inside of my mouth knowing that tears make you weak, especially when it comes to bullies. I told the detective that I had uncles who were police officers, my father was a veteran, and we were law-abiding citizens. "I know we look like hippies," I said. "But we're just peaceful musicians."

The uniform guys got a good laugh out of that but the detective, after not finding anything, told me that if my boyfriend was innocent he would probably be out by tomorrow. He also told me they were taking him to Van Nuys to be booked, and then just like that they were gone, leaving a huge mess to be cleaned up.

I didn't know what to do or who could help. I called his parents, and they were understandably upset and stunned. His father told me he knew his son was innocent and he would hire an attorney immediately. I remembered that my manager had some friends on the force in North Hollywood that he used to play in bands with, so I swallowed my pride and called. He showed up immediately and took me back to his apartment. Calls were made, an attorney was given a non-refundable retainer and all that was left to do was wait.

My manager was very protective and uncharacteristically kind that night. He told me I needed to rest and insisted, without much argument from me, that I take a couple pills to help calm me down. I had stopped partaking since moving in with Barny and I assumed they would do the job. However, I still couldn't sleep. I lay awake all night in a kind of pill induced fog listening to the clock tick, waiting to hear about the one man I had come to love with everything I had.

The next morning we got the call. The police soon realized after questioning him they had the wrong guy, but by then it was too late to process him out. He had agreed to a lie-detector test and had passed without any doubt. Now they were dropping him off at our friend's house.

We jumped in the car and arrived just as the police were leaving. I was so relieved to see him but had this thinly controlled righteous anger as I asked the officer why and how they could do such a thing?

He answered me by saying I should be grateful to live in America. Any other country wouldn't even care that he was innocent, and they would just let him rot in jail. The guy was so callous and had an obvious dislike for anyone who didn't sport a crew cut. I was thinking, "Man just because you wear a uniform doesn't mean you can't be a human being." We're not the enemy, buddy. I didn't waste one more minute but ran into the house to be with Barny.

We talked to his parents that afternoon, and they said they wouldn't be able to sue for false arrest because everything had been done by the book. The supermarket we went to the previous day had been robbed a few weeks before by someone who had long hair and was skinny. The grocery clerk observed that we looked out of place, and we left without buying anything. We weren't aware of it, but he followed us out and got the license plate number off the van and phoned the police. They showed up at our place thinking they were arresting an armed robber. They didn't give us any information because they didn't want to compromise the lie-detector test if administered. Barny said that after questioning him the detectives were sure they had the wrong guy, but he went ahead with the lie-detector to clear all doubt.

I was so glad to be back home together I couldn't stop hugging him. Barny just wanted to forget about it and get on with life. I however, kept thinking about how you can be sitting in your own little house, not bothering anyone, and be arrested because of the way you look. I also couldn't shake the memories of moving to Hollywood and encountering officers who liked to pull young girls over and make deals. I think I'll leave that one alone. I was still grateful to live in this country, but I didn't feel safe and that wasn't new.

Livin' on Love and Ten Dollar Gigs

Barny started turning me onto to music I'd never heard before. There was Leon Russell, Delaney and Bonnie, Edgar Winter, Joe Cocker and countless others. It was an instant connect, evoking the emotions I felt when I used to listen by the hour to Simon and Garfunkel's "Bookends" or Neil Young's "Harvest" album. It's like I had experienced this arrested musical development over the past few years, and now I couldn't get enough. We'd spend entire days just playing and singing together.

He introduced me to his friends, most of whom were musicians, and they'd come over and we'd jam for hours. These friendships turned into bands and bands turned into gigs. We discovered that it was easier to pay the $85.00 a month rent when we both did the gig.

One of his best friends, Bob Walden, was a killer guitar player. He lived a block over, so getting together to rehearse was no problem. We decided to form a band and call ourselves "Moonlite." Bob was a few years older than us, and we both respected his musical opinions as well as his business prowess no matter how lean the résumé. So when he thought it would be a good idea to dress up in our gig clothes, walk up and down Ventura Boulevard, hitting every club we could find to see if they would hire us, we got dressed and got in line.

He carried an empty briefcase thinking it made us look more professional. We had two songs in our repertoire, "Danny's Song" and "Dancin' In the Moonlight." I mean, how could they resist? Evidently it wasn't all that difficult for them, and not surprisingly we didn't get one job that way. We were however, an inspiring testimony to musicians everywhere who refused to give up.

Somehow we got hired to play a party that went well, and the word was out in the social circles that a new band was available for weddings, Bar Mitzvahs, Mormon dances, and club organizations. We actually played a dance mixer one time for the "Little People's" local chapter hosted by the "Tall Persons" club. Once the drinking commenced tall people were scooping up little people and dancing around the room. It was one of the funniest and yet oddly enough comfortable gigs we ever played. Talk about résumés!

We took as much work as we could get, and then signed on to a little more when Bob Shermer, who had a large casual band in the valley, gave us his overflow. We had also joined up with the Gary Hill Band playing local clubs and doing our best to balance our party gigs that usually paid a little more. We were recording on off hours at different studios in town for free and writing songs during the day.

"Moonlite" went to a whole new level when we hooked up with one the hottest caterers in town. He fed us as well as paid us and we were grateful. It takes a village, folks.

⭐ GARY HILL BAND ⭐

Sunday Nights
Are Party Nights!

COUNTRY
ROCKnROLL
9 PM TIL 2 AM
NO ADMISSION

Gary Hill Band

Palomino *Award Winning Country Night Club*

6907 Lankershim Blvd. — North Hollywood — 765-9256

VOTED NO. 1 COUNTRY AND WESTERN NIGHT CLUB
BY ACADEMY OF COUNTRY & WESTERN MUSIC

1965. 1966. 1967. 1968. 1969. 1970. 1971. 1972. & 1973

Shelter

"**S**helter! Shelter! Shelter!" From my perspective on stage, looking out into the faces of the crowd, I realized I was being paid one of the greatest compliments an artist could be paid. They were on their feet, banging their beer bottles on the tables demanding I sing a song that Barny had written for me entitled "Shelter."

Now, even though I considered myself an artist, in *this* band I was the chick background singer and Gary Hill was the Artist. He wasn't exactly thrilled about the attention I was getting. He had just signed a deal with Capitol Records, and a powerful producer was there that night to see him. Add to the mix that these were *his* crazy friends, and you can imagine how the dynamic was becoming a bit dicey.

This was at the famous Palomino Club in North Hollywood where we played as the house band on Sunday nights. I was underage and believe me, paid a price for my birth year every time I would show up to sing. For whatever reason, the doorman seemed to garner some sort of sadistic bullying charge out of harassing me, saying he wasn't going to let me in. Gary, who was first generation out of the Kentucky hills with a mama who could deliver a punch that would knock most men over and make them want to remain prone, would eventually threaten the guy. I would be escorted to the back room, which was where I would spend most of the night when I wasn't out on stage singing.

The Hill Family were not people you would want to mess with. Gary had a brother that was as big as a mountain and not only *loved* to fight, but lived to do so. Even the police didn't like to show up when he'd get into it at one of our gigs. They knew they ran the risk of serious injury and chose to come as a group. That man scared me to death. I'd seen him in action, and he was close to unstoppable.

I looked at Gary waiting for him to call the next song. He may not have been happy about the situation, but he knew there would be no proceeding until I sang "Shelter." He was also my friend, and I'm sure he felt conflicted by wanting to support me, but at the same time not wanting to give up part of his show. I understood that. But hey, what's a girl to do? So with a pitcher of beer in hand, he challenged everyone to a chug contest, then said, "Here she is boys, the ever lovely Miss Carter!"

The feeling up on that stage was incredible, singing with abandon and all those old boys and their girlfriends standing up singing along with me. Their unsolicited outburst and my passionate version of the song didn't go unnoticed by the producer sitting in the back, which would come into play further down the road. There were also a couple of other people in the crowd we didn't know. One would eventually become a band mate, while the other would be our road manager (Gordon Payne and Tom Bourke); both became our lifelong friends. You just never know who's listening.

I loved working with the Gary Hill Band. We'd rehearse out in the garage at his house where he and his girlfriend of several years were renting. Colleen was and is amazing. She worked as a waitress and was the only one bringing in steady money at the time. We'd drink beer and do music all day until she came home and fed us. There were always dogs in the mix, including our golden lab Beulah, who would play with Gary's dogs for hours while we worked toward making the music happen. It's also the place I was doused the first time by one of Gary's more questionable friends. Angel Dust ain't no fun.

From that old garage to the stages of the Palomino, we believed we were becoming a force to be reckoned with, and we were for a time. Our fan base shared a similar demographic with a couple of artists that were on the verge of turning country music upside down. Gary had recently tuned in to Waylon Jennings' "Honky Tonk Heroes" album, and the songs as well as the musical approach were resonating in a way nothing else had before. His music felt like home, and we spent many nights after long days of rehearsing, sitting around on Gary and Colleen's small living room floor, drinking beer and listening a little closer.

Angel Watchin' Over Me

L iving the carefree life of broke musicians wasn't all fun and games. There was still rent to pay and food to buy. Even though we didn't eat all that much, gasoline prices were continuing to soar, and most of our gigs weren't exactly right around the corner. L.A. is no small little hamlet, you know? Barny's trusty old van had gone out on him, and it was something that required special equipment that he didn't have and couldn't borrow, which is how he usually fixed it. The guy had inherited his father's ability to repair just about anything.

So, it was no easy decision when he bit the bullet and took it in to the shop for repairs. We had a couple of weddings coming up with "Moonlite," and between the money we would get for the two of us we figured we might just be able to scrape by that month. Our neighbors, who were also broke musicians, had loaned us their little VW and we were on our way to pay the big bucks and get the van back.

It was still light outside when we parked on the side street next to the shop, but neither one of us thought anything about it. However, by the time the paper work was completed it was dark. After telling Barny I would see him back at the house, I turned the corner off of busy Van Nuys Boulevard and started walking toward the old VW bug.

Almost instantly I sensed I was in danger. I noticed a car with a man driving and a woman in the passenger's seat. They were slowly following me. Immediately every recent news report about kidnapping and white slavery bombarded my consciousness. My first response was to run. Don't make eye contact; just run! Get the hell out of there!

There was no one around. The dealership on the corner had closed, and there were no salesmen on the lot. I was on my own. The car made an abrupt stop as the woman opened her door and was half way out. I started praying out loud, "Jesus, save me!"

All of a sudden, she jumped back in the car and slammed her door. She looked right at me and said, "You're one lucky girl. If it weren't for that big man over there watching, you'd be ours."

She pointed to the car lot as they peeled off into the night looking for the next victim. I started crying and looked over in the lot expecting to see someone, but there was no one there. I ran as fast as my legs would carry me down Van Nuys Boulevard and saw Barny stopped at the light. Screaming hysterically, I banged on the door, and he quickly let me in. I was shaking uncontrollably, but I was safe.

We drove back to our friend's borrowed car and saw that the dealership was completely quiet. There was no one there. Believe what you want, but I believe God sent an Angel and that's who the kidnappers saw as they started to make their move. I don't take such things lightly, and not surprisingly, after sharing the story with Mama, she completely agreed. Her prayers of, "Build a wall of protection around my children, Lord," had been answered that night.

Thank you Jeee-zus!

....

The Proposal

*What a strange day. Moonlite played for a wedding reception in Beverly Hills
tonight. It was beautiful. Little lights in the trees, limitless champagne for the
guests and the most amazing cuisine offered by Randy, the caterer who we now
work with on a pretty regular basis. Must have been a limitless budget because
he sure pulled out all the stops for this one.*

*A little different from the oil company gig we did last weekend with the
Gary Hill Band. After the company executive walked up on the stage to say a
few closing words to his employees, our drummer goosed him with a drumstick
and then stood up and said in a very loud voice, "Hey buddy, looks like you're
about a quart low!" The crowd, all dressed up in their fancy cocktail clothes,
was hammered by then and cheered so loud I thought the windows were going
to crack. Although it was side splittingly funny, my good friend Randy Farrar
(who was subbing on keyboards for Barny that night) and I were probably the
only people who felt it may have been a wee bit inappropriate. Well... the two of
us and the oil company executive that is. We won't be asked back, but at least
they paid in cash.*

*The music went over exceptionally well for the Beverly Hills party though
and all the musicians enjoyed the food Catering offered to us in the kitchen.
We were "puttin' on the dog" with little crab stuffed mushrooms, baby corn and
sweet peas. They call it crudités, but it's really just cut up veggies.*

*Barny seemed distant, kind of pre-occupied. I'd try to talk to him on breaks
and it was weird, like he was avoiding me or blowing me off. He never does that.
I started thinking of all the reasons he might be acting that way and the result
I came up with was not good. I'm one crazy ass liability. I have a past that just
won't go away, plus I have nightmares sometimes. He holds me and tells me it's
going to be okay, but I know I'm more than he signed on for. He had a good thing
going before I came into his life.*

*As we were packing up the van to leave the caterer came out and handed us
a bottle of champagne. He told us he had some more events coming up, and he
would be in touch. Gigs are always good news, but Barny still had his walls up.
On the ride home there was this gnawing, sick feeling in the pit of my stomach,
telling me to prepare for the worst. This had been a good run, but...*

*We arrived back at the house, and he never said a word as we unloaded the
Hammond B-3, Leslie speaker, and all the rest of the equipment. We have quite*

a routine that works well for a couple of skinny kids like us. Leverage. It's all in HOW you lift.

Once inside I felt awkward, almost like a guest who had stayed too long. I sat down on the bed, looking straight ahead out the window, waiting for the other shoe to drop. He came and sat down by me. My heart was beating right out of my chest as he spoke. He said, "I know why I've been feeling so bad today."

I tried to look in his eyes but his head was down. I swallowed and quietly asked him why? He took my shaking hands and held them for a moment, then looked right at me. "It's because I want to ask you to marry me."

I responded with, "What? Could you say that again please?"

He started to smile and said it louder this time.

"I love you, Carter. Will you marry me?"

I was in shock and must have asked him if he was serious and if he would repeat it again. The more he said it, the more we laughed.

"Yes! Yes! Yes!"

He stood up, went to the cupboard, pulled out two Pepsi glasses we had gotten for free from some gas station, and then grabbed the bottle of champagne from the refrigerator. He filled them to the top, and we didn't stop toasting until the glasses were empty. He called his parents, and I called Diana and then my parents. Our families couldn't have been happier for us. I still can't believe it.

I'm going to be Mrs. Clifford "Barny" Robertson!!!

I Do...

Even Though I Already Did

March 2, 1974 arrived in the middle of the gas crunch, bless your heart President Carter, and everyone was hard pressed to find stations that were open and willing to sell. Thankfully, Daddy had a line on a couple of local places to help our out of town guests, which included The Gary Hill Band. Some of them had driven up together in one of their vans and camped out at Pot Wisha, just below Sequoia National Park. A couple other musicians took their chances and hitch hiked, cutting it close, but still making it right on time.

There were blossoms brought in bags from the fruit trees in our yard back home, along with a few from the many orange orchards in Ivanhoe that had been pilfered along the way. The beautiful scent of spring scattered down the aisle and filled the whole church with its sweet fragrance.

The reception was being held in the church basement where we had it decorated with saddles, cow skulls and various other western articles. Caught a little flack for that but hey, it was *our* wedding. The cake was baked and ready to be put on the table along with the butter mints and mixed nuts. The virgin punch was in the church refrigerator staying cool until the moment it would be poured into the big crystal bowl. The plates, included in the price for the church rental, had a special place for your punch cup along with the napkins and forks.

Everything was all laid out nice and neat on pretty white lace tablecloths. The sweet ladies on the church wedding committee were lined up and waiting to serve us. For all they knew, we were good little chaste Christian young adults following in the tradition of countless others before us.

The funny and somewhat surprising part about all of it was that this was exactly how we wanted it to go down. No fuss no muss. No cooler than anybody else in the room factor, because neither one of us could or even wanted to take on that burden. Our plan was to stand in a reception line, thank everybody, and then let them eat cake! We figured we'd be able to wrap the whole thing up in about an hour and a half, and then it was VACATION time! We didn't much care for the word *honeymoon*.

It was a rainy day, and even though I had not been nervous up until then, I was now. Barny had already stared down his doubts and won a month or so before when he had hit a wall and questioned whether he could go through with it or not. I can't tell you how heartbroken I was, but tried not to show it. I chose rather to listen deep, to hear what he wasn't saying.

He wasn't questioning his love for me, or the good thing we had going. He was just feeling the weight of responsibility that comes with the choice of allowing someone else in your life and the commitment to that relationship forever. The last thing he wanted to do was get married and have it be a sham. Couldn't abide the idea of being a phony.

There was so much I wanted to say to try and persuade him. The very idea that he might walk away was sheer torture. I was crazy in love, maybe too in love if that's possible, thinking I had enough for both of us. In the end I chose to let him wrestle through it on his own terms. Within a day or two, Barny told me his heart was in too deep and he believed we were meant to be together. Both of us had been processing a decision that would not include a Plan B. We had been taught that marriage was a covenant with the almighty God, and neither one of us took that lightly. With that understanding, we held on to each other and never looked back.

Two months before the wedding, my manager made a last ditch effort to stop us by having braces put on my teeth. He was hoping I would be too embarrassed by my "under construction smile" to go through with it. Boy was he wrong. We weren't going to let anything or anybody stand in our way. Soon the ceremony part would be over, and we could get on with our lives starting with some much-needed down time at the beach. Now you're talkin'. "Damn the torpedoes! Full speed ahead!"

Barny's sister Raedena was a hair stylist in Sacramento and a very good one at that. When we announced our engagement, I asked if she would consider being my stylist that day. She was very excited and totally on board. She was also going to man the guest book for us.

Her husband was one of Barny's groomsmen and our friend and fellow band mate, Bob, was Best Man. Dave Laster, a guy that Barny had known since they met in the church nursery and had grown up getting into as much trouble as possible, was our usher-at-large. *He* wasn't large; it was just another one of those wedding title thingy's. From day one he accepted me into their circle and continues to be able to make me laugh like nobody else.

My sisters were both my maids of honor and bridesmaids. Pretty straight ahead. We didn't want any big fanfare or sappy wedding songs, so we hired the local pipe organist who was also the wife of the Minister who married us, to play classical music. She was awesome!

The night before our big event my sister Sharon, who had given birth to her first child less than three months before, prepared a last minute homemade lasagna dinner for everyone in the wedding. Somehow the planning of a rehearsal dinner had fallen through the cracks, and she and her husband Edd jumped in to save the day. I loved that about them.

That night, Barny left with his family to stay with them at a local hotel. As they were all sitting around laughing and catching up, preparing for the next day's big event, his sister decided to give him a nice little pre-wedding hair trim. She and his mom wanted him to look nice for all the wedding photos that would be cherished for years to come. They weren't big fans of his rock and roll lifestyle or look, but had chosen to curb their obvious dislike. Understand, his hair was past his shoulders when she started, and he was thinking *trim*. With the first cut of the scissors he knew the trim had turned into a full on cut, not much was left to do except let her finish.

I laugh when I think about it now, remembering a time when Barny asked if I could trim the front of his hair. All the other musician's "Old Ladies" cut their hair and he assumed I had those skills as well. You'd think the man would've learned by then. Well, not wanting to disappoint him and being overeager to please and impress him, I agreed to work my magic. I had cut my bangs before and had watched my mom cut our hair plenty of times. So with a comb and scissors in hand I put water on the front part of his hair holding it down and began cutting away. Much to my horror I hadn't taken into consideration that his hair had a lot of extra curl to it, and as soon as I released the scissors he had bangs that jumped up to his forehead making him look like Friar Tuck. "Oops" followed by an "Uh-oh" made Barny slowly respond with, "Carter, what do you mean, 'Oops'?"

I just stood there with my hand over my mouth trying not to laugh, knowing there was nothing funny about what I had just done. He took one look in the mirror and started laughing. He was such a good sport, but then that made me cry. Dear God, I did not deserve this man's patience! He started reassuring *me* and asked me to carefully finish the job. I think he wore a hat for a few weeks until his hair grew out. We were quite a pair, him with his monk bangs and me with my braces!

Anyway, the morning of the wedding, Raedena woke up, did Nana Alice's hair first of course, then Aunt LeVerne's hair, her mother's hair, her father's hair, and her husband's hair, while I sat and waited. By the time she got to me, I was supposed to already be at the church. With my ride revved up and ready to go downstairs in the motel parking lot, she worked as fast as she could all the while expressing her concern that she wouldn't get her own hair done, and now she was going to be too late to do the guest book.

After the last go around of hair spray, my brother arrived to help me quickly gather up the remaining wedding accessories and dump them in the car. I slid across the front bench seat as my mother burned rubber, and Norman slammed the passenger side door shut. When Mama wanted to she could make a 30-minute trip up the mountain turn into 20, and that's what she did.

I was still in my Billy Jack jeans with no make-up on hoping the bobby pins would hold the daisies that were delicately positioned in the uncooperative curls on top of my head. Sitting between the two of them, trying not to feel as rushed as we most assuredly were, I glanced over at my mother. Her hands gripped the wheel like a vice, and there was a wild expression in her eyes. She was going to get this troubled daughter of hers to the church on time if she had to blow past every CHP on the road. She was banking on the fact that she had connections in that department, as well as the zip code upstairs, if you know what I mean. There was nothing, and I mean *nothing*, going to keep her from this very important and crucial God-appointed task.

As I was taking this all in, it slowly dawned on me that she was wearing white. She looked very pretty with her up-do that the gal at the beauty parlor down the road had done the day before. She was all decked out in her stark white dress with her lime green high heels. I started to experience this sort of out of control laugh that started in my chest and spit from my mouth and came out more like a crazy kind of cry. My brother looked at me and in his formal sounding pastor's voice told me not to be nervous, this was all perfectly normal. Everything was going to be okay, Scout.

Okay? Really? Where have you been the past few years, Bro? This was insane. My off, off, off white wedding dress was hanging up in the backseat and my brown suede shoes with the red embroidered flowers and teeth marks where our dog Beulah had mistaken them for a chew toy was in the grocery bag from Daddy's store. I kept shaking my head and squeaking out a giggle that made one think it might be a good idea to have the guys in the white coats on call.

In a move that rivaled "Starsky and Hutch" Mom skidded to a stop in the church parking lot, and I jumped out of the car. Grabbing the dress and shoes, I bounded up the front steps introducing myself for the first time to some of Barny's very conservative side of the family. I could only imagine what they were thinking but hoped it could be explained later down the road. These people turned out to be the absolute best and found the whole spectacle quite humorous.

Barny had been there for a while just shootin' the breeze with his friends at the church, completely unaware that I was just now arriving. I ran into the room on the other side of the vestibule we were using to get dressed in and saw my sisters all ready to go, but wondering what had been keeping the bride. About a minute after entering the room while relaying the events of the morning, there was a knock at the door. When we opened it, the minister who had counseled us before we got married and who was now officiating the service, was red faced and annoyed. He told me I was late and that he and his wife had only paid for a babysitter for a couple of hours. So I had better get dressed and get down the aisle, or they were going to start this thing without me.

Sweet! This is just how I had always imagined my wedding to be. I think he had doubts about us, me in particular. He was a pastor on staff at the church where all the "stuff" had happened, and I'm sure had heard an earful about me. Add to that the fact that Barny and I didn't go to church and had no plans of changing that decision, and you can understand his frustration. He was taking a risk here, probably out of loyalty to Sharon and her husband, and didn't want his perfect officiating record flawed by a couple of crazy musicians.

As I slipped into my wedding dress, my sisters helped me with my make-up and before you could say, "Bobbity Boo," Mama had us in a circle holding hands and praying. Ahhhhhh...

The music started, and my sisters walked down the aisle one by one. I stood there holding on to Daddy for dear life, with my picket fence smile kind of frozen in an unnatural way, trying to remember if I was wearing any underwear. I was so skinny I looked like a child in my muslin wedding dress holding a bouquet of fresh white daisies that were now tucked up under my chin. I was shaking like a leaf. Daddy was cool as a cucumber and looked quite dashing in his brilliantly white loafers. Funny, my parents were the only ones wearing white that day.

"You nervous?" he asked almost laughing.

"Y-Y-Y-Yes." I stuttered.

He just shook his head, grabbed my hand, and squeezed it real tight.

"What are you nervous for, Carter? You been sleepin' with the guy for a year!"

Now I know this isn't exactly great father and daughter pre-walking down the aisle banter, but it was just what I needed in that moment. It wasn't the sentiment that we had been naughty by having sex for a year, but the reminder and clarification of why we were there in the first place. I loved Barny. Barny loved me. We were great together and had already weathered some pretty ugly storms to prove it. So there!

The doors opened, and I nearly fainted when I saw the groom standing there looking like a stranger due to his sister's generous wedding *trim*.

There are moments we still laugh about as we recall my sisters crying such loud happy tears that the minister had to lean over and whisper an admonishment. Then there's the part of the ceremony where we had planned to share the vows we had written to each other. It was Barny's turn up to bat and as he looked at me, I knew he had drawn a blank. After a couple of random, rambling sentences, and with a deer in the headlight expression he said in a clear voice, "Carter, you are my woman."

Which made all of the hippie musicians on one side of the church start to cry, and all the conservative family members on the other side of the church laugh out loud. The minister made sure we understood the gravity of the union we were entering into by explaining in detail what it meant for *me* to submit, and then pronounced us, "Man and Wife. You may kiss your bride."

Now we had practiced this. I'd told Barny to go easy, let's just make it a sweet little kiss and get out of there. He must have forgotten, or was so relieved to have it over, that he grabbed me and if the preacher hadn't stopped him, we might still be there.

At the reception Gary went up to Barny's dad, who has never had a drop of liquor in his life, and asked when the "drinkin' was gonna start," to which his dad responded in a very formal way, *"That's* up to Clifford," (Barny's given name) and walked away.

Gary also cornered Barny at one point and said, "Man, that preacher sure did tie the knot awful tight."

Guess he did. We're going on thirty-nine years.

Barny's dad gave us money so we could stay a couple of nights at the Madonna Inn over on the coast. I used to dream about that place when I was a kid and lived in Santa Maria. We would pass by it every time we were on our way to a C.A. Rally in Paso Robles. However, it cost over 40 bucks a night. That was half a month's rent. We made other plans, and with our dog Beulah in the passenger's seat, and me sitting next to Barny on the special bench he had made, we waved goodbye with a full tank of gas and "Hot Springs" and other classy sentiments written on the side of the old van.

Halfway down the infamous "Ridge Route" we blew the back right tire. By now it was dark and pouring rain. For those who have traveled that section of road, you know how dangerous it can be. We were sitting precariously on the shoulder of the far right southbound lane. Barny had managed to get us off to the side, but it was a narrow space with a drop off, and we were sitting slightly down hill. This posed a dangerous complication: the van didn't have a working emergency brake. So as my new groom lay in the gutter with a torrent of water rushing by, ruining his "going away" outfit, and with the wake of semi trucks nearly blowing us over the side of the mountain, I literally stood on the brake as he changed the back tire. And this was just the first few hours of wedded bliss!

Once we made it to the nearest gas station and were able to secure the lug nuts, we headed to our vacation destination—a simple house on the beach in Ventura owned by a friend's priest. Most of the time it was used as a church retreat. Hey, don't judge us, it was free! By then NOTHING could've dampened our spirits. We turned all the crucifixes and images of the Mother Mary to the wall and slept in the fold out bed, due to the fact that all they had were twin bunk beds. Good times, people. Good times!

Obsession Kills

After returning from our *vacation* at the beach, my manager began randomly showing up at some of our club gigs, saying that I owed him his inflated percentage. He didn't care where I played, or how much money I did or did not make, a large chunk of it was his, and he had the contract to prove it. The whole thing would have been laughable if it weren't so pathetic. Reality was this new marriage of mine was taking a toll on his ego and undermining his hold on me. The guys in the band didn't appreciate his little visits, and I think he got the message because he stopped showing up after awhile.

I still had to meet with him for career updates though, and he would make remarks from time to time that sounded like veiled threats. His obsession felt more like insanity, and the monkey on his back was growing into a gorilla.

One day, while sitting on the couch at his apartment listening to the latest dead end possibility, he sat down next to me and produced a long and very sharp knife from his briefcase that was filled with prescription bottles. There was a chill to his voice, and his eyes had a distant and hollow look to them. He told me to hold out my hands, palms up, because he wanted to show me how sharp it was. I instinctively tried to get up and back away, but he firmly took hold of my arm sitting me down once again and then placed the cold steel of the blade on my upturned wrist.

I was afraid to move for fear that the slightest deviation would have serious repercussions and escalate what had now turned into a very unsure moment. He held the shiny piece of metal there for what seemed like an eternity of hypnotizing seconds, moving it ever so slightly, telling me about the dangerous people that walked the streets near his office. The knife was his protection, and he assured me that he would not be afraid or ever hesitate to use it.

The glint of the blade kept me focused, and my mind was quickly working every possible angle. I knew he wasn't himself in that moment, and I knew I couldn't show fear. I stayed calm forcing myself to breathe and tried to keep my tone of voice even, acting as though what he was doing was completely normal. After about 30 minutes of this he seemed to come back from wherever he had been, and I was eventually able to talk him into putting the knife back in his briefcase for safekeeping.

Now, I would never consider him a violent or physically dangerous man, but I knew all too well that most, if not all humans, have the capacity to snap if they are frustrated and desperate enough. His business was failing, and he was in the beginnings of a nasty bankruptcy. Plus he knew he had lost me for good this time, and there was nothing he could do about it, contract or no contract. I left there that day and did three things:

1. I never met with him alone again

2. Barny and I hired an attorney to get me out for good, and...

3. I started doing something I hadn't done in a long time. I started praying.

Every night as I closed my eyes, I *begged* God to please rescue me. I was scared. It was a prayer based in a faith born when I was born. I couldn't ever remember not talking to Jesus. I just hoped He was listening.

A Night At The Troubadour

It felt great to be breakin' away, breakin' free, livin' in a world of sin and frankly, enjoying every minute of it.

"Bye, bye church."

"Bye, bye all you wolves in sheep's clothing I'd been chained up with."

I was running with a new bunch of crazies now. The effect of being the only girl in every band I was singing with was starting to rub off, and I was getting tougher. I may have been under age, but I could still party with the best of 'em and use the "F" word several times in a sentence. I was definitely *in*.

I was in love, and the creative climate Barny had introduced me to was absolutely intoxicating. Music was everywhere. "Hippie Country" was taking over and we were right smack dab in the middle of it when I scored a showcase at the infamous Doug Weston's Troubadour Club on Sunset Boulevard. My voice was finally going to be heard, and I wouldn't be the white chick background singer, or belting out some "clubby" Vegas standard at a wedding reception either. I envisioned a bidding war over who could sign me first was sure to follow.

Trouble is, I didn't know it, but right around the corner a dark cloud was brewing, and I was about to learn a very painful and important lesson. Word on the street was that Carter was striking out on her own and M&M, both of who I was in litigation with, were not happy.

The big day finally arrived and my naïve, grandiose expectations were contributing to a serious case of the nerves. Sound check went well, but the time in-between, not so much. The house was packed, and to take the edge off I had leaned into the Tequila a little bit. Good ol' Cuervo Gold.

After hearing the introduction, I grabbed every bit of liquid courage I could swallow and took my place on stage. Once the band cranked up, my nerves took a back seat, and I could feel the crowd was with me. But just when I started to lose myself in the music and be as good as I dreamed I could be, I made the mistake of looking at the faces. There, sitting only a few seats away, were the two men who on paper, pretty much owned me.

One guy had a perfectly manicured black goatee to match his perfectly manicured nails. He held a cigarette in a long holder with his thumb and index finger. The palm of his hand faced his lips, and he had his pinkie curled, blowing little smoke circles. Sure looked different than he used to when he was the *Minister of Music* at our church back home. He was finally out of the closet and had even freed himself from the bondage of his toupee. Just wanted to make sure I noticed. Oh, I noticed.

The other one was making a valiant effort just to focus. His hair was greasy, and his eyes were glassy and cold, giving away his addiction. He wore a familiar smirk reminding me that he could tell my future, and my future was about to crash. I would come back. That's what he was thinking. Shoot, I always had before. They were sending a not-so-subtle message that I belonged to them, and if they couldn't have me, nobody else was going to have me either.

As soon as I made eye contact, I knew it was over. I hadn't seen or heard from them in awhile, so my defenses were down, and I completely blanked, losing all concentration. My hands started to shake and my body felt like it was glued to the floor. I mean, who did I think I was anyway, a girl like me? I had no business being up on the same stage that had welcomed the greats like Neil Young, Kris Kristofferson, Tom Waits, the Beatles, you name it. All I wanted to do in that moment was run, but by then I had learned that most of the time the only way out of a mess is to just get through it.

So with more bravado than confidence, I went on to introduce the song "Stay All Night." I said I didn't know whose song it was but I grew up listening to my daddy sing it all the time. I threw in a few cuss words just to show 'em how tough I was and then dove in. By the time I sang the last note and walked off, I was ready to go back to Portland and become a Junior High teacher. No stress there!

While I was desperately looking for the exit, a fellow musician informed me that Willie Nelson was in the crowd, thought it might be a good idea if I went over and introduced myself. Well, why not? I bet he just couldn't *wait* to meet me. We met. I made no sense whatsoever, and in my defense, neither did he; not surprisingly, no great connection was made. As I turned to leave he said, "By the way, that song, 'Stay All Night?' Bob Wills did that." Which I interpreted to mean: "If you were a *real* artist, you would've known that."

As I said my goodbyes and walked out the door trying to hold my head up high, I was totally convinced my short career was over. I had my shot and blew it. However, there's no way I could have known that in less than two years the man who had sat there and willed me to fail would be the only fatality in a 50-car pileup just south of Bakersfield.

Nor would I have dreamed that I would be recording and touring with the great Waylon Jennings. I'd be the only girl in his band on the legendary Outlaw Tour with none other than Willie Nelson.

We'd be back, rockin' the Troubadour as part of the music culture that forever changed Country Music. But all I knew in that moment was defeat and confusion.

....

Better a Millstone…

"Hello?"

The silence that followed was more than enough to get my attention. There was somebody on the other end and they weren't talking.

"Hello, anyone there?"

"He's dead."

That's what she said. Diana's voice sounded strange. I was silent, couldn't make my own voice and air work like they were designed to work.

"Who's dead Diana? Who are you talking about?"

"Frankie's dead."

Did I hear her correctly? Did she just say my manager was dead?

"What are you talking about? How? When?"

My mind felt like a merry-go-round spinning out of control.

"Today," she answered.

"I don't understand. You're not making sense. Are you sure?"

"I'm sure, Carter, he's dead. He was killed in a freak accident on the 99 just south of the Grapevine. He was in Mr. E.'s car, sitting in the backseat of all places."

"There's gotta be some kind of mistake? He never sat in the backseat, and what was he doing with Mr. E"?

I was fighting to stay focused, swallowing all the emotions that were pushing my heart to beat faster.

"They were on their way to Bakersfield to check out another girl singer for him to sign. A farmer was plowing his field and a freak dust storm blew up. Caused a 50-car pile up...he was the only fatality."

A long numbing silence followed while my mind struggled to process the words just spoken.

"I don't know what to say, Danna. Are you all right?"

"...No, but I don't have a choice. I have to go fill his prescriptions for you know who, and then tell the funeral parlor what he's supposed to look like."

"This is crazy Diana! Come over here. You can be with us."

"I can't...she needs me."

Silence.

"Carter?"

"Yeah."

"The release for your contract arrived. He read it...but he wouldn't sign it, just left it on his desk. I'm sorry."

Silence.

"Me too. It's all right. I'll work it out."

"You okay?" Now she was asking.

"...No. This just all feels unreal. I prayed so hard, Diana. I didn't want him to die; I just wanted him to let me go. He's been so crazy lately."

"I know...we all know. Hey, listen to me, it's not your fault, you know that, right?"

"I hope not. I'm just...so tired."

"I gotta go. They're waiting for me. I love you Sissy."

Starting to cry, "I love you too, Danna."

Click.

Luke 17:1-2 King James Version

Then said he unto the disciples, "It is impossible but that offences will come: but woe unto him, through whom they come! It were better for him that a millstone were hanged about his neck, and he cast into the sea, than that he should offend one of these little ones..."

Part three

This Is No Dress Rehearsal

We are professionals and this is the Big Time

The Telephone Audition

"**H**ey, Carter! How high can you sing?"

"I don't know, pretty high I guess."

"Well, starting with this note, just go as high as you can."

"Okay."

And I did. That simple exchange was the beginning of one of my favorite "braggy, showbiz stories."

Barny and I were still living in our little one room house we called the Alamo on Valleyheart Drive, in Sherman Oaks. After the shocking death of my manager, and with the help of our attorney, the dark years of being tied up in the old contract had finally come to an end. The cost of freedom had not come without an emotional price tag that at times threatened my soul with bankruptcy. In life, there are some pretty outrageous psychological balloon payments that have a way of showing up and insisting on being paid in full.

I had lived for so long in that twisted reality that I was like a newly released prisoner, happy but guarded, relearning how to live. Fortunately I was young, and we were choosing to enjoy a simple life of embracing our art. For the first time we were able to dream of our future without restraint.

When the phone rang that night, I recognized the voice on the other end without introduction. It was our friend Loyd, one of the members of the group I had moved to Hollywood with. He had become an engineer and was working with several well known artists. He was a great vocalist himself, which I'm sure made him an even better engineer. He and Barny had become friends, and it was through him that we were able to do those off-hour recordings I spoke of earlier.

After hearing him sing the starting note into the receiver, I began singing my way up the scale until he stopped me and asked if I would do it one more time. I laughingly obliged. We were always doing crazy stuff like this, so I didn't think it was *that* unusual. When I was finished I heard a voice say something like, "That's good, cool." I didn't have time to ask any questions because Loyd immediately got back on the line and asked me if I knew who I had just sang for, to which I answered, "Noooooooooo…who?"

"James Taylor. He wants to know if you can come down to the studio and do a session for him?" Pause.

"Carter…Carter?"

Now, I'm not someone who gets star struck. However, James Taylor? "Sweet Baby James?" "Fire and Rain?" *That* James Taylor? Trying hard not to let the excitement show too much in my voice, I set up a time when I could come in. If Mr. Taylor had been able to see me after the phone call he may have changed his mind. I was jumping up and down like some little kid who's been told they get to go swimming, while Barny was watching me thinking I had absolutely crossed over to the other side. Loyd knew me well, or at least well enough to not tell me who I was auditioning for on the other end of the line. Good call, friend!

The session was booked for the Warner Brothers Amigo Studios in North Hollywood, and a few days later I was on my way. Driving there, in spite of my shaking knees, I kept telling myself this was like any other job, and I needed to be the professional that I had become. Then the little raspy voice on my shoulder would light a cigarette and say, "Yeah, good luck with that."

Not giving in to the fear, a slightly stronger voice would yank the cigarette out, extinguishing it with one snub, and remind me that life might just be getting ready to turn around. I mean, at that very moment I was on my way to do a recording session with James Taylor, for heaven's sake. Straighten up!

By the time I arrived at the studio, I was nearly dizzy from the crazy conversations with all three of my selves! I took a deep breath and walked in. Sitting behind the console was my friend Loyd and Mr. Taylor. Introductions were extended and his very low key, soft-spoken demeanor quickly put me at ease.

After explaining what he needed me to do, I turned and walked out into the studio. I stood there and sang one long note at a time working my way up the scale. These notes would later become part of a vocal choir that they were putting together on separate tracks to create the ethereal sound on "Shower the People."

When I was finished singing, I stepped into the control room to see if they needed anything else. Mr. Taylor told me he was pleased with what I had done and asked if I'd like to hear an example of how they were going to use the vocals. I was intrigued and sat for a moment while Loyd put it all together. Even though it was a quick mix, it sounded to me like a symphony of voices, and I told them so.

As I was gathering up my things, James said they were all going out for a drink and asked if I'd like to join them. I wanted to, I really did, but I didn't want to ruin something that had been so wonderful. Sometimes it's best not to get to know the people you admire. I shyly declined the invitation, saying I needed to get home to Barny.

Once back in the safety of the old van, I took a deep breath and told myself, "Well done, Carter, well done." Loyd called the next day to thank me. He laughed and told me I missed out on a good night, and that I should have come along.

Maybe. But home felt pretty good too. It *was* nice to be asked though.

When One Door Closes

After two albums and about three years of playing joints like The Corral in Topanga Canyon and rakin' in the big bucks at the Sundance Saloon for ten bucks a night and all the free tap beer you could drink, (which meant with those boys the club definitely got the short end) Gary's record deal with Capitol went south. There were whisperings that the "suits" in the company had grown weary of his up close and personal negotiating style. When things didn't proceed the way he felt they should he could be one very intimidating guy.

With promotion thin and radio not being paid off at the rate they felt they deserved, Gary and the rest of the band had to make some hard decisions. Keeping the lights on was a necessity that none of us could ignore, and reluctantly Barny and I started taking more and more outside gigs. It was a shame really, because Gary truly was a great country writer and singer.

One of the associations that survived the dismantling of the band was our growing musical partnership with Gary's producer, Ken Mansfield. He had an impressive history as a Capitol Records executive that included the Beatles, along with many others. When we met him he was becoming a "mover and shaker" in the "on the edge" country music scene in California. We used to love watching him sit behind the console late at night, eyes closed, listening to the music we had just recorded. I appreciate how overused this expression is but, it was a *magical* time. In fact it felt like there was no time at all, just space to take it all in.

After working with us in the studio on several projects, Ken caught the vision of what he believed we were artistically capable of and offered us a production deal with his company "Hometown Productions." Any mention of contracts would kind of put me in a tailspin and understandably so. However, a business relationship, as well as a friendship, was forged with him and his wife.

They had an amazing place in the Hollywood Hills previously owned by a silent film star. The whole front of the house had these big sliding glass windows that would disappear into the walls and could be opened up to the beauty of the outside. There was this very cool bar downstairs with autographs on the walls of some incredibly famous people from a long ago era, as well as the new. The place reeked with creativity and connection. Ken definitely knew how to create a vibe.

One of my favorite things to do during that time was to be invited to their house where we would smoke a little pot and listen to music for hours. Eventually we would make our way to their dining room to eat a special meal prepared by their housekeeper/cook that to this day rivals the best culinary experiences I've had the pleasure of enjoying. She would make this very simple meatloaf, with a hard boiled egg in the center, so that when sliced it looked like a work of art. Absolutely delicious!

After a long and relaxed dinner we would hop into our little brown Honda and head back to our one room mansion next to the Ventura Freeway down the hill...far, far away.

From time to time they would have parties that Barny and I would be invited to. We could hear the laughter as we walked up the stairs on the hillside, and once reaching the top, feel as though we were stepping over the threshold into a moment from the past.

I remember arriving at one of these Galas and being greeted by none other than the great Ringo Starr. He had a little instamatic camera and grabbed me to take a picture of the two of us. It was surreal to say the least. There were also smaller dinner parties where we were introduced to Dolly Parton and other icons of the business. It was a door that was opening to a world I had always dreamed about, and this time it was the real thing.

Mr. & Mrs. Honky Tonk Hero

In the spring of 1975 Ken opened another door for Barny and me that we stumbled through, only to have it quickly lock behind us. There would be no going back; forward was the only option. He had just finished co-producing an album with Waylon Jennings for his wife Jessi Colter on Capitol. She had a huge hit with "I'm Not Lisa" and it was breaking all kinds of records, "crossing over' where no Country artist had gone before. Ken, knowing the way I sang and the way Barny played, felt that we'd be a good fit for her band. So when she came to town for her debut at the Santa Monica Civic, we got the gig.

I remember having more than one conversation with Ken's wife wanting to give me an insider's "heads up" about the margin for error that was always lurking. It was a pretty rough and rowdy world of life and music on the edge, and I was still a few weeks shy of my 21st birthday. I think she felt like a protective big sister. She wasn't privy to some of the more tainted parts of my story, and didn't realize I wasn't quite as green as I looked and sometimes acted, but I appreciated her intent.

A rehearsal was booked for us in one of the studios at the famous Capitol Records building on Highland Avenue. Waylon and Jessi were late, and the band, who was set up and ready to go, were standing around waiting for them to arrive so we could dive into the music. There was a lot to get done in a very short period of time, and I was beginning to wonder how this was all going to work when we were alerted to their arrival. I remember Waylon had been *roarin'*, and everybody was walking around on eggshells. I overheard a few of the guys saying that he wasn't real happy about something to do with the record company. Shocker!

It's kind of funny thinking back to first impressions. I was this little California hippie musician, wearing jeans and t-shirts with no makeup and long blond hair. Since "shy" was my default mode, especially in new situations, I was more than happy to be the invisible background singer. Barny was comfortable behind the keys, and the guitar player, Gordon Payne, was one of those guys I talked about earlier that used to come out and see us at the Palomino before he joined up with Waylon. He hadn't been working with him all that long and was actually pretty quiet back then as well. Barny and I were more than a little guarded due to the unpredictable nature of the situation we were stepping into. Waylon's well documented no bullshit reputation preceded him, and working as Jessi's band was new territory for everybody.

He was the first one to enter the room, followed by an entourage of anxious looking people scurrying around to make sure the Boss was happy. He was a big man, and his swagger and energy made him seem even bigger. His hair was greasy, and he had a cigarette in his mouth. I could smell the Musk cologne he was wearing from across the room where I was standing. It took only about 30 seconds to conclude that it would be best for me to stay out of his way and not initiate any conversations. I was there to do a job, and I was going to do it. I was kind of half expecting him to look at me and fire me on the spot, just because he could.

Once he was through the door, Jessi and her people walked in, and I remember audibly taking in a big gasp of air. I don't think I'd ever seen anyone that strikingly beautiful before, and I'm not exaggerating. It was like everyone in the room couldn't take their eyes off of her. Where Waylon was big and commanding by his presence, Jessi was petite and incredibly glamorous and captivating in a very cool way. I'm sure you know what I mean if you've ever seen her in person, or looked at album covers. They both had a presence that was all their own, refusing to be diminished by a business that routinely ate up and spit out talent like a glutton at an ancient Roman feast. They were definitely a force to be reckoned with.

I hadn't been working with women at all, and the way I looked fit well with the bands I was a part of. But in that moment, I became very conscious of what I was or was not wearing.

The introductions were brief, and I wasn't sure either one of them could have picked me out of a line up later in the day if they had to. The pressure of success, and big success in particular, will wring you out, and it was evident in that moment that something was disturbing the force.

I had prepared myself for an intense rehearsal, knowing how very important this gig was for her, and frankly for me as well; you only debut once. We'd been working in situations where musicians and engineers would spend hours just tuning the guitar so I was resigned to a long and arduous day in the studio. I couldn't have been more mistaken. After chatting it up with some of her friends in the room, Jessi eventually sauntered over to the piano and sat down. She played for a bit, kind of getting the feel of everything, and then the rest of the band started falling in where it felt right.

My mind was trying to make every left turn with them, holding on like a hobo catching a ride. I had memorized the background parts off the album and did my best to fit with Gordon's vocals. At the same time I was using all of my past-learned skills to match her very challenging phrasing. It was one wild pressure cooker of a rehearsal, at least for me, anyway.

Every once in awhile, Waylon would explain things, and it was like he had his own language. The rest of the band had been with him long enough, and not only understood, but were fluent in their ability to converse. This was new to Barny and I, so we chose to listen close, absorb as much as we could, and then hope for the best.

As awkwardly as the rehearsal began, it ended. The two stars were swept up and rushed into their waiting cars for the next event of their long and demanding day. With the debut just around the corner, we went to the house and did our homework.

Interestingly for me, her big night at the Santa Monica Civic held an unexpected and truly spiritual moment. Barny and I didn't know Jessi very well yet, but we knew there were some personal issues she was dealing with. I imagined how crushing the pressure of both her and Waylon's careers must have been at times. She was trying to push these distractions aside and go out and give her much awaited live concert debut in hypercritical L.A. no less. I had seen her backstage earlier, and it was obvious she had an inner struggle going on.

I remember standing behind my mic and looking off stage, watching her, asking God to please help her. The crowd was ready and as the introduction finished I watched as she gracefully and confidently walked out and knelt beside her piano. It was like everyone was afraid to take a breath, not wanting to disturb this almost holy moment. She then sat down and played the single note intro to "I'm Not Lisa," a song that put her at the top of the charts.

From the first step she took onto the stage she held that audience in the palm of her hand. Her smile and the ease in which she presented herself and her songs melted the heart of every would-be critic in the room. All the nerves and "what-ifs" of the days leading up to this crossroad in time were gone and the band as well as Jessi gave themselves permission to enjoy the music. I get chills just thinking about it. This would be one of many moments that I would witness Jessi sing her heart out for those who had ears to hear and spirits to embrace her journey.

Gordon once referred to me as a singer that sticks to an artist's phrasing like flypaper. It was a compliment. There have been moments when rather than watching her, I would close my eyes and lose myself in the song, matching her phrasing better than I ever had with my eyes open. It's all about the *listening*... I am blessed to call her "friend."

From then on, whenever she was in town, whether it was recording or filming the "Midnight Specials" for TV, we got the call. It was a very exciting time.

Are You Ready For the Country?

By January 1976, Waylon was growing restless. Coming on the heels of his recent success of "Honky Tonk Heroes" and "Wanted! The Outlaws", he decided to join forces with Ken once more and shake Nashville up by recording an album at Sound Lab Studios in Hollywood. Back then that was considered Country Music treason. He'd been through a lot and had the scars to prove it. The days of trying to play nice with the record company and radio were over.

This is where the real meaning behind the title "Outlaw" came from. He refused to clean up or wear those god-awful rhinestone stage outfits. He insisted on using his road band in the studio, and fought for the control to record the songs *he* wanted to record, *how* he wanted to record, and *where* he wanted to record.

Record companies, especially out of Nashville, weren't partial to allowing artists that kind of say in their careers. Executives insisted they use a small group of "studio musicians." Now, nothing against these guys, they were and are incredible, but when you use the same musicians on all the records coming out of Nashville the music starts sounding alike. The "art" part of music often becomes stale, and all the passion that is experienced on stage with your road band never makes it to the record. Waylon was one of the first artists to stand up to the executives and call their bluff; as a result, "Outlaw" became a brand.

It's important to note that Waylon didn't name *himself* an "Outlaw." I think Hazel Smith coined the phrase, and RCA saw a marketing opportunity. The rest is history as they say. He just wanted the freedom to do his music the way he saw fit and then take it to the people, which is exactly what he did. It was undeniably a bold move and was a direct hit with his audience. California "Hippie Country" had been very well received, and now Waylon's demographic started expanding and embracing this younger rock crowd. Looking back, it was absolutely brilliant!

Ken hired Barny to play keyboards and hired me to sing backgrounds on the new album, which was "Are You Ready For the Country?" For the first few days I sat on the sofa below the console in the control room and just quietly observed. It was one thing to work with Jessi, but now I needed to learn how to merge into Waylon's musical dynamic and rhythm. It was kind of like learning how to play jump rope on the playground at school. You would bide your time looking for your point of entry. Watching the rope hit the ground; you jumped in with the other children clearing it as it circled above you.

His raw approach to getting the song on tape was very different from how I had been working. You weren't always afforded a lot of chances. Sometimes it was one shot, and if you weren't on the money he moved on, especially if you were singing background vocals. There wasn't a big tolerance for fine-tuning due to a reduced attention span brought on by special effects. He didn't want the music to get stale, and he liked the imperfections as long as they didn't distract from the song.

I appreciated his way of thinking and his commitment to keeping it real, but at the same time I wasn't blind to the dynamic and effect the drugs played in all of this. There were other times when just the opposite was true, and the band would play a song over and over again, completely missing the best take. Fortunately, most engineers kept the tape rolling and the red light on so they could go back and choose when they weren't under the gun so much. For me, it was added pressure to get it right, or at least right enough the first time.

He was in the iso-booth one night recording his vocals when he asked me to come out and sing with him for the very first time. My knees were knockin', and I was suddenly 7 years old. The voices of all the failures I had experienced in the past were on repeat in my head, and I was fighting for every bit of real or imagined confidence I could drum up.

The booth was small and he'd been...up for a while. The way he was moving around I wondered how the engineer, John Mills, would ever get a clean vocal. Standing in the booth looking back at the control room I could see musicians, movers and shakers, a few select celebrities, as well as Ken in the Producer's seat.

Waylon liked to throw you in. He figured you'd either sink or swim, and that was pretty much up to you. If you were going to run with him you'd better be able to make some mighty quick turns. I remember he looked at me with this kind of crazy smile on his face and said, "Ya wanna do it?"

I took a deep breath, stepped my now twenty one-year-old self up to the mic and simply sang. If I was going home it wasn't going to be because I choked. No sir, not this time. A funny thing happened once we started singing; all that was left was the music and the beginning of a friendship that, despite a few bumps along the way, would last for the rest of our lives.

After the first week of working on the album, Waylon came to Barny and me and asked if we would be interested in going on the road as members of Jessi's band. They were starting a pretty big tour and she was the opening act. We didn't know it at the time, but this turned into the infamous Outlaw tour with Tompall Glaser, Willie Nelson, Waylon and Jessi.

Here's a kind of embarrassing side note: neither one of us really wanted to go out on tour. We loved working with Jessi, but Barny was already road weary, and we weren't completely convinced that we'd be the best fit. Don't get me wrong; we were no angels, far from it. That was never the point, but we wanted to build a life in L.A. and all too often road musicians are not taken seriously. Their road gig becomes work for hire with no future. Plus, I had my own artist's career to think about, and had already started recording with Ken in hopes of getting an album deal of my own. I wasn't sure how all of that could continue if I was out on the road.

Waylon asked us to go home and give it some thought, and that's what we did. We decided to ask for a wage that we thought he wouldn't go for, thinking it would give us a gracious way out and we wouldn't be burning any bridges. We'd never been this bold and it felt a little risky, but it actually wasn't a lot of money—just more than we were making at the time. We were hoping we'd be able to record with him and avoid the touring part. Wrong! He didn't even blink, just told us we were in for a good ride.

We left that night in a kind of daze. On the one hand we were grateful for the much-needed income that was going to be coming in (we had just purchased our first home) and for the adventure we were starting. But we were also skeptical, not wanting to lose career ground in L.A. We told ourselves we would go out for this one tour and then find a way to back out. I laugh when I say this now. Sometimes our plans are such a joke, especially in the rearview mirror of life!

A few short weeks later we found ourselves sitting at the "Hall of Fame" motel in Nashville, waiting for the bus to leave on our first tour. That was the beginning of the "Outlaw Years" for us.

At sound check, time to reflect, on the stage

Hello Road

$\mathcal{E}$very time anyone stepped onto the old Eagle bus there was an awareness of stepping into history. A considerable amount of it had already been documented, but there was definitely more to come.

When we first joined up, Waylon and Jessi had the bed in the back room. With the addition of Barny and me there weren't enough bunks to go around, so the band had to sleep in shifts. My first night out I sat in a seat up front because I didn't want to seem all diva-ish and insist on a bed, plus I loved watching the sunrise. As each guy would leave to get in his bunk, he would offer it to me first, but I would politely decline assuring them that I wasn't sleepy and for them to go ahead and go to bed. Honestly, if I really felt the need to sleep Barny and I were still skinny enough to share a bunk. I was just fine.

When Waylon came back up front early the next morning, he asked if I had been there all night. I answered yes, with a big smile on my face. He looked at me and kind of tilted his head funny, then wanted to know if I was always going to be this happy and perky? Pretty much. For now, as new and awkward as it was, I was choosing to embrace the adventure. This was unknown territory for me and it was getting more and more interesting with every city limit sign we passed.

The guys in the band showed great respect for both of us right from the git-go. In fact, we sensed a sort of unspoken reserve that made it difficult at times to really connect. About a week into the tour, after a show, Barny and I were sitting around *decompressing* with the rest of the band. Rance, one of the rhythm guitar players out of Tulsa, spoke up and said he was glad to find out we were just regular folks. We were puzzled by this and asked him what he was talking about. They all started to laugh and then told us that right before we came out, Jessi sat them down for a little talk. She said we were a big deal in L.A. and a couple of very classy musicians. She wanted them to be on their best behavior, and above all else control their bodily functions!

I laughed so hard I nearly peed my pants. I guess both Barny's and my kind of shy demeanor had made us seem aloof and unapproachable. In reality, since I had been the only girl in previous bands, I could pretty much out-gross anybody there if I chose to, and I would do it with a sweet smile on my face.

When you live together in the very close quarters of a bus, you have more than ample opportunity to get to know each other up close and personal. At first there's this kind of idealistic romanticizing of the adventure. But after your first time of cleaning the on-bus bathroom, you either become family or you go to your other house.

I think it was Gary Hulsey, our band roadie at the time, who told me that just because I was a female didn't mean I was exempt from bathroom duty or, more appropriately, bathroom doodie! I wondered if this was some kind of hillbilly band hazing, but I went along with it and tidied up the "shitter"… once. Told them I wasn't the one makin' the mess and my aim was just fine, thank you very much. They all thought that was pretty funny and didn't really think I would do it in the first place. Another lesson learned.

The Siren's Call

There's an attraction to the road for most musicians that rivals any temptation they've ever given into before. I think truckers understand the *draw* about as well as anybody: new towns, new faces, crossing state lines and taking in the landscapes of America. Sunrise…sunset.

Daddy always dreamed of someday hanging up his produce apron and hittin' the road. He was born restless and could hear the Siren's call even when she whispered. I used to watch him after a long day at work, that for him started around 4 a.m. He'd come home, shower and then sit in his chair, letting the distant voices on the CB radio take him to the places he traced on the map in front of him. He knew their handles and they knew his. Breaker, breaker…

I never doubted the pull of my father's DNA and had lived the consequences. But now, once again, I was experiencing it in an undeniably powerful way. After just one week, I was hooked.

It's true that I was rarely disappointed at the prospect of going home at the end of a long tour, but especially in those first few years, once rested up, I was ready to get back out there. I suspect it had similarities to life under the Big Top. I wasn't the only girl on the road, just the only one in the band. If the other girls ever got together they could write a book that would make your head spin. Love 'em!

Sherry the t-shirt girl lives right down the road from us now. That was her title back then, "t-shirt girl." Today she would be the Merch person. She was so beautiful that those ol' boys would line up for blocks just to buy a t-shirt from her. Plus she could outdrink most and run a card table faster than you could say, "Whoop! Whoop!" She shocked everybody by choosing to do life with crazy Tom Bourke and they're still going strong today. Being in this band meant being a member of the family, and there's nothin' quite as sweet as family.

Speaking of family, and this is important to note, I knew what was my business and what wasn't. I had their backs, but I would never lie for anybody. If they didn't want me to know, then they ought not to flaunt it. With that said, it was all on the table and we went from there. Right around then is when Richie Albright (drummer, band leader, producer, Waylon's close business partner) named me "Mama Carter." Guess I have *both* my parents' DNA.

White Lightnin' and Hot Georgia Nights

I loved working with Jessi. Her mama was a strong Pentecostal woman like mine, and we had an unspoken understanding. She had tender memories that would pick her up and carry her through hard times and had not seen the shadier side I had lived through. She held a unique place in history as the female Outlaw with Waylon, Willie and Tompall and could yank a crowd to their feet in a heartbeat with one of her smiles. I was watching, learning, and soaking in the privilege of being in her band.

One early summer night in 1976, a spur of the moment invitation was extended, and my life once again forever changed. We were in Georgia at an outdoor, backwoods kind of venue. By now, Waylon had already asked Barny to play keys with him, and he was pretty much settled in.

The venue was sold out, and the air was so thick and muggy you could actually see it. We'd been spittin' bugs all through Jessi's show, and it seemed like every time I opened my mouth to sing I was batting another one away to dance in the spotlight around my face. I really didn't mind it that much though; there was something raw and earthy about the whole experience. We weren't trying to please any out-of-touch critics or easily swayed radio reps because Waylon's "give-a-shitter" had broken, so what was left was just down and gritty music.

The crowd was a mix of drug-crazed, southern rock-and-rollers that had jumped on board and were part of the growing momentum. Sprinkled in were a few older country music fans that enjoyed their own Saturday night vices and were never late for Sunday morning service the next day. There was an irony to it all that was definitely not lost on me.

That night some ol' boys right out of the hills, aiming to be hospitable, had brought a jug of their very special white lightnin'. They were going to pass it around among the few, the brave, and the stupid, of which I had already earned a lifetime membership. Having been doused once in Gary's band, I had learned to be selective with this kind of offer. But there was something about these boys that felt like family; maybe it was the overalls. I had finished Jessi's set and figured my work was done for the night, so I put the jug to my mouth and took a long healthy swig. Burned like hell all the way down but had a rather nice glow once it landed.

While I was basking in this little homemade buzz, the band left the makeshift dressing room and headed for the stage. For weeks my routine had been to stand out of sight over by the crew and watch the show. I'd challenge myself to find a part in my head and then silently sing along. Finding a niche wasn't easy because the guys in the band had most of the harmonies covered, and I knew one of the worst things a chick singer can do is step on somebody's part.

I pictured myself out there, soaking up the music and rhythm, all taking place on that exclusive piece of property we called the stage. Night after night I watched as my friends played their stories, unaware that they were making history and memories for the folks who had forked over their hard-earned dollars to be part of something that helped them forget, or better yet, remember.

As I was standing off to the side, waiting for Waylon to go on and feeling content with my ability to blend in, he walked up behind me, leaned in and said, "How 'bout you come out and sing with me tonight?"

I wondered briefly if that white lightnin' had hallucinatory properties in it. Once I recovered, I looked at him, told him I'd love to, then asked, "Which song?"

"All of 'em," he replied.

He smiled that smile with his cigarette kind of clinched between his teeth and hollered over his shoulder to the roadie, "Get her a mic!"

Uh-oh! What did I just do? Now, it's important for you to know that this wasn't a decision he had included the band in, or even told them what he was thinking before he walked on. I worked very well with these boys on Jessi's show but was also aware and respectful of the unspoken reality that the next hour and a half was pretty much a *man's* world.

"This is no dress rehearsal.

We are professionals and

This is the big time."

Yes, you can buy the t-shirt!

So, I'm following Waylon out there, feeling the stares of these boys all asking themselves the same question, "What's Carter doin' here?"

Barny kept looking at me from behind the piano, nodding his head, his body language telling me not to over-think it, just DO IT!

Taking my cue and confidence from my best friend, I stepped up to the mic and once again did what I had done a few months before in the studio—I sang. All those weeks of standing off stage in the shadows studying, soundlessly singing in my head, paid off. I was selective about which songs I felt I could add a little something to and chose not to sing on all of them. That approach worked, and by the end of the show history was made. Carter was a "Waylor!"

Looking back, that was a turning point. This big giant of a personality believed enough in me to throw me out there without a net for the second time, and somehow innately knew I would do more than simply survive, I would thrive.

The Photo Shoot

One afternoon while in L.A. between tours and recording vocals at Sound Lab, I received a call asking me to come be a part of the photo shoot for the James Taylor album that I had sung on. It was going to be for the back cover, and they wanted everyone involved in the album to be there. After checking my schedule, it was determined I would be in town, and I accepted the invitation.

I wasn't quite prepared for the enormity of celebrity and accomplishment that were represented in the room. There was Carly Simon, Art Garfunkel, Peter Asher, Jim Keltner, David Crosby, Graham Nash, Lee Sklar, Russ Kunkel, Danny Kortchmar, Waddy Wachtel; the list was impressive and extraordinary. My confidence had grown since starting to work with Waylon and Jessi, but it didn't always follow me back home to L.A. Walking into the photo shoot, I tried to act calm and convince myself that I wasn't crashing the party. I had been invited, but I still had to fight the urge to run. I found myself standing next to my friend Loyd and the famous producers, Lenny Waronker and Russ Titleman.

The photographer had us all arranged in a kind of semicircle, with James sitting on the floor in front. He was trying to get a cool candid shot but was having difficulty getting all these larger-than-life personalities to loosen up a bit. By then I was feeling more secure and removed in a good way. This wasn't *my* problem; I was just a lowly background singer. All I had to do was show up and smile when they said, "Cheese" right? Wrong!

For some crazy reason he tuned right into me and asked if I would come down where James was seated on the ground in front of the mass of egos, talent and fame. At first I looked behind me, thinking he was talking to someone else. But noooooooo...it was me. My face must have turned a zillion different shades of red. I was extremely embarrassed and suddenly felt like I had buckteeth, raggedy underwear and a hand-me-down dress on again. I was sure any minute somebody was gonna holler out, "Hey, I know you. You're that Holy Roller kid from Visalia!"

I was wishing I could just vanish and would have welcomed a timely power failure, but of course that didn't happen. As I knelt down next to him, the photographer directed me to fold my arms around the back of James' neck and lean into him. You've GOT to be kidding! So with that great cloud of witnesses looking at *my* backside for a change, I did the best I could under the circumstances to act completely natural. As I leaned in, James said in a quiet voice, "Hi, Carter, glad you could make it."

"Uhhhhh...me too." I know, pretty snappy comeback huh?

After a couple of incredibly uncomfortable shots, I was released to go back and stand with all the many icons that represented the music I had such deep respect for. I was so excited to be a part of the project that I told everyone I knew and every stranger willing to listen that I sang on the album. When "In the Pocket" came out, my name had been inadvertently left off; I was in the picture but wasn't given any credit for singing. This wouldn't be the first or last time my work would either be credited to someone else or my name left off completely. Ahh, such is the life of a *background* singer. Doesn't really matter though, because the memory is mine, and I have the album to prove it.

So...thanks for the memories, Mr. Taylor!

Picnic Anyone?

I don't know about you, but I love a good picnic. Growing up, my family enjoyed these outdoor feasts on a regular basis. However, when I arrived in Texas for Willie Nelson's Fourth of July event, I knew it wasn't exactly going to be a Yogi Bear and Boo Boo with their pic-a-nic baskets kind of day.

We were a few months into that first year of the "Outlaw" tour, and the shine was still shiny. I was in one of the hottest bands in the country, singing for thousands of people every night, and now we were going to be sharing the bill with some of my favorite artists.

Waylon and the rest of the band were pumped and prepared. Pumped because they were looking forward to hangin' out with old friends and doing music; prepared because they'd been to this dance before and knew it would most likely turn into a marathon. Most of the time Waylon insisted on Willie closing. He knew his friend's penchant for losing track of time while on stage and preferred rather to get on, get off, get on the bus, and get to the next town. Pacing one's self was an art form born out of experience, and extremely necessary if you planned to stay on your feet. You had to go with the flow, which is easier to do when your vice is of a slower nature. If you're on the other end of the spectrum, it becomes a bit more challenging.

I spent extra time getting myself all dolled-up for the big concert. I had bought a brand new pair of cloth wedge shoes that laced up my leg kind of sexy-like. I wanted to look good, and I was giving it my best shot. This was going to be one of the most exciting career moments so far. I was ready to embrace the moment and the opportunity to make a little history. Boy, was I green.

The leave time for the buses must have been set back at least four or five times before we headed out to the country to have ourselves a big time. I'd never seen anything quite like that before. There was an ocean of people. Everywhere you looked there were drunk, high, sunburned bodies dancing and giving themselves over to the music. As cool as the perception of it all was, I was glad I was on our bus headed for the backstage area. However, backstage had its own brand of crazy, and my capacity for integration into these kinds of rock-n-roll festivals was about to be expanded.

I believe it was late afternoon by the time we arrived. We were like children jumping off the bus at summer camp. We walked from bus to bus soaking in the music of our friends, not wandering off too far because we might be up next and had to stay ready. This held its own unique set of obstacles. We all needed to stay straight enough to do the show but loose enough to enjoy the moment.

Our individual methods seemed to work for a while, but after several hours of preparing to take the stage and then having someone else go on, our fun wasn't so fun anymore. It kind of felt like being strapped to some wicked carnival teeter-totter that wouldn't let us off: up and down, up and down.

In the wee hours of the morning, after multiple rain delays had caused a serious setback in the artist line-up, the hurry-up-and-wait routine came to a halt. Waylon drew a line in the red Texas mud and insisted that we either go on next or we were goin' to the house. They'd been holding us off because they wanted to keep their biggest acts until the end. There was an estimated 80,000 fans out front waiting for us, and all hell was going to break loose if we left. Waylon won and once again we suited up to do our show.

Leon Russell was on stage, rockin' it with his big white grand piano under the cover of a huge tarp, when the rain decided to make another appearance. This was no slight drizzle either. It came down in "everything's big in Texas" size buckets. He was completely wrapped up in the music and unaware of the seriousness of the storm. Just as ol' Leon was puttin' it all together and bringin' it home, that big stage tarp gave way to the weight of the water that had been accumulating for a few days and dumped a lake full right in the middle of his beautiful piano.

Miraculously, no one was electrocuted, but that pretty much ended the picnic. We all went back to the hotel like "gutted snowbirds" as

Waylon used to say, having never played or sung a note. That was my first Willie picnic.

And the Beat Goes On

By the end of 1976, Waylon's career was exploding. Where he used to play a club a year before, he was now going back to the same cities and selling out their arenas. We went from one bus to several, along with semis loaded with our own lights, sound, two grand pianos, and a Lear jet on the side. Hell's Angels were our protection, and money was being spent like water from a bottomless well. We were rock stars from a different zip code with an arrogance to match.

If you were an on the edge artist and considered yourself able to keep up with the best of them, you may have found yourself needing to redefine those parameters. That's exactly what George Carlin did before opening for us at the Hollywood Bowl once. Seems he did a little pre-show hangin' with the boys on the bus that definitely made him *do different!* There was a sense of being invincible that kept road managers awake at night and money managers chewing their fingernails to the quick.

When the clock struck midnight on January 1, 1977, we were full blown and you can take that however you want. Barny and I were making more money than ever and hardly spending a dime. Waylon was very generous and paid us each a set fee per gig, as well as all expenses. There were perks on top of perks, including flying first class, and limos waiting for us became the norm rather than the exception. We camped out in the studios, turning engineers into speed freaks just to keep up with us. Most of them are still around, but a few have chosen to sell insurance and honestly, who can blame them?

We'd taken up residence earlier that year in American Studios, literally recording around the clock. It was conveniently located next door to Waylon's office, 1117 17th Avenue South on Music Row. I remember sometimes, after a leg of the tour, the bus would roll in, we'd get off, and go straight into the studio to start laying down Waylon's latest songs for his newest album. Plenty of memories were made there, some more infamous than others. I'm holding most of them close to my vest, since I don't have a good poker face.

Chips Moman was the producer on this latest album, and unlike me had a very good poker face and played the game quite well. Hence the name "Chips." Back then, the honeymoon period with *any* producer didn't last all that long, and with Chips there was no exception. He had a song he and Buddy Emmons had written and wanted Waylon to put it on the album. Waylon wasn't exactly sold on the song (I think that had more to do with his relationship with Chips than the song), but he did eventually record it. I remember him complaining and saying it would probably become his biggest hit, forcing him to sing it every night for the rest of his life.

In April 1977, "Luckenbach, Texas (Back to the Basics of Love)" was released and by May 21st was #1 on the Country Charts, staying there until June 25th. It reached #25 on the Pop Charts and #15 on Billboard Top LPs and Tape Charts, skyrocketing the album "Ol Waylon" to not just gold, but platinum status! Yes, Mr. Jennings had to sing that song pretty much for the rest of his life. I believe a peace was eventually brokered between the two men, and they both benefited greatly from their association. In fact, Chips later was the producer for the legendary "Highwaymen" which was made up of Waylon, Willie, Johnny Cash, and Kris Kristofferson.

As much fun as the studio was, we were doubling it out on the road. Along the way the Crickets joined the tour, bringing a cachet of iconic music history and stories with them.

Those guys are some of the funniest people I have ever known. J.I. Allison, who was Buddy Holly's drummer, has a twisted sense of humor and rarely stops smiling, but he's definitely nobody's fool. Drummers are their own breed. Joe B. Mauldin, Holly's bass player, looks like this regular guy but is so cool and has a book's worth of stories. And then there's Sonny Curtis. He played guitar for Holly, and I could listen to him sing, talk and laugh forever. They wrote some of music history's biggest songs, and I have a tremendous amount of respect for them.

I was just a young kid, and they treated me as an equal, engaging me in their music and conversations. If you look these guys up on the internet you better make sure you have plenty of paper in your printer because their influence in this industry is monumental.

It was my good fortune to introduce them every night on the road. They were the act before us, and I'd go out there and bring them on. One night after a show, J.I. called and asked me to come on up to his room. I knocked on the door, and it was just the three of them in there. They said they had something to give me in appreciation for introducing them and handed me an envelope with the following written on the outside along with their individual signatures:

We really dig it

The way you announce,

So us ol' Crickets

Scored you an ounce.

Now that's pure poetry, folks! I was taken back, to say the least. They told me to open it up which I did, and pulled out a beautiful African gold Krugerrand. I still have it tucked away in a very safe institution.

I love these guys' wives, Joannie, Jane, and Louise, as much as I love them, and a few years later even named my first daughter Rebecca Louise after Sonny's wife. When I called Daddy to tell him I had a baby girl and what we had named her, he didn't skip a beat, just said, "Oh, Becky Lou!"

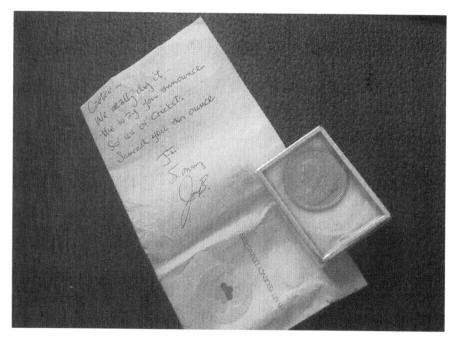

A little surprise gift from the Crickets

Shoot the Moon

Not long ago Barny and I celebrated thirty-seven years of marriage... together...in a row. We did something kind of strange that day. While still in our pajamas and holding our coffee cups, we listened to my album "Shoot The Moon" on full blast and danced around the living room. I was an artist with ABC records eons ago, and this was the first time in about thirty years that I had been able to listen to it. You may ask yourself why didn't you listen before, and why on your 37th anniversary? Can't say I have the answer for the last question, but the first? Well...

After signing a deal with "Hometown Productions," my schizo-phrenic career continued between Nashville and L.A. Whenever Barny and I were in town between tours or recording with Waylon, we'd go into the studio to work on our own music. We'd record whatever song of the day that sparked that certain "something special" response. That's one of the drawbacks about being a vocalist who can sing a lot of different styles and enjoys doing so. There's no clear direction. Plus, whether I wanted to admit it or not, I was still in a place of always want-ing to please, so it seemed as though I didn't have much of an opinion.

The Sound Lab in Hollywood was where we found ourselves most of the time, and the production company was racking up huge amounts of billable hours. The result was a lot of random recordings and a stu-dio bill that was demanding payment, so a plan of action was put into place.

Ken introduced me to rock impresario Alan Pariser. I was told he had managed Delaney and Bonnie, Dave Mason, and had enjoyed long associations with a list of who's who in the rock world, including Eric Clapton, the Beatles, the Stones and countless others. He was also the man behind the infamous Monterey Pop Festival and co-produced the cult classic, "You Are What You Eat," directed by Barry Feinstein. Look it up, it's CRAZY!

Alan and I entered into a management agreement where he would procure a record deal for me, helping Ken to at least break even on his investment, and hopefully get something going for me solo-wise. In 1977, I signed with ABC Records and began the insane journey of putting out an album.

Up until then, I had lived a lifetime of acquiescing, passing the ball off to someone else. Believing, or at the very least hoping, they would *get* me and open the doors for the artist that was just waiting inside to *wow* them. Even though I was writing back then, I wasn't taken seriously or encouraged to follow through on being a writer.

Sometimes I wish I could just go back and shake some sense into that girl! I would have told me, "C'mon, stand up for yourself!" But I didn't. So, when the record company decided they needed a white dis-co-type singer to fill the gap in their artist roster, I said "yes" and got in line. In that moment my art lost its voice. I agreed to be whatever and whomever they needed. Honestly, I was feeling the stress and pressure of Ken's investment and didn't want to be responsible for making him lose money. I had already lived that story and didn't feel like repeating it. Now *there's* a recipe for success.

Musicians were called that read like a "who's who" in the recording industry. There was Steve Cropper and John Hug on guitars, Duck Dunn on bass, Dallas Taylor, Ed Greene and John Raines on drums, Jim Horn and John Klemmer, Klemmer, Klemmer (that's what we called him) on sax, not to mention Clydie King, Vanetta Fields, Shirley Mathews, Donna Washburn (Leon Russell, Mad Dogs and Englishmen tour) Carolyn "Pepper" Watson and Dennis Brooks on vocals. Whew! The list goes on and they were *all* incredible.

New songs fitting the new criteria were chosen and the studio booked. It was time to record and then make decisions on what would actually become the final ten songs for the album.

The Night the Walls Closed In

One night, after being in the middle of the back and forth decisions of how to approach some of the new songs, the walls started closing in. I can look at it now, and the "why" is abundantly clear. Reflection was not a choice I made for myself back then. I either didn't have the time, or simply chose not to make the time, to process some of the events in my life that had nearly taken me out. That decision worked for a while. Thing is, burying the *stuff* doesn't come with a guarantee that it won't surface again and probably not at a very opportune time.

Yes, I was having a great time. Our careers were definitely improving. We were part of a music movement that was literally blowing the minds of traditional country, shaking up the executives, and threatening their grip on the artists they had oppressively controlled for years. We may not have been liked in the boardrooms of Nashville, but their financial departments were becoming addicted to the money that was rolling in from the phenomenal success of the Outlaw Movement. Waylon's thinking was: they could either get on board and ride the train with us, making more money than they had so far, or they could stand there and watch us go. One thing was certain; the train wasn't going to wait for anybody. It was their call.

We were enjoying the fruits of success and could indulge in pretty much anything our little hearts desired. I weighed about 98 pounds and for the first time in my life bought expensive stage clothes and make-up without batting an eye. I was working in this world with all the trappings and seductions that make you actually believe you're irreplaceable. While at the same time trying to promote an artist career in L.A., where nobody seemed to care who I thought I was.

I remember being home for a week in between shows and going to Sound Lab to record one night. Alan was pushing to get the project finished so everyone could get a return on their investment. The pressure at times felt suffocating. It wasn't *my* music, it was music that had been assigned to me, and I felt like a background singer on my own album.

There are certain things about that evening I recall in almost snapshot detail, even down to what I was wearing. I had left the house anticipating a productive time in the studio. This may not have been the album I wanted, but I was going to do my damnedest to make it the best possible showing of my vocal and artistic abilities.

Walking out to the iso-booth after listening to a play back, I began to feel a little shaky, but told myself to just concentrate on the song. This was no time to be weak. People were counting on me. Just as I finished adjusting my headphones and started to sing, I suddenly felt as though the walls were pressing in. My heart started racing, and I broke out in a cold sweat. I kept telling myself, "Not now, Carter! Push through, you can do this, it will pass." The fact that I was completely straight and hadn't been partaking of anything on the speedy side contributed to my fear because I didn't have an explanation for this very physical manifestation. I tried my hardest to ignore it, thinking it would go away. But every time the red light signaled that the state of the art 24-track was going into record, I froze.

Barny knew I was in trouble and told the guys in the control room to turn the mics off so he could go out and talk to me. By the time he walked through the door, I was having difficulty breathing and felt as though I were going to faint. It was clear there would be no talking me off the ledge this time. We had a very real problem.

Needless to say, the session came to an abrupt halt. John Arrias, who was the engineer on the session, said that I might be experiencing an anxiety attack. Barny scooped me up and put me in the car. I cried all the way home, terrified that the very thing I had been running from for so long had finally caught up with me. I had lost my mind, and we all know that a mind is a terrible thing to lose.

We headed out to our cute little older suburban house, in our very sweet little neighborhood in the San Fernando Valley. The closer we got, the calmer I became. My heart started beating in its steady rhythm, and I didn't feel quite so fuzzy anymore. Our big ol'dogs Beulah and Beuford met us at the door with so much love it literally knocked us over.

After putting on some jeans and a t-shirt, I sat there hugging myself and asking if I was cut out for this business. Hey, the "Betrayers" study group said I wasn't and maybe they, along with all the other naysayers in my head, were right after all.

We decided to take the rest of the week off and just do *normal* things before catching the plane and meeting up with everyone for the next leg of the tour. We spent afternoons at the beach and worked in our yard. There's something about digging your hands into the earth that reminds you of the deeper connection.

All those years, even though the band and crew were counted as some of my closest friends, I never told them how much I was struggling. It felt too risky. It's a gift and a curse to have *functioning* depression. I don't know if that's even a real term, I just know I never let those episodes take me out of the game. If there was an expectation of people counting on me to come through, no matter what that looked like, I would show up smiling. I'd been trained by the best since childhood. One thing I couldn't completely bury that night in the studio, though, was that I knew deep inside I had broken. Humpty Dumpty had nothin' on me.

Tulsa Ain't No Place
For Sissies

As calendars would have it, July showed up again and with it another Willie Nelson picnic. This one had a similar result but with a little bit different back-story. Our tour was out in California, maybe Anaheim or somewhere like that. There was no way the buses could get us there in time, so the decision was made to partner up with the band Lynard Skynard and charter a plane out of Burbank. They were giggin' in California and were booked for the picnic the following day as well. The flight would get us into Tulsa in time to rest a bit, shower, and then head out to the venue.

Waylon rarely, if ever, chartered a plane for his band because of the tragedy he had lived through with Buddy Holly early in his career. We either flew first class commercial or from time to time a few of us went on the Lear with him and Jessi. I don't think he was exactly comfortable with this night's arrangement, but his back was up against a wall and somebody in the organization signed off on the jet while he and Jessi took the Lear. It was INSANE! I think the plane was a 727 with two pilots and a few stewardesses. Don't get mad, now; that was their title back then before the current vocabulary of "flight Attendant" was adopted.

The merging of these two bands and crew was a mistake of epic proportions. The cabin looked and smelled like the inside of Willie's bus. The drink cart was unlimited, and one of our new road assistants decided to create a little ambiance. He lit a stick of incense and then waved it around my head while we were preparing to take off. Understand, I am a mild mannered person at heart. I have a pretty tight grip most of the time. But when I'm tired and someone else's stupidity threatens my space and well being, the dark side makes an appearance.

I very calmly told him if he didn't put it out immediately it would find its way into his favorite cavity, and I wouldn't even blink. Oh and by the way if he had a problem with that, I had a few rather large friends who would find it *sporting* to hold him down for me. He quickly extinguished the smoking, heavily scented irritant.

The doors kept swinging back and forth in the cockpit, and it seemed to me that all this misguided "let's make a road memory" bullshit was intent on proving that you could break every flight safety rule there was and live to tell about it. I wasn't so sure, and found myself praying for God to save us. He didn't have to save *all* the crazy occupants in this flying cabin of extreme mirth if He didn't want to, just Barny and me, and the people I loved. The other yahoos could do their own praying!

The pilot came on the intercom while we were sitting on the tarmac and informed us that the plane was overweight. He said he was going to have to, "back this thing up in the weeds to make sure we have enough runway to achieve lift." Grrrr-eat! God once again was gracious, and we eventually landed safe and sound in Tulsa.

It just kept getting better, though. Richie and Nancy, his wife at the time, were about as spent as Barny and I were. We needed our rooms at the hotel, and we needed them right then. However, our whole bunch had arrived early, and the rooms weren't ready. Of course they weren't. No problem. The four of us walked into a room that had two unmade beds and told the maid not to bother us for a couple of hours. The way we looked was convincing enough, and Richie and Nancy took one bed while Barny and I took the other. I was sleeping on someone else's sheets, but I was too tired to care. Wasn't the first time either. I did put my t-shirt over the pillow, though. Sometimes you just have to make adjustments. After awhile our road manager found us and gave us the keys to our clean rooms.

Once we got a little sleep and were able to freshen up, all the grievances from the night before faded. We were ready and more than willing to jump on the bus and head out to the country. We were excited and hopeful about the prospect of doing a little pickin' and grinnin' with people like Bee Spears, Willie's bass player. He and Richie were best friends and their crazy road exploits hold a legendary status to this day. I surely do miss that boy...

If I had thought that the previous picnic had a bunch of crazy fans, I was completely shocked by the conditions at this one. The spirit of Woodstock was alive and well and dancing up a storm in Tulsa. As far as I could see, there were people. It was like they were their own nation. Scenes from Alfred Hitchcock's "The Birds" flashed in my mind, and I hoped we didn't draw too much attention as we slowly and carefully drove through the masses toward the back-stage.

Security was on high alert and they did make me feel somewhat more at ease. However, once we parked and a few of the team had left to go check things out, word came back that the crowd was getting more and more unpredictable. I don't remember the numbers that were there but some, if not most, had been in the scorching heat without enough water or facilities for days. Concert promoters have thankfully learned a lot since those times.

We were told to be on guard, ready for anything. Many of the veteran players had experienced the phenomenon of a crowd that loves your music suddenly turning dangerously ugly when pushed to this limit.

Boomer, one of the Oakland chapter Hell's Angels, and a few other security guys walked Jessi and me to the stage. I don't really remember feeling scared—just kind of excited about the energy and opportunity to sing in front of that many people. However, once on stage and after dodging a couple of beer bottles, I got to thinking that this might not live up to my little romantic musical fantasy.

Security at the venue had constructed a tall plywood barrier in front of the stage. On one side was the massive crowd; while on the other were as many big strong bodies as they could get who had no problem with being ruthless. Each one held a large stick. As the fingers on the hands of the fans would creep up over the top of the barrier preparing to make the leap on stage and into infamy, whomever was closest would bring that big stick down with a decisive whack, sending the wounded, inebriated fan into the arms of the front lines below. It was nuts!

I kept trying to get that vision of reality to match up with all these bodies laughing, dancing and singing along. So, tell me again...why were they throwing beer bottles? Our very seasoned crew, made up of several tough Vietnam Vets, told me not to worry. It was just something that happens in a mob. They were actually having fun, making memories to share with their grandchildren someday. Really?

Once Waylon came out on the stage, he made an instant decision that Jessi and I would not be joining them for this show. I wanted to be out there so badly, but nobody argues with Waylon. Security never let Jessi and me out of their sight, but I did get to stay on stage as long as I stood over to the side. I vaguely remember talking him into letting the crew set my mic up far enough away from the front line, so I could sing on a couple of things. It was just one more interesting Willie Nelson Picnic. That's rock n' roll boys and girls!

The last picnic I played was with Jessi after Waylon left. We were on the bill with Bob Dylan and a few other heavyweights. That one went off without a hitch, and Jessi brought the house down. Guess third time's a charm.

Jessi and Carter at the Willie Nelson Picnic, Fort Worth,
TX. 2005

"Subtly" Sexy Album Shoot

I haven't always been a very good communicator. My skills and ability to articulate have definitely improved over the years. Much of that progress was due to the tendency I had to get myself into hot water or the necessity to stay out of bubble baths…

With the music finally recorded and the songs chosen for my album, it was time to come up with the title and vision for the front and back covers. One of the songs we'd recorded was "Shoot the Moon," and after meeting with both Ken and Alan, we all agreed it would make a great title. With that decision tucked away, we were free to then conceptualize about the look of the cover. I wanted something subtly sexy. I'll say it again…*subtly* sexy.

We kicked around some ideas about what I would wear and decided to go with the very cool look of a shop on Sunset called "Tenderness." They specialized in soft, very snug fitting suede dresses that had a sultry, yet earthy and sophisticated appeal.

The next step was to decide on a photographer. Alan spoke up quickly with the recommendation of his cousin, who was an up and coming in that field. I was told he had shot several Playboy Magazine covers and was in great demand. Again, I made it clear that I wanted something *subtly* sexy and was assured we were all on the same page.

I don't exactly have a love affair with cameras, and knowing the situation would make me feel self-conscious, I told Barny I wanted to do this on my own. He wasn't at all disappointed and sent me out the door with a kiss, saying he knew it was going to be great.

It was a night shoot at a studio inside of a warehouse, and all the way there I kept telling myself there was no reason to be nervous. I arrived, dragging in my wardrobe and enough accessories to outfit a chorus line. As I walked into this very large, hangar-type building filled with various crew, my line of sight was immediately drawn to a lovely bathtub. There were bubbles floating in the air like lazy wishes, then popping on the strategically placed lights above. I kind of stood there for a few minutes, thinking what part of *subtle* did I not make clear?

The team was in place, quickly relieving me of the massive amount of clothes I was holding and then taking me to an area behind a screen, which would serve as my dressing room. There was a make-up artist, hair stylist, wardrobe person and an assistant who was a very happy, *straight* male, whose job was to make sure all my body parts lined up the way they should. They'd just done a wrap on the next Playboy cover, and my shoot was next. What? Maybe I should've had Barny come with me!

I looked over on the rack to confirm that my chosen outfits were there, and they were all hung up nice and neat. However, right next to them was this piece of short, filmy, white material, and I was wondering if we were going to use it as a scarf or something.

The coordinator told us they'd be ready for me shortly and to go ahead and get dressed. I reached for one of the soft suede dresses just as the wardrobe person handed me the "scarf." I smiled and said I wasn't sure that was going to look very good with what I was holding in my hand. She returned my smile and in an unmistakably patronizing voice while reaching for my outfit and hanging it up behind her, explained that the flimsy piece of see-through material WAS the outfit.

Uhhhhhhhhhh…huh? I called for Ken and Alan, showing them the "scarf" and telling them, as if they needed to be told, that I wasn't a Playboy Bunny, I was a singer. Looking at Alan, I demanded to know what the plan was. Again…SUBTLY sexy!

Ken seemed uneasy and thankfully left, leaving his wife to hold my hand. Alan said it would all be very tasteful, and I should make the most of my attributes. He went on to remind me that it's not easy for new artists to sell records. He assured me this was going to be worth it. So, I put my big girl panties on and, wait a minute…I took my big girl panties off, took a sip of a little somethin', somethin', and had them turn the music up loud. For the next couple of hours I pretended to be someone else while Alan's cousin worked his photographic magic. After that the other shots in the leather dresses were a cinch.

I packed up and headed home, trying to think of how I was going to explain all of this to Barny. In reality, he's actually a lot more open-minded than I am about such things. He was sure that the finished product would be perfect, and he was proud of the way I had handled it all. Okie, dokie, then. If you have a copy of my album or have seen the back cover, just know it wasn't my big fat idea!

Years later I was asked to be the speaker at a Christian business-women's luncheon in Nashville. It was sort of a last minute request, and I agreed. They needed a picture of me for the brochure that was going out, and I directed them to Waylon's website which has a solo picture of each member of the band. Somewhere along the way their Internet GPS took them on a detour and after receiving a copy of the organization's online flyer, I opened it up and was shocked at what was staring back at me. There, in the upper corner next to my bio, was the Playboy-ish picture from the back of my album.

I started laughing and could barely control myself as I picked up the phone and dialed the woman that was handling the booking for the organization. Once the Southern pleasantries were out of the way, I asked where she found that particular shot. She had evidently Googled my name, and this was one of the pictures that came up. It was pretty much thumbnail size and to her I looked like an angel in the photo, so she thought it was appropriate for their function.

Biting the inside of my mouth I proceeded with caution, explaining that I was naked under that little white angel looking dress. Much to my surprise she started laughing as well. She reasoned that I was being asked to share my story, and that photo shoot was part of the story. Besides, the picture was so small no one would ever know.

Thank God for people who embrace a good sense of humor. Now, any time I start to take myself too seriously I just remember the naked angel and I come down off my high horse real quick!

Oh, and don't go tryin' to find one of those albums folks cuz I got 'em all safely stashed underneath my bed!

I think...

Yikes!!

Beware of the Piper

It's said that great songs and stories are born out of real life experiences. I believe that to be true and on August 24, 1977 we were all about to take that to a new level.

Barny and I were nestled all safe and sound at our house in Southern California for a rare few days of respite between tours. We were giving ourselves permission to relax a little and enjoy the simpler side of life with lazy afternoons and long dinners. It was all about good food, good friends, good wine and beer.

While we were basking in the sun, the Piper came knocking at the door of American Studios in Nashville all dressed up as Federal Narcotics agents. Waylon himself tells the story best in his book, "Waylon: An Autobiography," by Waylon Jennings and Lenny Kaye. I highly recommend reading it if you haven't already. He's incredibly honest and transparent in his recollections of that night. I wasn't physically there, so I can't add anything to that part of the story. What I can talk about is what happened afterwards.

We'd been running all around the country playing our shows, unaware we were creating an underground movement that changed the way mainstream Pop looked at Country Music. When we were together, whether on the road or in the studio, it was like we were our own city, accountable to no one but ourselves. We weren't trying to hurt anybody, and we sure as hell weren't profiting from anything other than a musical experience and fun. It's well documented that drugs were a part of the culture, but they weren't the whole culture. Incredible songs were written. Unforgettable nights of music were performed on stages across the U.S. of A. and magical moments were captured for generations to come on the old analog machines of the time period.

However, when Waylon was busted for possession of cocaine that night, the deceptively fragile balloon we had all been holding onto so tight developed a slow leak. Paranoia sat at our tables and listened in on our phone conversations. It followed us in unmarked cars and showed up in the faces of strangers. I probably did the least amount of anyone out there but still checked under every bed and took every hotel phone apart. I can't confirm it, but I'm convinced our home line was tapped for a while. Waylon used to call us on a regular basis, and to think we were exempt would have been naïve.

From what I understand, some rather glaring mistakes were made that Wednesday night, and the prosecution was left holding an empty bag. When arresting him for possession and asking about the drugs Waylon replied, "Where I come from, possession means 'got it,' and you ain't got it."

$100,000 later the charges were dropped and the dust settled. Waylon made every penny of that money back and more when he wrote, "Don't Ya'll Think This Outlaw Bit Has Done Got Out of Hand?" He had a little better idea of who his real friends were and his popularity on the streets of America and around the globe went through the roof.

Wisdom would tell a person after such an event that it was time to re-evaluate, maybe cut back a bit or stop altogether. But Waylon was one of the most confusing people I had ever met. On the one hand he could be tender, kind, compassionate and genuinely empathetic. On the other hand he had the capacity and fortitude of an army and could bring you down without even so much as a blink. The kinder side would show up when he would dry out. But his addiction fed a darkness that only he knew the depths of.

"I've always been crazy but it's kept me from going insane" wasn't some made up lyric. He lived it, and after the "Piper" went home Waylon's drug use increased, along with his web of security. Our love and loyalty at times was misplaced, and regrettably for a while enabled him to continue that dance with death. It's a common story, played out on the front pages of newspapers and around the clock coverage of the latest person in power or celebrity's downfall.

I watched as he became a cult hero representing the injustices of the world. Thing is, I knew all too well that doing drugs and being an addict begins with a choice. I've seen true injustice, and I'm not so sure the transference of people's pain to that particular event was all that well placed. I'm not alone in that thinking, by the way. Waylon himself acknowledged the same in conversations, as well as through his actions later in life after he made the courageous and loving decision to get clean.

But back then it really didn't matter what I thought, and most of the time I kept my opinions to myself. We were all in and at the time would have paid any price to patch up that big balloon and keep it soaring. See, it wasn't the drug culture that tied us together. It went deeper than that. We were a family, and families close ranks and protect each other.

From that moment on I was more on my toes, but my casual affair with recreational drugs became more of a love/hate relationship. In a sense, the blinders came off and I had a difficult time reconciling what cocaine was doing to my friends as well as myself.

Long Way To Fall When Your Heels Are too High

Waylon and Willie's popularity continued to soar, and by 1978 their duet album, entitled "Waylon and Willie," hit #1 on the Country Charts. It remained there for the next ten weeks. "Mama's Don't Let Your Babies Grow Up To Be Cowboys" not only held the #1 spot, but earned them both a Grammy Award in the "Best Country Vocal Performance by a Duo or Group" category. Life had settled in, and our rock-and-roll lifestyle became the new norm.

Back in L.A., my record was finally finished and we were ready to move on to the marketing process. Like most artists' first album, Side One consisted of the most commercially on target songs for the chosen demographic. Side Two consisted of five songs we recorded before the record deal had come into existence. Three of those were Barny's, including "Shelter", leaving the old blues song, "Who Will Your Next Fool Be" by Charlie Rich and "I'm Through With You" written by our old friend and best man, Bob Walden. So, in review, Side One was kind of disco-ish R&B, while Side Two had a more organic quality to it, kind of country blues-ish. How's that for clarity? Gee, I wonder why it didn't sell millions!

The single was "Something's Up", complete with Ian Underwood's synthesizer, disco strings and effects. Some of the smaller markets picked it up along with American Airlines onboard radio, and a few music critics gave it a passing grade. However, the question of the day was why someone who was touring with the biggest act in Country Rock would release an album that had no obvious appeal in that market? Excellent question, my dear Mr. Watson!

The record company sent out "Regionals" every once in a great while that were supposed to be promoting me to the local radio stations. Most of the time they were no-shows, or when they did make an appearance just wanted me to get them backstage passes so they could meet Waylon or Jessi. The majority of them had no idea who I was. Add that to newspaper reviewers getting my name wrong or assigning something I sang that they liked to another female singer who will remain anonymous, and it's not at all surprising that the record started tanking and my confidence with it.

After hearing the album, Waylon and Jessi took me aside and explained the benefits of being a big fish in a little pond as opposed to an itty-bitty fish in an ocean. I didn't at all disagree, but this album had less to do with me as an artist and more to do with Hometown Production's risky investment.

Please know I now have a more mature understanding of how stressful it was for Ken, and I appreciate all that he introduced me to back then. I was just really young and incredibly green, feeling responsible for everybody's wellbeing.

Anyway, I was relieved and they were happy to get the money from ABC so they could pay Armen Steiner for the outstanding studio bill. They threw a big party to celebrate. So I guess everything worked out in the short term.

In the middle of ABC's brilliant no-promotion policy, Alan got the company to book me for a radio convention at the Century Plaza Hotel. They tried to prepare me for what to expect, but I had no idea what I was getting myself into and should have listened more closely.

My assumption was that it would be more of a *listening* group because of the new music that was being showcased. They might be a little drunk but hey, what crowd wasn't? Whenever Ken or Alan asked if I felt confident, I did my best to put their minds at ease. They told me it was probably going to be my most important concert so far, and I needed to knock it out of the park. No problem, boys.

We put together a band with Ron Tutt on drums, who was in Elvis Presley's band. Sherman Hayes played bass; John Hug was on guitar and Barny on keyboards. They sounded great, but I started realizing a little too late that I needed more time to actually be able to develop a good live show. I knew how to back somebody else up, but it's a whole other ballgame when you're the artist. I was beginning to see just how far behind the curve I was on that one. With a couple of two hour rehearsals under my belt, I was expected to deliver a wildly successful performance that would give Ken, Alan and the record company what they needed: a homerun.

The dressing room was first-class, complete with wine and flowers. When Ken stepped in to check on me, I could tell he was nervous as a cat. I tried to be as convincing as possible, acting like I wasn't the least bit concerned. However, everybody else's nerves were starting to put me on edge.

Alan had befriended the famous astronaut, David Scott, 7th person to walk on the moon, pilot of Gemini 8, Command Module pilot aboard Apollo 9 and the Commander of Apollo 15. Oh, *that* David Scott! He had an entrepreneurial spirit and spoke with me on one occasion about wireless mics before there ever was such a thing. He was interested in how that new technology would affect an artist's live performance. Well, that was another reason Ken stopped by. Mr. Scott was their guest and looking forward to a great show. With my album entitled "Shoot the Moon", Alan thought it would be a very cool tie-in and wanted me to be sure and introduce him from the stage. Uh-oh, we have a problem, Houston!

From my dressing room, I could hear my label mates, the Oak Ridge Boys, bringing down the house. These guys were veterans and could have phoned in their show and still been incredible. Tell me, how do you follow that?

Now it was my turn. I was wearing the leather dress from the album cover and the very high, high heels as well. I had never worn them other than for the album shoot. The band played the intro, and as I walked on to the stage I immediately realized it was freshly waxed and very slick. Carefully, almost in a skating motion, I moved to the mic, and with that damned phony smile frozen on my face, began to sing.

The crowd was made up of a bunch of jaded, cynical male radio programmers. They'd seen it all, experienced it all and had the multiple alimony payments to prove it. I was eaten alive. I sang fine, even though I had difficulty hearing, and the guys played great. But the crowd was already so drunk and loud that I wasn't even background noise. I didn't exist. I stood completely stiff, not moving an inch from the mic for fear I would fall down, but still having to do my twenty minutes. Ken and Alan had their heads down, not wanting to make eye contact, and I wouldn't even venture a glance at David Scott.

As I hit the dressing room, I could hear Denise LaSalle putting on a show for the same crowd that had just ignored my existence but who were now on their feet. She was a true R&B star and had been working these kinds of events for most of her career. She had every one of those radio boys wrapped around her little finger from the first downbeat.

My performance, or lack of, was nothing short of painful and pathetic, even worse than my showcase at the Troubadour. It would have taken the strength of the Hoover Dam to hold back my tears, and I hate crying. I didn't want to talk to anybody, see anybody, or be anybody. I just wanted to go home.

The memory of that night would haunt me and be instrumental in my decision to drop my pursuit of being an artist a few years later. The voice in my head telling me I was no good or, at best, not good enough, couldn't be silenced or persuaded; that night's performance was a fatal career wound.

Honestly, in that moment, I wasn't good. I sucked. But it shouldn't have been in any way, shape, or form, the end. It could just as easily have been the beginning if I had understood the value of failure. Barny recently said in one of our morning coffee conversations that, "Failure is not screwing up, failure is *giving up*."

What I had to learn, but didn't understand then, was that I would eventually become more comfortable being *Me*. Embracing my art, my story, being true to who I was created to be. I was never meant to be a compilation of what the studies say a certain record company needs to fill the gap. Nor was I created to be what some other person needed to make them feel good about *their* art and position in life.

It's ironic that I was right in the middle of a movement that was fighting the very thing I was experiencing, and yet it wasn't helping me one bit.

I met some good people back then. One guy in particular, who was part of the A&R department at ABC Records, was Bob Kirsch. He was always kind and felt genuinely bad about how things had played out. He believed in my talent and wished me only the best. It all became a moot point when in 1979 ABC Records was sold to MCA because of insurmountable financial problems. The ABC label was officially discontinued March 5, 1979 and all but a few high performing artists were dropped. That's Showbiz, for ya!

Welcome to Vegas, Baby!

I've been told I'm the worst at receiving a compliment. My first response is usually one of deflection. One night while singing a solo with the Waylors at Red Rocks outside of Denver, I was given a standing ovation. I kept looking around assuming that Waylon or Willie had walked on stage. It took a while for it to register that the applause was for me. Nearly knocked me over. Given what you've read so far the next story shouldn't surprise you a bit.

The *Boys* in Vegas decided to gamble on our show and had invited us to bring our rowdy friends and their money along with them. We didn't hold back a lick and even though the crowd stretched the maitre'd's patience, the casino was making so much profit they let the antics of the fans ride. They'd jump up on the tables and hoot and holler like they were at a Willie Nelson picnic. Eeeee-haaaa! And this is where Connie Nelson, Willie's wife at the time, cooked up a little surprise for me.

One night, about fifteen minutes before I was supposed to take the stage with the "Waylors," she came up and said she had someone who wanted to meet me. No problem, I had plenty of time. I asked who it was, assuming it was another musician or writer. She just smiled and chatted about nothing as she walked me over to a group of people who were standing in a circle. When they saw Connie and me approaching, the circle opened up and standing there, in the flesh, was the one and only Robert Redford. He and Willie were in town filming "The Electric Horseman."

Now, by this time I had met a lot of celebrities and famous influential people. I respected them, but I didn't worship them. If anything, I usually felt uncomfortable and looked for an opportunity to quietly escape.

I remember Connie saying, "Bob, this is Carter. She's the back-up singer in Waylon's band I was telling you about."

Mr. Redford flashed that million-dollar box office smile, stuck out his hand and said, "Hi Carter, nice to meet you."

To which I responded in a voice that was barely audible, and extending my own hand that was visibly shaking, "Hi...(awkward pause with goofy smile plastered on my face). Bye."

I turned around and walked back to the stage, desperately wishing I could look over my shoulder and say, "Just kidding!"

Barny had followed us over and heard Mr. Redford say, "Well okay, then." The two of them were introduced and in the wake of my silliness, a good laugh was had by all. Happy to be of service folks.

Later that night I caught up with Connie to apologize, but she was still laughing and assured me all was well. One of the actors, Tim Scott, that worked in several of Mr. Redford's films during that time, was in the circle that night. He later became a faithful supporter of mine in L.A. as I worked to get my solo career up and running. I decided that Robert Redford must be a pretty nice guy if he had friends like Tim Scott. So there ya go.

Strike 1-2-3—I'm Outta Here!

There are parts of Texas, or at least parts that I was sequestered in, that are not exactly where you might want to spend a romantic wedding anniversary. Despite all the Doubting Thomases and the nearly insurmountable odds of a marriage surviving in that atmosphere, Barny and I found ourselves waking up on our fifth anniversary, and still in love. Go figure!

We had a show that night but were determined to make the best of it. If I remember right, we were headed to a larger city and thought we might have an official celebration there. Everybody, including Waylon, knew it was our anniversary and were making the usual jokes while giving us big family hugs.

The show had been its own brand of Texas crazy, which always happened anytime we were within spitting distance to where Waylon had grown up. Now, back at the little roadside motel we had all taken over, Barny and I were waiting for the call to tell us when the buses were moving. The crew almost always ran ahead of us unless there was a day off in between since they had to be at the venue to set up, but the band bus and Waylon's bus would run together more often than not.

This night there was a shift in the sanity meter, however, and Waylon's not so better self was showing up and reeking havoc. Every thirty minutes or so we'd get the update that departure was delayed, so just hang tight. Thing is, as tired as we were, we couldn't go to sleep because any minute we might be leaving. So we sat and waited, dressed and ready to go, *all night long*. Waylon was flexing his, "Don't forget who's in charge muscles" and had collected all the keys to the buses, not even letting the crew bus leave. Everybody was pissed!

My long fuse had been doing a slow burn all night and by the time morning arrived had burned clean out. By then Tom Bourke was road manager and called to say it was time to go put our stuff in the bays and hop on the bus. It looked like we were finally going to be heading to the next city.

Now that phrase, "I was so mad I could hardly see straight," didn't apply. For me that day, I saw with a clarity that I had not given myself permission to see with in a long time. As I sat there and listened to everyone bitchin' and complainin', that old Walker rage rose to the top. So when Waylon entered the bus and parked himself behind the wheel telling all of us that he was the boss, and we would leave when he was good and ready to tell us to leave, I snapped.

I walked up to the front to have a serious chat with the man. Told him I didn't care who the hell he thought he was, he had just treated a bunch of people who would do anything for him, and some had, as though he owned us. And just to make it crystal clear, he didn't own shit! I think he was in shock because he just kept staring at me with his mouth open.

Now, I'm no fool. I know I was able to get by with this because I'm a female, and in that moment I used that little bit of reality to the best of my ability. I went on to remind him that the previous day was my anniversary, and I didn't appreciate being hung out to dry all night. Furthermore, I wasn't EVER going to put up with that kind of power play again, AND if he had a problem with it I highly recommended he fire me on the spot. Go ahead, fire me now, because frankly I'd rather be home than out in some Godforsaken country with *him* behind the wheel.

Strike one…

At a birthday party my family had for me at our house after Waylon had passed, we were all sitting around reminiscing when Sonny Curtis' wife Louise reminded us of that story. We all had a big laugh, and I'm sure Waylon was laughing along with us. I mean, picture it: I was only 98 pounds, but in that moment I felt like I was 350 pounds of pure muscle.

So what did a big Outlaw star do when his little chick background singer called him out in front of the boys? To his credit, he laughed and laughed big. It was like instant relief of all the pressure that had been building up for us out there, Waylon included. He had proven his point; he *was* the man in control even if his drug habit was calling the shots. But he hadn't hired a bunch of "Yes" people that were going to stand around and watch him go down the tubes and take us with him. He weren't no Elvis, folks.

....

Life on the road was crazier than ever, and our stays in the studio were legendary. Which was where strike two came roaring across home plate from out of nowhere. I was struggling to keep everything in my L.A. world from burying me and made the mistake of taking my eyes off the ball, the ball being...Waylon.

I had just turned down a pretty sweet deal to sing on an album in L.A. for one of my favorite rock artists. Waylon had insisted that I be with him in Nashville, even though I could have come in a day or two later to do my vocal backgrounds. I was disappointed, but it didn't really bother me that much because I loved making music with all my friends.

By the time we landed and hit the studio, he was already a couple days into one of his infamous round the clock *roars* and wasn't about to wait on anybody. Time to get on board, children. I couldn't run fast enough to make the leap, and I'd grown tired of watching what the drugs were doing to my friend. Plus, true to form, I didn't sing my first note until about 3 a.m. two days later. I was fighting that claustrophobic feeling of a life out of control, and that scared me to death. Add to that my album crashing and burning and the record deal along with it, and it's not a stretch to see how emotionally spent and vulnerable I was in that moment. Not a good combination.

What happened next was so petty and Junior High that it's hard to understand why it would lead to Waylon and me getting so mad at each other. We got into a fight over a football game. That's right, a football game. It was so stupid: an argument that wasn't an argument and a fight that wasn't a fight. There was a build up of events and dynamics in our relationship that became such a strong current I just couldn't fight against it anymore, and I ended up letting it carry me way off shore.

The L.A. Rams were playing the Dallas Cowboys and even though I didn't really care that much, after hearing all the trash talk about the Rams I suddenly grew some loyalty for them and added fuel to Waylon's fire. He'd rub it in every time the Cowboys scored, and I'd do the same for the Rams. At first it seemed to everyone else that it was just a bit of good-natured ribbing between Waylon and "Mama Carter," but by the 4th quarter it was clearly about something besides football.

When the Cowboys won, of course, Waylon was impossible. He wouldn't stop taunting me, and calling my team "losers." Every time either one of us would walk back into the room we'd start back up again. I was dishing out just as much as he was and finally reached my limit. I turned around, looked him square in the eyes and using my favorite word back then told him what he could do to himself *and* his little Cowboys!" Then I walked out of the studio and went back to the hotel.

He'd already evoked this kind of a reaction from me once and had let it go, but not this time. He didn't speak to me for the next two weeks, which made the time on stage pretty miserable.

It's funny what we choose to expend our anger on when we can't bring ourselves to address the real issues, and it's best that some of those stay with me. But one thing was clear, I was tired of being controlled, told what I could and could not do. There was a big ol' elephant in the room that had made friends with the monkeys on our backs, and now it was beginning to smell a whole lot like a third-rate circus that had stayed too long.

The stalemate was finally broken when Richie was talking to him one night and said, "C'mon Waylon. It's Carter. You can't stay mad at Carter."

Sometimes when we back ourselves into a corner, it takes someone else to paint the door to get out. Richie must have channeled Rembrandt that night because the next day it was as though nothing had ever happened.

But for me it was Strike Two.

....

Like recording tape on the end of a reel that picks up speed, so were the days leading up to the infamous 1981 break-up in Las Vegas. What had begun as the adventure of a lifetime had succumbed to the ravaging of a drug that pulled off a coup, imprisoning all who *chose* to stay and the rest who didn't have the strength to leave. The following lyrics of the song written by J.J. Cale and recorded by Eric Clapton were our mantra.

"She don't lie, she don't lie, she don't lie...Cocaine."

Are you kidding me? All cocaine does is lie. She's a crafty and cruel mistress with deceit dripping from her lips. She tells you she's just there to help you tap into your best self, your most creative side. And then when she gets you hooked, she constantly whispers in your ear telling you you're no good without her. Nobody's going to listen or like you unless you bring her to the party. Bitch! It was time to take her off of my "call a friend" list and send her packing.

Barny and I decided to start a family. Our plan was once I was pregnant, we'd give notice and go back to L.A. to pursue our careers. Most everybody was experiencing a slow crash and burn of some sort, and Waylon's habit was out of control. He was canceling gigs and making wild decisions. I could see what it was doing to him, as well as Jessi, and the people who loved them both. Not living in Nashville made it possible for us to stay away from the office drama. We had no idea just how bad financially things had become for his *organization,* and I use that term loosely.

When Waylon was straight, he was a completely different person. We always looked forward to seeing him when he came back after cleaning out for a time. The sad part was that his intentions weren't to kick anything, just to clean out long enough so he could start back up and once again feel the high.

I'm not revealing anything new here, so you don't need to get nervous. All of this is well documented in his own biography with more detail and candor than most celebrities allow. He and I are of the same opinion. If you spin, marginalize, and homogenize the dark places of your life, you do an ultimate disservice to the generations to come. Redemption is the thread that holds the tapestry together and makes it truly beautiful. Well, it wasn't beautiful yet, but it was coming.

For two years Barny and I tried to get pregnant. The old emotional teeter-totter showed up in a big way every month. While many unplanned pregnancies were happening to friends around us, and some unwanted on top of that, I remained barren. After tests and an unsuccessful round of fertility drugs, I was told my chances for having a child were close to nil. I was devastated.

However, Mama and my sisters never stopped praying for us, and right before Christmas 1980, God gave us a miracle. A little life was able to hold on and was now growing into our very own baby. If all went well, we could expect our first child in August. Barny and I were absolutely ecstatic. Waylon and Jess and the whole road family joined us in our excitement.

The first couple of months were a bit rocky. But once that was over, I started feeling great and my spirits were soaring in spite of the insanity that continued to build on the road. I had stopped doing any kind of drug long before I got pregnant. I wanted to keep my body and mind healthy, which probably contributed even more to my desire to leave. It's hard being straight when everything else is so crooked around you.

I was very much aware of this growing sense of autonomy and freedom, and it was stronger than anything I had felt up until then. We had a baby coming! As we were soaring, Waylon was plummeting, and that's how all the ingredients for the perfect storm came together for me in June of 1981.

By now Shooter was a little over two years old, and Jessi had created a pretty cool world out there for him. She was blessed with an extraordinary woman named Maureen, who was their nanny, housekeeper, executive assistant, chef; you name it, she did it and she did it with excellence. As an artist, mother, and the wife of Waylon Jennings, there's no way Jessi could have kept all those plates in the air all by herself. No one could.

There was talk of Barny and me hiring someone like Maureen, so we could stay and continue working with them. We knew the invitation had come from a place of friendship, and we loved them for that. But we also knew we had to do what was best for our own little growing family.

So in March I gave notice that the Vegas date that coming June would be my last. It was bittersweet and not going to be easy to say goodbye. But everyone seemed to understand and was completely supportive, celebrating this miracle of life with us.

By that summer, Vegas had become my least favorite place to play. When we were there early on, it was fun and kind of dangerous. We were breaking down barriers and taking no hostages. But now it just smelled and needed paint. This was right before millions of dollars were invested turning "Sin City" into the desert's family friendly vacation Mecca of the 80's and 90's. We played two shows a night, which for the band meant we were on our feet until 2 or 3 in the morning, and by now I was six months pregnant.

Our last night of a long week at the Riviera Hotel and Casino finally came to an end, and the band and a few crewmembers were in the dressing room backstage. We all knew things were dicey, but it was the end of a long tour, and experience had taught us that it was time for everybody to go home and rest up for the next round.

I was feeling a little sad at the prospect of leaving these friends, but I was incredibly excited for what was in my future. Diana, who lived with us for about three years and helped manage things at home, used to come out on the road every once in a while. She was there to celebrate my last show and had joined Barny and me along with the band in the dressing room.

Just as I was getting ready to go around and tell my friends goodbye and promise to see them soon, Waylon stormed through the door saying he was shutting everything down, and firing everybody. He was obviously higher than a kite, but he was also more serious than I had ever seen him. For the official story, I refer you once again to his autobiography. I'm just going to tell you what happened from my perspective.

He was raging, not making a lot of sense. In that moment, I saw my dad, and my initial reaction was one of fear and self-protection. However, those feelings were quickly booted out by a much stronger person who had taken up residence in me: the mama lion.

Everything became incredibly clear and focused. I watched him and listened to him, taking in all the faces of the guys I loved so much. I felt ridiculously protective of them. The Kingdom had come undone. He never once made eye contact with me. He knew that I *knew*, and while I was feeling a rage build inside, it was also tempered with a deep sadness.

When he left the room, all hell broke loose. This was a family he was breaking up. These were people who had put their lives on the line for him and were now being dismissed as though they were disposable employees. Every band member in that room was denying the hurt and allowing the anger. Some of those details fall under the category of "What happens in Vegas stays in Vegas." All I knew was that I was done.

I told Barny and Diana that I would meet them at the room, but first I had a little errand I needed to run. They both knew me well enough not to try to stop me and said we'd talk when I got back.

I took the elevator to Waylon's room and knocked on the door. Deakon, who was his bodyguard and one of the top members of the Oakland Hell's Angels, answered. Understand this was someone you would never want to cross. I told him I needed to speak with Waylon, and he stood there like a giant Redwood tree with his arms crossed, not saying a word. It's strange, looking back. I don't remember feeling fear or intimidation, just total calm.

I flashed to a recent outdoor concert near Salinas when some of the club, wearing their colors, rode onto the fairgrounds. They were impressive and scary, to say the least. I was about five months pregnant, and there was this Barney Fife kind of rent-a-cop who I guess never looked at himself in the mirror because he was walkin' and talkin' with a swagger that could get his 125-pound self in serious trouble. I could see where this was headed and quickly walked over putting myself between Deakon and the Mini-Me cop. I told him these guys were with us, and they were cool, trying to diffuse the mounting volatile situation. Thankfully the guy woke up in time to see who he was facing and walked away. Deakon looked at me and starting laughing, he said, "Man Carter, I don't know what we would have done if you hadn't come along and rescued us!" The sound of his big laugh was something I will never forget.

Now here I was again, and it was clear that the pregnant lady wasn't going to back down. Out of respect for Waylon and his friendship with me, he stepped aside and let me walk through the door.

Waylon was in the room pacing. He immediately tried to assure me that what had happened in the dressing room had nothing to do with me, and he hoped Barny and I would come back. I just stood there looking at him. In that moment so many of the incessant patterns learned from my childhood of always trying to keep people happy, clean up their messes, make them like me so they wouldn't hurt me, played like a movie in slow motion. It was as though I were waking up from a long winter's nap.

Finally in a very calm voice, I told him this was goodbye. This was the last way I ever wanted to leave him or this family of musicians I had grown to love, but he left me no choice. I reminded him that he had known since March this would be my final night. If our friendship meant so little after everything I'd gone through with him, then it was over for me. I wished him and Jessi well, then looked him straight in the eye and said this was my last goodbye. I was leaving and never coming back...never. Without waiting for his reaction, I turned around, walked out the door, and quietly closed it behind me.

Still in this very composed state of mind, I went to our room and after telling Barny what had happened began to methodically pack up all of my stage clothes. He and Diana both tried to convince me to stay until the next day and get some sleep. They said we could leave after breakfast and be home by late afternoon. By then it was after four in the morning and I just couldn't take one more second of the stench of that hotel and what it represented. At that point I was so mad, I never wanted to see Waylon again. So, we packed up the Blazer, headed for the house and a whole new chapter in our lives.

Strike 3, I'm outta here...

Part Four

Reunion and Redemption

One more time around

Never Say Never

'll never forget the feeling of walking through the door of our house and knowing I was home to stay. It's one of those "puzzle piece" moments in your life, where not only does the piece fit but completes another part of the overall picture. It was time to plan with abandon. Time to celebrate!

Barny and Waylon used to laugh, calling the next ten years the longest maternity leave in history. Honestly, I never thought we'd see each other again. The blow up in Vegas was the final straw for me, and it couldn't have been a better time to move on. Barny went out for one final tour with everybody after that, but I stayed home, which had always been the plan.

Things with Waylon and the rest of the band smoothed over enough for show commitments to be made. There were so many aspects of Waylon's business that I had no clue about, and didn't become aware of until years later. Our connection had always been one of music, art, and friendship first; business was secondary.

For the next several months, whenever the band was in town they'd call and come over to the house for a visit. I'd fix them dinner while they did their laundry. We'd laugh as we caught each other up on our families, and then spent time remembering the best days.

Once, while Jigger (aka Jerry Bridges, the bass player that had replaced Sherman Hayes) was there, he passed on a message from Waylon asking us to please consider coming back. I didn't even have to think about it. The answer was "No" in Vegas; it was "No" now.

I had recently found Jesus. Actually, it wasn't like He had been lost or anything. I'd just been looking in the wrong place all that time. He'd always been there with me, and waking up to that reality on May 12, 1982 was not only a heart-changer but a life-changer as well. The birth of our precious, healthy daughter helped me to take all of those spiritual questions, church wounds and bitterness off the shelf and look at them with new perspective. I've always been a seeker, searching for the meaning of things. Now for the first time in my 28 years on the planet, I was asking the hard questions that I had chosen to defer for another time.

I remember lying in bed one night and deciding to pray. I said, "I'm so confused right now. I don't know if I've been talking to the ceiling all these years, or if you're like the Force in Star Wars, but I've come to the end of this road and I'm ready to make a turn. I have a precious little girl I need to raise, and I want to know if what I've been taught since childhood is true. If you're *real*, God, then prove it."

The next morning I woke up around 5 a.m. to a crying baby. Becky had a pretty significant case of colic and cried most of the time she was awake. I fed her and much to my surprise, she went back to sleep. I laid her down in her little crib and went into the living room. I was restless. Barny had worked a club the night before and wouldn't be up and around for a while, so I started dusting, which is a miracle in itself. As I was cleaning my old bookcase, one of the titles caught my eye.

A few years before, Waylon's bass player, Sherman Hayes, had been let go. One of the reasons was that he had become a Christian and tried to save all of us. I loved his heart, but at the time I wasn't interested in his message. I'd been there and done that. Before he left he'd handed me a book, and told me he thought I might like it. I thanked him and quickly forgot about it. Now, there it was staring back at me. I opened the old bookcase and picked up the book. It was *Evidence That Demands a Verdict* by Josh McDowell. My heart started to race as I cracked open the pages and began to read. Question after question was answered and the ones that weren't became a desire to know more. Once again, God answered the honest and desperate prayer of a girl who'd gotten lost but was trying to find her way home.

I understand that this profession may make some of you uncomfortable. That's not my intent. I see my story as one of hope and redemption. God has been patient with me. He let my leash out as far as was necessary, until I learned to stop running *from* and start running *to* the one whose love will never let me go.

I'm still a reluctant churchgoer at times, but I love Jesus and I make no apologies for that. Sometimes our wounds leave a limp, and that's not necessarily a bad thing. It serves to remind us of where we've been. From someone who's lived in darkness and now knows the light,

I can honestly join all who've gone before me that have said, "Amazing grace, how sweet the sound, that saved a wretch like me. I once was lost, but now I'm found. Was blind, but now I see!"

I tried briefly after having Becky to pursue a solo career, but at that time my association with Waylon had become a liability in L.A. The bridges he hadn't burned were at the least severely scorched, so, instead of my association with the whole Outlaw phenomenon being an asset, I faced door after door being slammed in my face.

Over the next several years, we would not only welcome one beautiful, healthy daughter, but two more: Emily and Joanna brought the grand total of little miracles to three. Our lives were beyond anything I could ever have asked for or imagined. Barny worked hard, allowing me to stay at home to raise our girls. It wasn't easy and, again, not what he originally signed up for, but God faithfully provided for us. In that ten-year period, he recorded over fifty children's albums, garnering the coveted "Grammy" award in 1992.

We never spoke with Waylon or Jessi that entire time, and never told our children about the people we used to work for or what we had been a part of musically. They were too young to grasp all that anyway. We gave them the best life we could and even though it didn't come without a price, every moment was worth it.

By the end of 1991, Barny was working for a Christian record company producing children's albums and found himself once more in Nashville on a business trip. He was at the airport and had some time to kill when he decided to get in touch with Richie. They had a great conversation, and toward the end, Richie urged him to give Waylon a call. Said he had changed a lot and would love to hear from him. So Barny dialed the number and waited to see if Maureen would pick up. She didn't...but Waylon did.

I guess it was quite a reunion there on the phone. Waylon was so happy to hear from Barny. When he asked him what he was up to, Barny told him he was producing children's albums and happened to be in town. Waylon asked him to come by, but Barny told him he was at the airport waiting for his plane.

Waylon said the timing of the phone call couldn't have been better because he was there by himself with Shooter, working on a concept for a children's album. Jessi had recently done one, and now he had an idea. He was wondering if could he talk to Barny about it sometime.

That phone call broke through a barrier that had been constructed to never be breeched, but it's amazing what happens when God allows healing to take place. The two of them set up a time to talk, and then Barny boarded the plane and flew home.

I suppose somewhere in the back of my mind, I expected him to have a story or two about meeting up with the guys in the band. But I never imagined he would come home and tell me he had talked to Waylon, and that they were kicking around the idea of working together on an album.

I asked a million questions and then asked them all over again. Seems that Barny and I weren't the only ones who had made life-changing choices. For the past ten years, while we were building our life in L.A., Waylon had gone cold turkey and kicked his cocaine habit. The love he had for Jessi and Shooter proved to be stronger than his destructive affair with drugs. Once he was able to think clearly, he went on to receive his GED and often spoke on campuses across the country, encouraging students to stay in school and get an education. He also wrote some of his best songs, partnered up with Willie, Johnny, and Kris as "The Highwaymen," acted in movies, did guest spots on Sesame Street, and entered into a world of genuine sobriety.

He was a man who had survived more than most, and when given the opportunity and strength to change, he took it, mending bridges and making peace with the people who were willing to take the extended olive branch. This new embrace of health enabled him to accomplish an endless (and at times anonymous) list of philanthropic endeavors. He was actually more consistently productive after drugs than he ever was when he was on them. Life, when lived honestly and simply, holds more beauty than any vice could ever promise you, even in the short term.

Over the next few days Waylon and Barny had a few more good conversations, and then Waylon said that he and Jessi would love to see us again and meet our three little girls. They were going to be in town soon, playing the Universal Amphitheatre with the Highwaymen, and wondered if we'd like to come out? Barny said he'd make it happen, and the plans were put into place.

It had been ten years, and I was more than a little nervous as we walked down the hall of the Beverly Wilshire and knocked on the door of their hotel room. Since it was a school night, we decided to only bring Becky with us. As soon as Jessi opened the door and saw the three of us standing there, she flashed that smile. Instantly, all the distance and years melted away. We were back with our friends.

She looked beautiful, of course, and Waylon looked better than I had ever seen him. His eyes were clear, and his sense of humor was not only intact but sharper and funnier than I remembered. We literally picked up where we left off, minus all the crap. It was like coming home. Waylon told us that over that ten-year period, any time they were even close to Southern California, he would scan the audience to see if we were there. That still makes my throat feel tight.

The night couldn't have gone better. They treated Becky like she was a little princess, and Waylon dedicated the song "Amanda" to her during the Highwayman show. She sat by us in the audience, falling in love with her new hero, and I remember marking that moment as the only time I had been at one of Waylon's shows and not been on stage singing with him.

They eventually came back with Shooter, which was so much fun. He was a real whiz at computer games and actually liked what I had prepared for dinner. How 'bout that? Joanna ran around calling Jessi "Grandma", and Emily ran out into the cul-de-sac and in her loudest voice said, "Waylon Jennings is at my house for dinner!" Waylon thought that was pretty funny.

A few months later he was again playing in California, and he surprised them one Sunday morning by showing up at our little church. It was the first time Barny and I had ever seen him in anything but jeans. In the old days, he would wear them for days at a time and then wonder why his skin itched. But here he was, all dressed up and sitting in the back, surrounded by our three little girls. When the pastor asked if there were any visitors, we introduced Waylon to the congregation.

Our daughters thought he hung the moon, but there's no way their young minds could have fully appreciated that very large show of love and affection for them. Waylon was NOT about church, but he put that aside to embrace our family in a way that is difficult to articulate. I will always love him for what he did that day.

The Little "Grammy" That Could

In 1992, Barny was nominated for a Grammy in the Best Album for Children category. We were beyond shocked and totally out of our minds with excitement. This project had been extremely difficult to produce and the record company had not exactly been supportive. Alex McDougall was executive producer, and it was his brainchild. He brought Barny in to make it all happen and the two of them made an amazing team.

To everyone's surprise, Barny and Alex's album, "A Cappella Kids", was in the same category with industry heavyweights Sir John Gielgud, Danny Glover, Dom De Luise, Carol Channing, Gerald McBoing Boing, Jonathan Winters, Taj Mahal and Mark Isham. We asked all of our friends who were part of NARAS to take a listen and then vote their conscience.

Money was scarce, but we scraped together every bit we could and left for New York via Nashville. We thought we might as well make a little vacation out of it. After all, there was no way we were going to win, so we'd do our own brand of celebrating. A dinner at the Sunset Grille in Nashville was planned in our honor by the one and only Tom Bourke.

The whole family showed up, including crew, the Crickets, the Waylors, Waylon and Jessi, everybody's wives, and even a few of their children. Having that time to reconnect with our old friends was pure joy.

As we left that night, each one came up to us and told Barny that he was coming home with the Grammy. I loved them for their support but didn't for a minute really believe that was possible. I did, however, make Barny put together an acceptance speech. That trip was like a fantasy; it couldn't have gone better if I had scripted it myself.

The night before the Grammys, there was a party for all of the nominees at Tavern on the Green. I felt like Cinderella as we walked around with all the beautiful untouchable people. There were lights in the trees and the best food and drinks imaginable. Again, pure magic!

As we dressed for the awards show the following day, I made Barny go over his speech, and we were both laughing because what everyone says in these situations was true: it really *was* an honor just to be nominated. As we sat in our assigned seats at Radio City Music Hall, I couldn't help looking around and realizing that this world I had worked in for so long wasn't as big as I once thought. There we were, rubbing elbows with the stars. My, my, my, makes a soul believe that just about *anything* is possible.

Alex and his wife Linda held their breath, and I held Barny's hand as they read off the nominees in his category, preparing myself for the "oh well" smile. When they said…"and the Grammy goes to…Barny Robertson for Accapella Kids," I hollered like I was at a Waylon concert, and Barny was in shock as I pushed him to his feet. I watched as he and Alex walked on stage to accept the most prestigious acknowledgement the peers in our industry can bestow.

I remember seeing him reach into his pocket and pull out his short acceptance speech. There was no deer in the headlights look this time, and he didn't stutter or stammer once. His speech was flawless, and I could no longer hold back my tears. He had worked so hard and overcome so much opposition, and now he was standing in front of the whole world, giving thanks and credit where credit was due.

I wish I could say that the Contemporary Christian community embraced this miraculous honor, but sadly, it didn't. In fact, it was glaringly ignored. The record company was at odds with the distribution company, and instead of seizing the opportunity, they ended up shelving the album in a warehouse somewhere on the moon.

When the company was asked to put the Grammy award winner stickers on the product to help with the marketing, their response was stupefying. They wouldn't stand in our way if we wanted to contact NARAS, or go to all the little stores and put the stickers on the CDs ourselves, but they would not pay a dime for it.

Oh well, who knows? Maybe someday when space travel is more affordable, Barny and I can take a trip to the moon and bring it back for all you earthlings!

Barny's around-the-clock work on that album produced a timeless vocal masterpiece. There is something so special about listening to those children's beautiful voices singing his brilliant arrangements that moved an industry to honor him with its highest recognition.

Just a note to all of you engineers and producers out there, this was before the convenience of sampling or pitch-shifting had hit the market. He had spent one whole week just recording "oohs."

Our daughter Emily was so excited when she heard that her daddy had been awarded the Grammy that she ran around telling everybody he had won a million dollars! We had to convince a few folks with a sure-fire investment plan that the little gold-plated gramophone didn't come with a check.

Our friends and family celebrated this incredible accomplishment and loved us in a way that no amount of money could ever do. The Grammy now sits on Barny's grand piano and testifies to just how sweet God's good gifts are.

I'd like to thank the Academy...

Sweet Forgiveness

The concept for Waylon's children's album took time to put together, but in the fall of 1992 Barny and I found ourselves once again on a plane for Nashville. I wasn't telling anyone, but I was scheduled for surgery the week of our return. Four ruptured discs in my lower back had me battling a serious case of chronic pain. The thrill of our restored friendship, however, was better than any meds I could have taken, and which I had turned down when my doctor insisted on writing the script. I kept thinking, "Doc, you don't know my history."

Friendship after friendship was renewed on that trip. We stayed with Waylon and Jessi, and Maureen welcomed us with open arms, like we were their favorite, long lost family members. Jigger played bass, good old Sonny Curtis was on guitar, Robby Turner wowed us on the pedal steel, and Jeff Hale played drums. It was one of the coolest reunions ever.

But I have to say the most poignant moment came while we were recording in 1111 Sound, previously known as American Studios. Over the years we had made more memories on that corner of the block than any book could contain, and now here we were, making new ones.

My back was killing me, and the sciatica in my leg was relentless. Everyone was in the control room, listening to a playback, and not wanting to draw attention to myself, I quietly slipped into the small room leading out into the studio. It was kind of like a little kitchen area, with a refrigerator, table, and chairs. I had sat at that very table so many times, waiting to be called up to record my vocals in the wee hours of the morning. Now, a decade later, I still couldn't escape all those pictures floating just above my head, waiting for me to reach up and pull one down.

Waylon interrupted this impromptu reverie as he walked through the room and out into the studio; he was kind of looking back over his shoulder and smiling. I was sitting, staring at the door he had just walked through when it swung back open. He stood there looking at me, and I knew it was another one of those rare, almost holy moments that you don't want to disturb.

After a while he found his words, and his voice had a slight, uncharacteristic quiver to it as he said, "Carter, I need to ask you to forgive me. I put you through a lot back then and gave you a pretty rough time. I've had a lot of years to think about it, and I want you to know that I was sorry from the moment you left. Drugs make a person do things they normally never would. It means everything to have you and Barny back with us again."

Waylon didn't like seeing people cry, but my vision was starting to blur, and I was biting the inside of my lip real hard so I wouldn't give in to that very thing. I stood up and gave him the biggest hug I could, not even feeling the pain in my back. I told him we both had a lot to be forgiven for, and I was glad we were all together again. We smiled, then he went out and recorded "Cowboys, Sisters, Rascals and Dirt" —one of the all time best children's albums—Waylon style!

Life never ceases to surprise me. If you had told me at that moment that within two years Barny and I would move our little family to Franklin, Tennessee and go back out on the road with Waylon and Jessi, I would have insisted that one of us was delusional. Yet in November 1994, that's exactly what we did.

....

A Prayer in the Night

Lord, I'm tired. I know this isn't news to You, because for the past several months those have been the first words out of my heart when I finally get the girls to bed and can just be still.

What do You want from me? I feel like the Apostle Peter sometimes, and You're giving me second and third chances to make up for all the times I denied You. But did I really deny You, or just the crazy culture that surrounds Your name? Oh, I don't know, maybe that's a conversation for another day. Right now I'm so weary from the hits that keep coming into our lives, I can't even sleep.

So...what now? Is it actually possible that You want us to uproot our little family and leave this house we've built, thinking we would watch our children and grandchildren grow up here someday? Surely not. We were born and raised in California. Our parents are here, our sisters and brothers and nieces and nephews, and what about all of our friends? We love this little community, so quiet and wholesome...but there's no work.

I do want to thank You for the great time we had in Nashville last week. Being with Waylon and Jess felt right, and staying with Alex and Linda was sweet. They live in a very cool neighborhood, and if I could take everyone I love that lives here back there, maybe it wouldn't be so bad...

I'm still stunned by the phone calls tonight. We had three projects, Lord, all lined up for the rest of the year, and now all of them have been canceled. What are we going to do? Every company Barny works for has moved to Nashville. How many more garage sales can we have?

Help...please help us, Father. Show us the way. Make it unmistakably clear, like when Mama used to put out a fleece. I'll be honest, because it's pointless to be anything else with You, but...You're going to need to change my heart because I don't want to leave my home. I choose to trust You right now, even though it feels like You're not listening to me.

Forgive me. Please help us...

Can't Argue with an Earthquake

We were all tucked safely and snuggly in our beds on January 17, 1994, when at 4:31 a.m. an unknown fault under the city of Northridge in the San Fernando Valley, about fifteen miles down the road from where our house sat on a hill, ruptured, registering a 6.9 on the Richter Scale. For the longest thirty seconds of our lives, it violently thrust the crust of the earth in an upward motion.

This wasn't the first earthquake we had experienced, and like most Californians we considered ourselves experts at gauging the severity of the shaking. We'd hold onto doorways or railings, saying, "That's around a 4.7 or 5.3." However, none of us had been through a ride like this. Most of the time they felt like a wave, as though the floor were rolling. This one was vertical, slamming furniture up and down. People's handprints were later seen on their bedroom ceilings from being tossed in the air like children on a trampoline.

When the dust finally settled and our little family was safe in the backyard, we watched from our vantage point on the hill as transformers continued to explode down in the valley, followed by flames reaching as high as several-story buildings.

Neighbors checked on neighbors, going house-to-house and making sure no one was hurt. A temporary mini tent-city sprung up in our backyard for friends whose houses were not safe to go back into. They held their children close, riding out the subsequent aftershocks that were on a magnitude of a regular earthquake. None of us wanted to alarm our kids, so we made a game of the rolling motions, all the time keeping a close eye on the walls and lampposts that swayed with each movement.

We were without electricity and telephone service for days, causing fear and anxiety for friends and families all over the country. Even though Nashville was in the middle of a disastrous ice storm, Waylon tried relentlessly to get a call through to us, without success. We didn't own a cell phone back then and relied on the kindness of strangers who were able to get through to our family outside of Southern California and notify them that we had survived. By the time we were able to talk to Waylon, he was chompin' at the bit for us to move our family to Nashville. Ice storms were no fun but neither were earthquakes, especially one this size.

We had to depend on the generosity of the Miller Brewing Company for bottled water. They had gone into emergency mode and turned off the flow of beer and instead filled their beer bottles with good, clean water. Our girls *loved* drinking from those bottles and always wanted to go with me to the park, where I would get in line with the rest of the residents to have volunteers fill our trunks with the amount allotted for each family.

It would take weeks before roads were cleared enough to drive south, and months before the freeways were back up and running. We eventually found out that Diana and her family were safe but had lost their home. It was a catastrophe that California had not seen since the 1906 earthquake in San Francisco. According to news reports, it would hold the distinction of having the strongest ground motions ever instrumentally recorded in a North American urban setting.

Due to the Martin Luther King holiday, casualties remained relatively low, but statistics don't bring much comfort when you're the one planning the memorial service. The natural disaster was big enough, but the economic disaster was the second in a one-two punch. More than 681,000 people would eventually apply for much needed assistance from federal and state governments, and insurance companies would be stretched to the breaking point. And that's where we found ourselves in 1994.

We were fortunate that our house did not have any structural damage, just mostly cosmetic cracks and flooring inside, stucco and concrete damage outside. I stopped asking God to make it clear and began praying that He would help us to sell our place and find another in Tennessee.

Waylon and Jessi extended an invitation to stay with them while we began our search. They were sad for the hard place we were in but were thrilled at the prospect of us moving back. Their generous hospitality was definitely a soft place for our little family to land each night as we wrapped up our day's adventure of finding a new home.

We were looking in the quaint little town of Franklin to see if we could find a house that would take a contingent sale. No one wanted to even consider such a deal when the house waiting to be sold was in the massive earthquake destruction zone. It didn't matter that our house had come through with flying colors; the zip code spelled disaster, and the only people who were going to be buying houses in our area for awhile were other earthquake victims. We had to accept the reality that within thirty-one seconds we'd lost over one hundred thousand dollars in hard-earned, self-employed musician's equity, and that's not counting its inflated California value a month before the quake. That stung!

Finally just choosing to take the proverbial leap of faith, we put some money down on a lot in the same development that our friends Alex and Linda lived in and began the process of building a home clear across the country, even as we worked tirelessly to get our own home ready to sell. We were praying that the best case scenario would happen: a sale in the spring, making it possible to move during the summer and have the girls all settled in for the coming school year. The last thing I wanted was to uproot them once school started.

My prayers are not usually answered as per my script. That fall, after Becky began her 8th grade year at Arroyo Seco Junior High, we received one offer and one offer only on our beautiful home in the hills outside of L.A. We swallowed hard, hoping it would be enough. It's expensive to move not only your family thousands of miles across the country, but your business as well.

The stress level was palpable, and we were about a month away from closing when we realized the math didn't work. We wondered how we would be able to pay for the movers, and the house in Franklin was running a few weeks behind, which meant we were going to need to rent a small apartment until we could take possession. Plus, where would we store our belongings until then?

It's a wonder Barny didn't have a heart attack. On top of everything else, he was finishing up one last project, and the deadline was looming. He would be wrapping the night before the movers were scheduled to arrive. We needed every bit of cash we could scrape together.

The company we were insured with had sent out an adjuster after the big quake, but we had yet to see any check. We had chosen not to wait, but to go ahead and do the repairs on our dime and repay ourselves once the money arrived. However, the insurance companies started to get real tight with these checks and sent out letters telling everyone they would release them incrementally to the contractors and homeowners. This was very bad news for us, and the clock was ticking.

A week and a half out, I woke up determined to find a solution. I had a serious conversation with my "Abba" Father and laid out our situation. Even though I knew He was already fully informed, I reminded Him I was on board now. I'd let the doubts go and was doing everything I could to make this move happen, but as He knew, we had hit a wall and needed His intervention.

I felt good after I said "amen" and picked up the phone to dial the insurance company's 800 number. I must have talked to five or six representatives, who told me there would be no bending of the new rules, and my problem wasn't their problem. Exasperated, I told them that I would just continue to pursue this everyday until they let me talk to the top person, and that's when I met her.

She was cordial and professional, showing sympathy but as immovable as the Rock of Gibraltar. Just as we were getting ready to hang up for the last time, out of a "what have I got to lose" moment, I asked her what her first name was. She hesitated a moment, then told me. I asked her if she had a family and children. She said yes and then was quiet. I told her the names of my children and their ages. I strongly suspect she knew where this was headed. Then I told her I needed to talk to her…woman to woman. Thankfully, she stayed on the line. I said, using her first name, "My family needs our money and we need it now." Her end of the line was quiet for about ten seconds and then I heard the words that paid our way to Nashville: "Mrs. Robertson, your check will go out this afternoon. You should have it in a couple of days. Good luck to you and your family." I thanked her, hung up the phone and danced like Sister Alvin at a revival meeting. Thank you, Jesus!

Waylon and Jessi insisted our family stay with them until our house was ready, and for the girls it was like living in Wonderland. Their every whim was catered to, which was definitely *not* how they were raised. They ate it up. Even after the house was finished, Waylon tried to convince us to let the girls stay with them, offering to drive them back and forth to school everyday while we put the house in order. That would be about a forty-mile round trip, twice a day.

Their offer was sweet, but there's something about the adventure of moving into a new place that kids love, at least ours did, and we needed each other more than ever to process our new home thousands of miles away from family and friends.

A couple of weeks later we found ourselves sitting in Waylon and Jessi's living room preparing to enjoy one of Maureen's sumptuous Thanksgiving feasts. The girls were dressed in their finest and Waylon was allowing himself to be totally charmed.

As we stood up to walk into the dining room, he stopped us and asked if our family knew a song of thanksgiving. Without hesitation the girls started singing a song they had learned at church. Their voices, complete with harmonies, were sweet and pure, evoking an emotional response by the adults in the room. I couldn't help but acknowledge the contrast of a long ago Thanksgiving in Hollywood, when I had given in and given up. In that moment of clarity, the realization of all I had to be thankful for was almost overwhelming. Nothing, and I mean *nothing* is impossible with God.

One funny note: when filling out the emergency contact information for school, Waylon insisted we put him down as first call. You can imagine the bustle *that* caused when the secretary realized it was *the* Waylon Jennings.

The Real, Real World

For those of you who think musicians who have had a modicum of success continue to rake in the bucks, you may find this enlightening. We had several gold and platinum albums in the studio at our house. Barny's Grammy sat on the grand piano, and our résumé at times read like a who's who in the industry. But if you were someone who had worked a steady job with a moderate salary, you were light years ahead of us financially. The life of a professional musician is definitely a journey of faith. Most of the time we live month-to-month, which is pretty crazy when you are providing for a family.

Barny and I had made a tough choice to gamble on a future in Tennessee. The decision was based on as much data as we could gather, and then we just had to step out and do it. We had seasons of just enough, some of a little extra, and then some with next to nothing at all.

By now I was doing some vocal contracting and conducting for the children's projects Barny was producing for several different publishing companies. This was challenging, to say the least. Barny is an educated and trained musician, while everything I've learned has been from simply doing it. I have a good ear, but I don't read music. Some of the kids who were singing on the projects had more of a formal musical education than I did. I had no choice but to force myself to get better at it.

During one of our next-to-nothing income seasons, and for the first time in my adult life, I had to find a straight gig to help supplement our income. Starting to work in the real world was incredibly foreign to me. Here I had all these great music creds, but I had never filled out a simple job application before. It was more than just a little intimidating. Much to my surprise I landed a retail job my first time out and ended up staying there for about a year and a half.

It was during this time in the late 1990's that Waylon's health began failing, and he started giving up. He wasn't touring anymore and nothing seemed to be able to light that old fire buried inside of him. He enjoyed his family and all of his friends, but there was a weariness that seemed to cover him like a shroud. This broke all of our hearts, and it seemed that there was nothing to be done.

One day we all received a phone call from Linda Albright, Richie's wife. She told us that Waylon had been chosen to receive the "Chetty Award" from Chet Atkins, and the event would be held at the Ryman Auditorium. She had spoken with the powers that be and set it up for Waylon's old band to surprise him by backing up Mark Collie, who would be singing some of his songs.

We agreed to hide backstage until it was time for Waylon's award to be presented to him. I remember all of us walking out together and seeing him sitting off to the side, next to his old friend Johnny Cash. He was kind of leaning on his cane, but as soon as he saw us he started to smile and sit up a little straighter. We played from our hearts that night, and by the time we were done Waylon was on his feet. That old fire had been re-lit.

After the show, we grabbed our daughters and started to head over to the party in Waylon's honor. As we stepped into the alley behind the Ryman, we were met with a bunch of fans asking for our autograph and pictures. The girls were shocked by what they were witnessing and began to wonder who in the world their parents really were.

Now, the Grateful Dead, who we had done concerts with many years previous, have fans called "Dead Heads." Outlaw fans are known as "Hoss Heads," and they were out in force that night, asking us questions about how we were and naming our children. To some musicians this may seem a bit intrusive, but these folks had followed us for years and were continuing to cheer us on.

The next morning, after signing as many autographs as I could the night before, I found myself at the big home improvement store where I was employed. No spotlight, no applause, no Hoss Heads, just another hardworking employee, greeting the customers and handing them a cart as they came through the doors. I had to laugh!

Waylon called me a couple of days later to see if I would come over the next morning and watch the sunrise with him and Jessi. I had never told either of them that I was working for grocery money and to pay for the girl's piano lessons. They thought I had taken the job because I was bored and needed some outside interest. That's the difference between artist and sideman.

I had to be at work by 9 a.m., so I fixed the girl's lunches the night before and had Barny make sure they got off to school on time. By 5:15 a.m., I was dressed for work and on my way to their house. It was a beautiful morning, and we sat and talked quietly about life and family. Waylon loved hummingbirds and had a few feeders placed around his patio. They were kind of independent and didn't always show up to get their fix of sugar water. But that morning they did, and we admired their beauty as we watched the sun come up on a new day.

I'm so glad I didn't hesitate to take him up on his invitation that morning, because it's one of my favorite memories. We started reminiscing about the old days, and I told them I hoped I got another chance to do the kind of music that makes my heart beat. I wanted to show my girls that art has nothing to do with age, gender or socio-economic status, but rather everything to do with our God-given DNA.

Shortly after that morning, Waylon called all the band members. He said if we had the chance to go out and do this thing one more time, if we could get paid a fair wage and do it on our terms so it would just be fun, would we be interested in playing together again? Guess I wasn't the only one wanting to do some music. There were plenty of voices with the same opinion, and it was just the push Waylon needed. There was no hiccup, no pause, no, "let me think about it." Simply, "Yes!" And that's exactly what we did. The family was back together.

On the Road Again?

The last few years we all toured together was a whole new ballgame. Drugs no longer played a part in our decisions. We'd all been there and done that and then moved on, encouraging the next generation to learn from our mistakes.

The first trip back out after joining up as the "Waymore Blues Band" took us to a casino in Mississippi, where we were breaking in the new act. On the way there one of Waylon and Jessi's friends,—we call her "Miss Elsie"—came along for the ride. Miss Elsie is one of the most beautiful, genteel southern women I have ever met. Carl Smith, country music icon and one of Waylon's heroes, and the rest of the band, were at the front of the bus, while Goldie Smith, Jessi, Miss Elsie, Nikki Mitchell and I were in the backroom, laughing and carrying on.

Jessi suggested we play some cards to help pass the time, and we all thought that was a fine idea. Miss Elsie said she had never played cards before, but it sounded fun to her as well. We played a hand, and I think Jessi or Goldie won. But then Miss Elsie spoke up, saying it might be more fun, since we were on our way to a casino, to play for money.

As I write this it seems obvious what was about to take place, but trust me, her engaging drawl made you forget everything you thought you knew and you anteed up. Of course, that was the last any of us saw of our money in that back room. Miss Elsie just kept saying how surprised she was and that it must have been beginner's luck.

She speaks with that captivating and hypnotic Georgia accent that immediately puts you at ease, and if you are doing business with her, at a distinct disadvantage. A person would never presume that she is one of the most successful businesswomen around. She can smile while taking all your money and you'll thank her as you're walking out the door. She's a good woman to have on your side.

It was just pure, unadulterated fun to be back with everyone again. Not only had Waylon put the old band together, Richie: drums, Jigger: bass, Rance: rhythm guitar, Barny: keys and me: vocals, but he had recruited a few of our good friends to join us as well. The one and only Reggie Young wowed us on guitar every night with his melodic genius. Robby Turner played steel in a way that made Mooney proud. Jenny Lynn joined us on fiddle and cello and became one of my dear friends. Jim Horn put together a rockin' horn section with himself, Steve Herrman and Charles Rose. Our old friend Greg Kane mixed monitors for us, and the amazing Wes Delk worked his magic mixing the house.

Many of the folks who came out to see us those last three years were old fans that had been part of the "Outlaw" phenomenon. They had their own stories to tell, and now it was as though they knew this might be the last time they got to see and hear their hero sing. City after city, town after town, I'd see from the stage the faces I had seen so many years ago. They knew how hard Waylon was fighting to keep going, living out his passion for the music that was more alive than ever.

Those last few years of touring, he had to sit during his show on stage. He'd joke with the audience, putting them at ease by saying, "Don't let this chair thing fool ya. I can still kick ass. You just gotta come up here for me to do it!"

I remember walking off the stage after our show that first night. I was surprised to see a long line of fans over by the dressing rooms, waiting to get an autograph and have their picture taken with Waylon. Looking at Tom Bourke, who had signed on for the latest adventure, I asked what all of this was about. He smiled and said, "Times have changed. Waylon enjoys taking time with people now."

I was struck by how different everything was. We were laughing, enjoying ourselves to the fullest. But unlike the "Outlaw" years, there was nothing reckless about it. We had not always been awake to the fragility and temporal reality of life. When we were younger, we consumed our opportunities like cheap candy bars, always thinking we could buy another one. Now we had lived long enough and through enough to know better. We treasured each minute of being together, knowing there was an expiration date on the moment, but not the memory.

Waylon and Waymore Blues Band at the Ryman Auditorium, Nashville, TN 2000

When You Mess Up, Fess Up

f I had a dollar for every story somebody has told me about his or her wild night of drinking with Waylon, I'd have my retirement sown up. In my humble opinion, there's been some misrepresentation surrounding this very issue that has become more folklore than fact.

All the years I worked with Waylon, I only saw him drink a couple of times, and then it was one or two at the most. It's well documented that his vice was of a speedier variety. He had a very low tolerance for sloppy drunks, and I was around him a lot.

When we all reunited those last few years, we chose to enjoy ourselves within reason. As I said before, drugs were not a part of our lives by then, and hadn't been since the old days, but we had no problem indulging in a little good-natured drinking every once in a while.

We made quite a few memories touring together those last three years. A few times a month, we'd meet at the airport in Nashville, usually leaving on a Thursday and returning on Sunday. Waylon would be sitting quietly with Jessi, waiting for us all at the gate. It was obvious that the time in between tours was rough on both of them and was taking a toll. But with the arrival of each one of us, his energy would return, and it wasn't long before we had taken over a whole section of seats, laughing and joking.

If you were on any of our flights during that time, I apologize. It got a little loud and a wee bit tipsy for a few of the boys in the band. We almost always flew into the city the night before the gig so we could have dinner together. Now, we didn't head to Cracker Barrel, although we love Cracker Barrel. We always went to the nicest restaurant in town, and it was all compliments of Waylon.

There was one particular restaurant we went to where things turned a bit rowdy. I'm not pointing any fingers, but the over-serving of drinks on the plane didn't stop when we sat down for dinner. Our servers were patient and the food was amazing, but the language and behavior, well let's just say, it wasn't up to our new grown-up standards. Waylon never said a word, just paid the bill and tipped big.

Jim Horn was not happy with the evening, and after making sure some of the culprits were safely locked in their rooms, went to Waylon and apologized for how it had gone down. Waylon was incredibly gracious and generous in his response. These boys were just letting off steam. They hadn't done anything that the rest of us hadn't done more times than we could remember, literally! He was proud they were in his band, and now he had something to give them a hard time about.

That would have been cool enough, but the next night he took us all back to the same restaurant, asked for the same servers, and we were the classiest table in the place. The manager could hardly believe it was the same rowdy party of fifteen that had been there the night before. They loved us and all came out to have a great time at the show, compliments of Waylon, and THAT boys and girls is how it's done!

Waylon and the Girls

I used to enjoy watching Waylon interact with kids. I've seen grown men nearly faint when they met him, but the children by their sides were totally at ease. My daughters were no exception. From the moment we told him we were leaving California and moving to Nashville, he and Jessi made it their mission to make the transition as smooth as possible for our little family.

During the summer we sometimes brought them out on the road with us. Waylon would take them on impromptu adventures on his bus to fun places he had scouted out. He'd have flowers waiting for them when they joined us for dinner and made sure they were watched after when we were all on stage. They had a blast, and even though his strength wasn't what it used to be, he dug deep and found the energy to make a memory they carry with them to this day.

He didn't like the fact that they were growing up and becoming teenagers, and when they started dating he relished the opportunity to give them a hard time. One evening while Becky was getting ready to go out, and Waylon was at the house, her date showed up only to have Waylon Jennings be the one who opened the door for him. The look on that kid's face was priceless. He was trying not to react, but we could tell he was visibly shaken. He came into the house and was officially introduced as he waited for Becky. When they were getting ready to leave he casually put his arm around her. Waylon, in a booming voice said, "Get your hands off of her!" The poor guy nearly fainted. Waylon laughed that laugh that said, "I'm just kidding...not really, watch yourself." I have to say, Barny and I thoroughly enjoyed this. Hey, who needs a shotgun when you've got Ol' Waylon around?

He used to tell me that our middle daughter, Emily, thought she was invisible. He called her "angel eyes" and at times it seemed he could see right through to her soul. She was a free spirit and at times liked to push the envelope. When she started to date, I decided to try a bit of that Waylon intimidation myself.

As she was getting ready to leave the house, I gave her date a thorough grilling: "How old are you? What kind of car do you drive? Have you ever had a ticket? What's your cell phone number?" You know the drill. Anyway, I told her I just wanted to give her a heads up. Waylon heard she was going bowling and I didn't want her to worry if she saw a car following them. It was all cool. Waylon just had some friends who were going to look out for her tonight. She was like, "Mom, you're so kidding, right?"

I answered by telling her of course I was, but it wouldn't matter if I wasn't because he said they would stay out of sight. It was kind of fun messin' with her. When she got home, early by the way, she said she was nervous and kept looking in the rearview mirror the entire time. Mission accomplished!

I smile every time I remember Waylon and Jessi, along with Carl and Goldie Smith, showing up for one of Joanna's birthday parties at the above-mentioned bowling alley. She had no clue that the people she considered family and who had signed her bowling pin were some of the greatest legends of Country music. Joanna has such a brilliantly twisted sense of humor and could make Waylon and Jessi laugh with total abandon.

There were Christmases when Waylon would come over in his pajamas and cowboy boots with a Santa bag slung over his shoulder filled with presents for them. I still laugh when I think of the time Becky had the lead in "Little Shop of Horrors" for Centennial High School. He came in through the side door and sat in the front row with some of the extended family taking up the rows behind him. A few still have not mastered the ability to whisper, so at times the whole audience could hear people saying that Becky was the best and all these other kids needed to go home. I was more than a little uneasy, thinking of ways to smooth it over with their parents. In one of the scenes, Becky's character was getting ready to be kissed and just as the guy was leaning in Waylon said, "Uh-uh-uh, hold it, Hoss!" It was hysterical.

He doted on them and listened to their every word. When the girls messed up and I grounded them, he'd argue with me the entire time we were out, trying to convince me to let up a little. He had insight into each daughter's personality and would call and talk to them about what was going on in their lives. If we weren't home, he'd leave really long and funny messages on our old answering machine about making a legend wait for them. We have a pretty valuable "best of" tape with some of those cherished calls.

At the end of one of our short tours, he planned a special dinner for the girls at a nice restaurant in town. By now Becky was in college, and Joanna and Emily were attending high school. He arrived in his suit and brought each girl a gag gift. Barny and I knew he was fading and had watched his decline over the past couple of years. But that night he dug deep and found a strength that charmed all of us.

He may have missed out on the first few years of their lives, but he was making up for lost time. Our whole family loved him and Jessi with a depth that makes the words on this page look too small. This history helps explain what happened next...

Part Five

The Goodbye

Choices

Do you ever feel like you have Post Traumatic Stress Syndrome when it comes to telephone calls? I do. Now, most of the time when the phone rings, it's good; you know, routine stuff, but then there are the other calls. Raising three daughters, no matter how delightful they may be, is not a job for sissies or the faint of heart, and it was definitely more than I bargained for. Note to young parents: just because you go by the book and do "ABC" doesn't mean that the rest of the alphabet will follow suit. Just don't lose your sense of humor.

There are the teenage car accidents, flat tires, locked keys in the car, running out of gas and stranded at two in the morning. They're not *all* that benign, but when it comes to my family, I think I'll just keep the more difficult ones between us. The thing I hate the most is the interruption of *normal*. Life happens at some of the most inconvenient times.

March 22, 2001 was a day at the beach, a *beautiful* day at the beach, actually. It was Friday, the last day of our Spring Break vacation, and the plan was to leave bright and early the next morning to head back home. We'd had a blast and were all kissed by the sun, wishing we could live there year round.

It had become a tradition to have dinner at one of our favorite restaurants that was within walking distance from the condo. The food was excellent, and the good company of friends put us all in a place of sweet relaxation. We felt renewed.

Barny and I were looking forward to the week ahead. The following Monday, Waylon and the "Waymore Blues Band" were going into S.I.R. to get ready for our upcoming shows. We'd been off for a while because Waylon had suffered a slight stroke and needed some time to recuperate. Everybody was wondering how wise it was for him to keep going, but it was obvious there was no stopping him. Truth was, all of us being together, doing the music we loved with the people we loved, contributed heavily to keeping his illness at bay, at least for our short weekend jaunts. Going in that week wouldn't be without its special set of challenges, but we were ready.

Barny and I, along with our youngest daughter, Joanna and a couple of her friends, arrived back at the condo from dinner and were beginning the long process of packing everything up when the phone rang. It felt a little odd, because we'd shared that number with only a select few, but there were other families there with us, and I thought most likely it was one of them.

As I heard the voice on the other end I knew *"normal"* was just about to be re-defined. It was Diana. Daddy had suffered a massive heart attack and was in intensive care in Visalia. She was in route from L.A. and would get back to me as soon as she had more details, but suggested I look into finding a flight out of Pensacola, at least to see what was available. I couldn't help but think of all we had shared over our lifetime bringing us closer than most sisters, but at the same time I remember hanging up and feeling oddly disconnected.

After letting Barny know what was going on, we started checking into flights. If Daddy was okay maybe I could go out for a quick trip and be back on Tuesday, only missing one day of rehearsal. Our friends prayed with us, and then we waited. Once my sisters arrived in our hometown to assess the situation, they called with an update. Daddy was resting comfortably, and there was nothing more to report that night. They encouraged me to get some sleep, and they would call if there were any change. Sleep? I don't think so. I spent the rest of the night finishing the packing and then finally laid down, watching the phone.

Saturday dawned and there was still no word. I decided to check in, even though it was two hours earlier on the West Coast, knowing that once we got on the road, it would be difficult to reach us. I also needed to know if Barny would be taking me to the airport or if I would be making the drive back to Nashville and flying out from there.

The news was good; in fact, it couldn't have been better. Daddy was awake and alert, teasing the nurses and raising his own kind of good-natured hell. He was quickly becoming the favorite patient on the floor. My brother and his family had driven in, and they were all there, laughing, reminiscing, and generally enjoying the deep breath they were all being given after the scare. My sisters told me there was no need to fly out. It looked like he was going to be around for who knew how long. Probably would outlive us all! There was so much going on in his room that I wasn't able to talk to him right then, but I sent my love via my sisters.

When I hung up the phone, I felt divided. On the one hand I couldn't have been happier that Daddy was going to be okay, but on the other hand I felt left out. I missed my family and wished I could be there with them.

We arrived home later that night, and on Sunday afternoon I was finally able to get a call through. Again, the family was there and Mama answered the phone. Her voice sounded excited, kind of like it did when we came home for the holidays. She asked me if I wanted to talk to my dad, and I was thrilled. I could hear him in the background asking, "Who's that?"

She told him it was Carter and then handed him the phone. I could tell he was distracted and didn't really want to take the call. My dad HATED talking on the telephone, but he was making an exception because I was out in Tennessee and not there with the rest of the clan.

I asked him how he was feeling, but his answers were short, like he couldn't wait to hang up or pass me off to someone else. I tried so hard to engage him, but the laughter in the background was a greater pull than the daughter on the phone.

I remember having to talk loud like you do when you're at a party with a lot of noisy people. I told him I loved him and missed him. Then I added for some reason, "You know Daddy, that Jesus loves you too, right?" His reply was quick and simple, "Yea, yea, yea, here's your mom," and then he handed her the phone.

Now, I didn't want to overreact or be a sap so I let it go. He was going to be fine and we would both live for another day when we could have a real conversation.

Monday morning I sent the girls off to school and Barny and I headed into town to have some fun with our *other* family. The time we all spent together that day couldn't have been sweeter. We laughed, played music and hung on Waylon's every story. He was back! We were back! He'd get tired a little more quickly but we took our time, knowing that after being together all these years we could fill in any blanks that needed filling. I had gone from the timid background singer to his friend that shared his stage, up front and right next to him.

It became apparent that this last stroke had been a thief, and had robbed him of some of his ability to remember lyrics. I stayed close by, ready with the next word to feed him. We had this great natural stage banter that went back and forth.

What the audience saw was two old friends having a blast, and that was true. What they didn't see or hear was me singing the next line in his ear, checking on him to make sure he was feeling okay, and if he wasn't, letting Jessi and the offstage people know. It had worked before and it was going to work again. When we left that night the whole band was riding high.

As soon as I got home, I called to see how Daddy was doing. Mama said my sisters and brother had left because there was no reason for them to stay. He would probably be in the hospital for another few days but would most likely be going to Westgate Gardens Convalescent Center by the end of the week, more good news.

I hung up the phone and prepared for the next day's rehearsal. We were scheduled to fly to Austin on Friday for a concert with Willie and all of our friends Saturday night. Even though it was March, the cumulative excitement made it feel more like the kick off for a summer tour. I was tired but relieved at the same time, and as I laid my head down on the pillow all the previous days' stresses and events melted away, and I fell into a deep sleep.

Tuesday morning in the wee hours, I woke up with a start. My heart was pounding, and I knew something was wrong. I went upstairs to my office and sat still breathing in and breathing out. That's when the phone rang. It was Mama. Daddy had suffered another heart attack in the middle of the night, and the hospital had called, telling her she needed to come in right away.

When the elevator door opened on the intensive care floor, Joanie, the daughter of Frances who had been tragically killed so many years before and who was now the charge nurse for the whole hospital, was there waiting to give her the latest medical update on my dad. It wasn't good. He wasn't going to make it this time.

Joanie encouraged my mother to go sit with him, help him to make the journey over. She did. She held his hand and prayed for him. She told him she loved him and always had, no matter what they'd been through all those years. She told him it was okay for him to go. Jesus was there with his friends and family waiting for him on the other side. Then she did something that chokes me up every time I think about it. She sang to him. He used to love to hear her sing, but over the years she had lost her voice. That night and in that moment, love won and Mama sang Daddy into the arms of Jesus.

The early call had awakened Barny, and he was now in my office waiting to hold me as soon as I hung up. There were plans to make, flights to figure out, funeral arrangements for my sisters to schedule so everyone could get there. My mind was buzzing when all of a sudden I remembered the rehearsal and the Austin gig. Well, death is not something we have control over. They were just going to have to do this one without me.

All the years I had worked for Waylon and Jessi I only missed two shows. One was early on in Minneapolis, when I had a raging fever and had to be forced to stay in my room, and the other was when Barny had his emergency appendectomy in Nashville a couple of hours before the bus was supposed to leave. This was going to make it three, but there was nothing I could do about it.

The phones started ringing as soon as the word got out. I believe Rance called me first. He'd always liked my dad and especially appreciated the fact that he was from Oklahoma. He and Gordon used to tease me all the time about being the "Direct Descendant" of an Okie.

A year before we had all flown into Sacramento, California after being delayed in Dallas for a day, thanks to American Airlines. We had to make a mad dash, dodging every car and truck on the old Highway 99 to make a concert in Stockton on time. By then Daddy was a full time resident of Westgate because his medical needs were too much for my mother to handle on her own. Diana and Sharon had checked him out for a couple of days so he could come see us play with Waylon again.

The morning after the concert, my sisters and I were all sitting out on the motel patio drinking coffee before the van left to take us back to the airport. Barny's family lived in Sacramento, and he was going to stay a couple of days and do a little visiting with them and had left the night before. It was a genuinely sweet morning, one I will always treasure.

When it was time to take off, I hugged my sisters and then went to my dad. He held my hand and hugged me longer than usual, then told me goodbye, more like, "See ya later alligator," and gave me a kiss. Even then, my heart was so starved for my dad's approval and love that when I sat down in the van and waved goodbye, a floodgate opened that I couldn't shut. My tears wouldn't stop, and the harder I tried to swallow the emotions, the more intense it became.

The guys in the band had never seen me cry, not once in all those years, and now I couldn't stop. Every once in a while I'd feel a pat on my back, but the only sound was the short breaths my body forced me to take in between the tears. After a few minutes, Rance, who was sitting behind me, became my surrogate big brother and reached forward putting his arms around me. He said in that great deep one-of-a-kind voice of his, "You miss your daddy, dontcha baby." I shook my head, staring straight ahead swallowing the memories and dreams of the little girl I used to be, and thinking I miss the one I never got to know.

Now I was hearing Rance's voice again, only this time through the telephone receiver. His words were kind and brought a gentle comfort. We'd all known each other for so long and loved each other's families. When one of us hurt, we all hurt.

Waylon and Jessi were so sweet, telling me they loved me and to take all the time I needed. Jim Horn, who was eloquent and kind, along with a few of the other band and crew members, called to express their condolences and telling me to hang in there. Their love and support was undeniable, but I couldn't shake or dismiss the question that remained unspoken, "What was going to happen this weekend?"

The phone rang again, and this time it was Richie calling. From the very beginning he held a special place in both Barny's and my hearts. In the old days he was the bandleader and Waylon's undisputed right-hand man. The buck stopped with him. He was old school when it came to comforting someone, a man of few words whose presence said all that needed to be said. This was an extremely difficult call for him to make, and from the moment he spoke, I knew what was coming and that I had a choice to make.

He told me how sad he was for me and how much he and all the boys loved me. Then he got quiet and finally said, "You know he won't do it without you. We talked this morning and he's canceling the rehearsal. He's leaning on you a lot for these shows. I hate to ask this and I hope you'll forgive me, but...is there any way your family can schedule the funeral so you can fly into Austin for the Saturday concert?"

For the next few seconds, which must have seemed an eternity for Richie, I thought of all the events of the last few years, all of us reconnecting, the incredible restoration and redemption of relationships, Waylon working so hard to be healthy enough to be with his friends and do music again. Life never promised to be convenient, and if I were going to choose to be honest with myself in that moment, Daddy would've told me to do the "dadgum" show!

"It's all right," I said, "Tell Waylon I'll be there."

There are some things about God's timing and sovereignty that I completely don't get, and that week is one of them. I had just started to feel better from the aftereffects of an upper respiratory infection I'd been fighting for a couple of weeks, and now the day I was flying home to join my family and begin the process of saying goodbye to my dad, it showed up with a vengeance.

I ran to the doctor and got some medication for the cough and all the other yucky stuff that is associated with that and headed to Visalia, California. No major airlines fly into Visalia, so I had to go via the Fresno airport, which is about forty-five miles away from my childhood home.

As often happens with family deaths, it became a reunion of sorts. Cousins reconnected, siblings sat around and remembered when, and old friends dropped by to catch up. My sisters and brother had been given the opportunity to say their goodbyes and were much further along in the processing part than I was. My short day and a half there was filled with helping make decisions about the memorial service.

I wanted so badly to be able to sit in that living room that contained so much of my own history and come to terms with the things I hadn't allowed myself to think about for years. I wanted to hear the laughter that used to bounce off of the walls as the four of us, as children and teenagers, would sneak into the living room late at night once we thought Daddy had gone to bed so we could watch the Johnny Carson Show. Maybe if I was real still, I could hear Daddy reading the Christmas story and laughing when he came to the word *espoused*. "Espoused," he'd say. "What the heck does *es-poused* mean?"

Yes, those walls had heard and seen a darker side as well, but for me in that moment what I longed to hear more than anything was the laughter. The Walkers knew how to have a good time.

However, the tyranny of my schedule wasn't allowing for reflection. On Saturday Barny and I drove back to the airport, boarded a flight for Texas, played the show in Austin, (which went great, by the way, Waylon rocked!) and then got up before the sun the next morning and flew back to Fresno. We drove to meet up with family in Visalia, then on to Dinuba, where the funeral parlor was and the viewing was taking place. Whew! You tired yet? I am. Oh and by now I was sicker than ever. It was Sunday, April 1st, April Fool's Day, and I was wishing it *was* some kind of crazy, elaborate cosmic prank.

That night as I lay in the bed at the motel, I remember thinking of my dad's last words to me, "Yea, yea, yea, here's your mom," knowing in my mind that he didn't mean it to hurt me, even though it did. I wanted a daddy in that moment so badly, I *needed* a daddy so badly, and yet there wasn't one. I felt abandoned.

I was too tired and sick to fight or process what any of it meant. It was like I was this tree whose roots went down deep but now half of the root system had been yanked out of the ground and life was crooked and unbalanced. I think that whole weekend I only got a few hours of sleep.

The graveside service on Monday was beautiful. Family and a few select friends were invited to share their stories of remembrance with us all as we sat on our folding chairs looking at the flag-draped coffin. We laughed at some and cried through others, none of us really wanting to say goodbye to the man who had been such a huge part of our lives.

Even though he was struggling through his own dire health issues, Daddy's kid brother, "Uncle Marlin" showed up, along with his daughter Leisha, who's like another sister. He had always been our favorite. He was so funny and distinguished all at the same time. The Walker men had a way of charming the staunchest critic. Listening to him speak in that one-of-a-kind Oklahoma/Central California accent gave me a momentary connection to my dad, and I was grateful.

The memorial at the church was filled with people from the different stores he'd worked at and church folks who pretended to know the stories behind the story. Our beloved Pastor Kumpe spoke and brought a comfort that only years of being in our lives could bring. All of the grandchildren sang and then choked their way through their individual tributes to the man they knew as "Grandpa Walker." There were moments in their remembrances that made me wish I knew him like they knew him…

Early the following morning, Barny and I and our three girls left to fly back to Nashville. Life isn't often generous in these situations, allowing those who are grieving the luxury of time off. According to my dear friend Tess's husband Dean, most of the time you just have to "Suck Up and Rock On."

As I lay my head down on my pillow that night, I asked God to help me with this new tilted part of life. I knew I didn't need to figure it all out right then or that I may never figure it out, but at least I was finally able to sleep.

Choices…

Daddy and Waylon, two of my favorite outlaws

Live ? Tonight
"The Sisters"
Dance Concert ?!
We Got It ?

Carter's Chord

never imagined when I left all those many years before, confident the Waylon part of my life was over, that my three little miracles would choose to follow in their parents' staggering footsteps. I had been determined that my daughters would never be exposed to the temptingly seductive world of pimping out your art to pay the light bill. I foolishly believed I was stronger than their DNA and could protect them from the hits this business inflicts on the best of talents. I was wrong.

I remember the three of them coming to Barny and me and telling us they wanted to explore the possibility of forming a group. They had been writing and singing separately, and now they wanted to pool their talent and see where it might take them.

I have to be honest, at first I felt almost like I'd been socked in the gut. I know that's dramatic, but it's difficult to explain just how protective a mother I was back then. I tried not to react on the outside, and Barny started asking them questions. The number one question was, "Are you crazy? Haven't you seen what your mom and I have gone through?" They laughed and said, "Exactly! That's why we want to do it." Evidently they appreciated the challenges we had lived through but believed the blessings far outweighed any of the hardships. Barny and I raised them to be independent, critical thinkers. What did we expect? The reality was that no matter what profession they chose, they were going to experience struggle. Every job has its own set of frustrations and challenging relationships.

One thing my girls knew was that I wasn't interested in being a "Stage Mom." This was going to have to be one hundred percent their journey. But they also understood that no matter what path they chose, they had my complete support.

Waylon was very proud and protective of them as well. So much so that when writing his 1996 biography, he told Barny and me he was leaving some stuff about us out of the book. He said he inserted a line saying we weren't into the drugs and tolerated the rest of them. He didn't want the girls to get the wrong idea about their parents and made us promise we wouldn't let them read his book until they were older.

He loved their harmonies and had them record one of his last songs with him. It was a tribute song he had written for Mohammed Ali, who was a dear friend of his. In the late 70's we had all been a part of the great fighter's retirement show at the Forum in L.A., with Richard Pryor going on before us and Billy Crystal closing the night, bringing the house down with one of his famous routines. We also all celebrated together at Waylon & Jessi's house in Nashville for Shooter's christening, with the great Civil Rights minister Will Campbell officiating.

Now when I listen to that recording it evokes an emotion that is difficult to express. They sound so young and his voice has a depth of life that can't be imitated or mimicked by anyone. The musical journey has come full circle.

While Waylon was going through recovery and treatment in Arizona after his amputation surgery, the girls recorded a version of the old hymn, "Jesus I Am Resting", and sent it to him. David Hampton wrote a new melody for the old lyrics and it had become one of our family favorites. A few days later Waylon called to tell them he had the doctors put it on repeat so he could hear it over and over. He loved listening to their voices and said it had been a source of comfort and strength for him. I wish he were here to see the girls and Shooter today. He would be so proud and probably kickin' some serious industry ass.

I've watched my daughters from the sidelines, cheering them on, encouraging them when they were so tired and exhausted they could barely keep their heads up. I've clenched my fists, bit my tongue, and fought the rage that comes from years of dealing with the corruption of this oxymoron we call the "Music Business." But through it all they have proven to be women of integrity, driven by their passion for art. They have a work ethic that puts many of the *suits* to shame, and as their mother, and as a female who has worked in this industry most of her life, I couldn't be more proud. They made the decision to do what makes their heart beat. They *chose* to be "Carter's Chord."

I've been blessed to be a part of an artist's story who insisted on standing up and shining a light on the inequity and restraints that have driven many incredible artists and songwriter's underground. For years, I've held my head up high, walking through the back door and just doing music. The acceptance came from my fellow musicians. The stage was the place for encouragement and embrace.

Which has lead me over the years to conclude...if you can sing, sing. If you write, write. If you act, act. Whatever your gifts, whether on the stage, your living room or front porch, spend them lavishly. The culture around you will be richer for it and the great family of artists will be standing somewhere and applauding!

．．．．．．．．．．．．．．．．．．．．．

Dadgum It, Waylon

Less than a year after saying goodbye to Daddy, and after wringing every bit of fun and memories out of our last go round, I found myself saying, "Dadgum it Waylon, why'd you have to go and do a thing like this?"

It was late afternoon, and we had just left Jessi and the rest of the family at their home in Arizona. Earlier, we had celebrated Waylon's life and then said our goodbyes. Even though it wasn't totally unexpected, I think we were still in shock. We had tried to be strong and steady in our behind-the-scenes-love and support for both of them and now, like everybody else, we were each going to have to find a way to let him go.

I knew he had fought a valiant fight and had no say over when he left us. That's in the control of someone much more powerful than even Waylon believed himself to be. Life had not come easy for him, and when he had trouble staying on track, he just built a different line and ran his train down that one. But I guess all tracks have to end somewhere. I'll always be stunned by the sequence of events that brought an awkward, shy Holy Roller kid from the San Joaquin Valley into the story and onto the stages of not just a musical revolution, but a family.

Thank you, Jessi, for how deeply you loved him and how hard you worked to take care of him so he could keep going. There's no one like you on this planet and Waylon was blessed to have you by his side: such a true love story.

Thank you, Linda, for having the vision to get us all back together and for fighting for us all along the way.

There are volumes I could say and have actually written and then erased, deciding some things are best left for those who were there. Our hearts will always know and words, as powerful as they may be, can never articulate the depth of the stories we lived. I'll never forget...

Thanks old friend for not laying down, but for getting up and fighting back the effects of a disease that was hell-bent on stopping you. I hate diabetes! But most importantly, thank you, God for not taking him before we all had one more round. Redemption Rocks!! (Cousin Leisha's term)

"If I can't go down rockin'
Ain't gonna go down at all..."

Waylon Jennings, "Never Say Die" album recorded live at the Ryman Auditorium

Waylon and Carter, old friends on stage, 2001

"Tell Daddy I Love Him"

Mama died for the last time on Tuesday, March 22, 2005 at 3:25 in the afternoon, Pacific Time. Four years to the day after I had received the first call informing me of my father's heart attack. It was a sunny day in Visalia, California. Sharon and I were with her, so was Diana, the one who killed her the first time around. I guess Jesus must've finally said, "C'mon in to stay this time, Emma. You've been a good and faithful servant. No need to worry about the kids anymore, I'm taking care of them, and they're going to be just fine. You raised them the best you could…you *and* Bill." I bet she was smiling her big smile when Jesus told her that Daddy was standing right over there waiting for her. Imagine…now that's grace *and* mercy.

I was talking to my sweet friend Nikki Mitchell the other night about those who've gone before, one of which was Waylon. We were both missing him real bad and agreed that perhaps heaven and our loved ones aren't necessarily as *vertical* as we've always thought. Maybe it's more of a reaching through rather than a looking up. Sometimes they feel so close, like you could put your hand out and touch them.

I struggle at times, wrapping my head around the picture that somehow my spirit is encased in this skeleton covered with skin. Scripture calls us "jars of clay." I like to think of our stories shining through the cracks of these fragile jars that have at times been inflicted by blows designed to make us shatter. Instead, what was meant to destroy us only gives us opportunity to receive and extend God's sweet grace that embraces our vulnerability.

Wrestling with hard providences that don't make sense isn't really all that surprising; we were made for the Garden of Eden, after all. The mystery at times seems so profound, and yet somewhere I sense that when I finally see face to face the God I have been talking to all these years, it will actually be astonishingly simple. There's so much we *don't* know…

Seems the longer I live the more puzzling things are, and there are fewer and fewer parts of the story that I am able to tie up in a nice neat bow. Kind of like the ribbon I'm using is too slick and shiny and keeps coming undone.

I always thought Mama and Daddy would live as long as their parents. Grandma Ennis lived well into her nineties, sneaking into neighboring residents' rooms late at night, standing over their beds, stealing their precious belongings, and waiting for them to wake up so she could do what she did best: terrify them. Monroe (Daddy's daddy) was riding a horse when he was like 93, fell off, and broke his hip. Both of these people were tough and were responsible for some pretty substantial generational sin, but they were granted a long life. Neither one of my parents made it to their 80th birthday, and I don't like that.

Mama made no apologies or excuses for finally feeling free after Daddy died. She'd lived a tougher life than any of us will ever know, and he was a big part of her pain. We buried him in the same cemetery that his family is buried in. It's where I want to be buried if my family refuses my first request, which is to prop me up under a tree and let my spirit soar. He has a nice headstone and Mama's name is on there too with the wrong birth date. We told her we'd fix it once she was gone. I always figured she'd be around till Jesus came back.

But I guess Jesus wasn't just a "Hey Neighborin" when he said in Psalm 139: "All the days ordained for me were written in your book before one of them came to be." Because a short three and a half years after Daddy left, Sharon and I found ourselves sitting with Mama in an oncologist's office waiting for the results of some tests.

They weren't good. Non-Hodgkins Lymphoma. She had something called Small Lymphocetic Lymphoma. A silent thief that travels around in your body while you go to church and the grocery store and your Senior Sunday School class Luau with your friends. You hug your grandchildren, get on your grown children's every last nerve and head up the prayer chain, praying fervently for the needs of others while it steals your own life and you never have one symptom. By the time you notice the lump in your side, you're stage 4 and trying to decide on quality or quantity of life.

At first she was leaning toward letting it all just take its course. She was in God's hands, and for her there was no more secure place to be. But Mama was also a fighter, so when her doctor encouraged her to do chemo because it could maybe give her five more years, she didn't hesitate.

We were planning on her coming out to Tennessee so we could pamper her a bit and she could enjoy all the red Cardinals that she loved so much. Maybe take a quick trip down to the Gulf so she could walk on the beach with its sugary white sand and pick up seashells while the friendly waves chased away the birds. It was going to be a short visit before she started treatment, but she kept hearing the ominous ticking clock and decided not to waste any time.

Two weeks past her first treatment, after talking to Mama on the phone, Diana jumped in her car in L.A. and drove the normal three-hour trip in a little over two. She made a quick assessment once she walked through the door of our old house on Frank Road, and then without any hesitation rushed her to emergency at Kaweah Delta Hospital. She never came home to stay again.

I would fly out every three to four weeks just to sit with her in her hospital room. I *loved* her like only the baby of the family can. She wasn't afraid to die, or so she thought. What she was afraid of was dying like her insane grandmother who she had been named after.

I captured her voice on my little recorder as she told how for years she hated her name. We talked for hours about her life, and I would listen to her tell me the stories I had heard so many times as a child and now absorbed them as though it was the first time. She was amazing. I told her I was writing a book, and she not only gave me her blessing but also charged me with finishing it. She knew me well. "Tell the story, Carter. Tell the story."

We'd pray together, and I'd do my best to reassure her by taking the lead the way she had taught me to do all those years growing up in her spiritual shadow. The crazy thing was that for the first few months, *she* was the one encouraging *me*, and not just me either. Doctors and nurses on the cancer floor would come in at the end of their shift just to be still and have Sister Walker pray for them.

My sisters pretty much set up a vigil. They put their lives, families and jobs on hold to take care of her. Even though Diana lived in L.A., she was still the closest. She spent weeks at a time in Visalia being tag-teamed by Sharon, who lived in Northern California and was an elementary school teacher. They were spending more time in Visalia than they were in their own homes. They received a swift and not so willing education in Medi-Cal and Medicare; what's covered what's not. Words and phrases like neutropenic and DNR became familiar parts of our conversations with her and each other.

As the cancer raged on and the morphine and other drugs made her a slave to the clock, we watched as our mother fought to keep control of her mind and spirit. The change was excruciating to observe. She became paranoid and at times, downright mean. When her surgeon told us that the tumor was inoperable and there was nothing more that could be done, her oncologist wrote the prescription for Hospice.

Thankfully, through the recommendation of a friend, we were able to put Mom in a beautiful facility. They had fresh flowers and soft music in her private room. It actually smelled really nice. She could look out of her window onto the patio and nicely manicured lawn.

The week before her 79th birthday, as many of the family that could get there, all gathered around her bed. Now, to say that Mama was a bit dramatic would be a colossal understatement, and she didn't disappoint us on that day. She had decided that this was it; she was done with this ol' world, and today was the day she was going home to be with Jesus.

My brother Norman sang "Down from His Glory," and we all joined in on many of her favorite hymns. Each one of us had a private moment telling her goodbye with words of wisdom spilling from her heart. My pregnant niece Katie was there, and Mama laid her hands on her belly and blessed the generations to come.

For those who weren't there, a phone call was made. Barny was the recipient of one of those calls while out on the road with Steve Green. Even my nephew, who is a California Highway Patrolman, was tracked down at a traffic accident so Mama could tell him goodbye. We all hugged and swayed and waited…and waited…and waited.

After a while, family members started to quietly leave. They had jobs to go to and miles to drive. They leaned down and whispered into Mama's ear, promising that they would be back soon to see her, and if she left before then, they would see her in Heaven. She kept her eyes closed as though she had gone into some kind of sleepy coma. We told each other not to worry; she was in God's hands now. She had raised us well.

One by one they filed out until it was just Diana and me, sitting beside her bed and looking at each other, wondering what was going to happen next. I guess once again Jesus didn't get the memo because pretty soon Mama opened one eye and looked around the room. She kind of sighed, disappointed like, sat up and said, "Well girls, I *am* kind of hungry." She threw her skinny little legs over the side of the bed, and we walked her out to the dining room, where she sat and drank her special milkshake. That was the beginning of the most bizarre, humorous and torturous weeks of our lives with Mama.

All of our mother's fears about how she would die, unfortunately, were fulfilled. She literally lost her mind. She was moved to the *dementia* side of the facility because in one of her psychotic states she actually walked out of her room wearing little to nothing, slapped the owner of the hospice, and threatened others. I guess some of her grandma's toxic DNA had been hiding for a while and now had decided to come out to play.

Finally, through some hardball plays by my sisters, she was moved back to the sweeter side. She slipped into a couple of comas and each time we prepared ourselves for her death. I suppose God knew she still wasn't as ready to cross over the river Jordan as she thought, because she kept coming back and each time a little crazier.

My sisters were at the breaking point, and I once again packed my already packed suitcase and headed home to California. Hospice had had it. They were kicking her out! Can't really blame them. She wasn't leavin' easy.

We were sleep deprived and desperate when Diana and I arrived late that Sunday afternoon. Sharon had been on the phone all weekend to see if we could get her into Westgate, the facility that Daddy had been in. A transfer was in the works.

I'll always remember what she looked like when we walked into her room. She had gotten herself out of bed and was walking toward the bathroom, skin and bones, her face so thin I had to squint to see if Mama was in there. When she looked at me, I wasn't sure she knew who I was and my heart broke, but by then so much had happened that the necessary emotional detachment was already in place. Her vacant gaze tuned into my sister and in a barely recognizable voice she said, "Diana, don't leave me."

Those were the last words she spoke.

Diana helped her get undressed, all the while reassuring her that Danna-Carter was there, and we weren't going to leave her, ever. I found a clean soft nightie that we had taken the scissors and cut up the back so we could place it on her without pulling it over her head. By then, just about everything hurt, but she seemed grateful for our tenderness.

While we were looking after her, one of the hospice workers put fresh flowers on the dresser and clean sheets on her bed. My sister and I sat there like grown-up little girls and watched as our mother lay in the bed, breathing in, breathing out. Taking care of business had become a fierce tyrant to be reckoned with, and we were caught in the quagmire of how we could possibly maneuver the system to get her transferred to Westgate. All of this was making our blood boil, but both of us knew we didn't have the luxury of blowing up.

I can't even begin to articulate all the hoops families have to jump through to get insurance companies and other agencies to pay for what the patient has already been paying for, for years. There's a secret protocol, and if you don't abide by the latest up to the minute specs, they'll deny your claim in a heartbeat. It's broken and so wrong.

While we were exploring our dwindling and not so optimum alternatives, the main caregiver/nurse walked through the door with a stethoscope around her neck. She went over to my mother lying so still and looking so small in that bed and listened to her heart. She took her pulse and counted her breaths. Then she turned and quietly informed us that there would be no need for an ambulance or a trip to the hospital, and we didn't need to concern ourselves with moving her to Westgate. Mama had slipped into a deep coma this time, and in all of her experience she had never seen anyone come back.

The tone immediately changed. All of my mother's insane flare-ups were forgiven. She gently went through what we could expect, preparing us for what was most assuredly coming and then left us to the quiet vigil of waiting on death. Once again, Diana and I were together facing what neither of us wanted to face, the reality that soon we would be orphans.

We called Sharon first, giving her the latest update. She had just left Mama a few days before and was now throwing *her* already packed bag into her car. She told us she would leave early the next morning and meet us there. Her voice had a fatigue and weariness to it that had become regretfully familiar. Between the two of them, Diana and Sharon had sacrificed more than any of us will know. It's astounding what we're capable of when the options run out. I will always be grateful to them both for what they accomplished and the care they facilitated for both of our parents.

My brother Norman was the principal of a private Christian school in Southern California and wasn't able to take off work. He and his wife Denise had been with Mom over the weekend and said their goodbyes then. He told us to keep him updated. By now we'd had so many close calls that unless you were there it would have been difficult to see that this time was going to be it. Now, we waited.

After a grueling drive down Highway 99 from her home in Northern California, Sharon arrived around ten the next morning. She immediately gathered us in her arms and held us tight. The reinforcements had arrived.

It's funny how birth order shows up in times of crisis. Diana and I were completely capable women who had experienced some very difficult situations and survived. But there were moments, when you could see Sharon feeling a weight that had somehow been assigned to her at birth. She was the next in line, and with that position came a responsibility, real or imagined, that the outcome was on her shoulders. Diana and I had been in that room for nearly twenty-four hours, and we'd had time to process. Slowly, Sharon began to let go of the fight and open herself to the next step, which was release.

As we covered ourselves in the crocheted blankets from the volunteers, we reminisced about our childhoods. We laughed at old family stories we'd heard a thousand times but yet found a sweet comfort in the familiar telling. Our family has always embraced laughter even in the darkest of times. As the night wore on and the exhaustion increased we grew quiet, not sleeping, just quiet.

About five a.m. as I was laying in the recliner, listening to the death rattle coming from my mother's worn out body and counting the breaths that were becoming fewer and further between, I experienced a coldness, like *steel in winter*. I was angry, but too tired to be mad. I was flooded with memories and pictures of the past, all she had survived, all she had fought so hard to purge from her own soul and ours was now mercilessly dogging her in death.

I was haunted by the memory of a month before, sitting on the bed and reciting the 23rd Psalm with her at her request, then watching her tremble with fear because she would get stuck in the same place every time. Somehow in her altered state, she believed God would bar her from heaven because of this failure to perform. She never did really understand grace.

I remember the caregiver encouraging me to go home and get some sleep that night after I had watched her slip into a full-blown agitated episode. No amount of sedative or push of the morphine drip could bring her peace. To watch your mother in that kind of excruciating agony and be completely helpless to bring her back to reality and a place of calm rips at your soul and your faith in your Abba, Father.

I had a rather messy conversation in my head with God. I told Him, I knew He was all-powerful and could obliterate me in the blink of an eye, but surely He could see how wrong all this was. I whispered the words audible only to myself and God, words I had cried out numerous times in my life, "It's not fair!" I said I knew Mama wasn't perfect but, shoot, neither was Daddy, and he didn't do this kind of suffering.

All my life she had told me the gruesome details of how the grandmother she had been named after had died in the asylum strapped down because she was criminally insane. I can't erase the details she shared, although I truly wish I could. Here she was, Sister Walker, who had tried so hard to avoid this kind of death and yet the past few months had been like some kind of sick generational pay back. Why? Why, God? What possible purpose could there be?

I was internally quiet for a while, half expecting the roaring lion to come through the door any minute and devour me with a holy chomp. But Mama's breathing rattled on and the cold air coming through the cracked window, filtering the stench of death, made me bury my face and breathe through the yarn of the blanket. It would take weeks before that deathly sweet fragrance didn't assault my sense of smell.

I didn't feel comfort or even anger anymore, just the cold. After some time had passed and while my sisters were quiet, I simply said, "I need to know you're good. That's all. Please God, just let me know you're good."

Around 3:15 that afternoon, the main caregiver and another young nurse dropped by the room to check on us. After taking Mama's vitals they started sharing stories about her. Some were poignant and sweet, and some were downright hilarious. We found ourselves laughing out loud, and then they would tell another one. It was like we were at a reunion of some sort, rather than in the room of a woman dying in the bed a couple feet over. It was a wonderful release. Sometimes humor is the best medicine.

One particular story struck us all so funny that we started laughing and couldn't stop, abandoning all sense of what could be perceived as appropriate. We knew Mama would be giggling along with us if she could, appreciating the comedic timing of the details.

As we were looking over at her, all of a sudden she opened her eyes and smiled. Sharon was at the head of the bed to Mama's right, I was at the foot of her bed and Diana was in the middle. Mama was looking right above me. Her eyes were clear and her smile was sweet.

From my left I could hear Diana's exasperated voice saying; "OH-MY-GOD! She's coming back...AGAIN!"

Sharon's leaning into Mom, saying, "Go to Jesus, Mama! Go to Jesus!"

I'm standing there, waving frantically like a child watching her mother backing out of the driveway saying, "You see Jesus, don't you Mama? Tell Jesus I love him! Tell Daddy I love him, Mama! Tell Daddy I love him!"

It was the craziest, most wonderful, beautiful forty-five seconds of my life. Mama may have sung Daddy into the arms of Jesus, but we laughed her across the bridge, waving the entire way.

She still had a slight smile that looked like total contentment as she closed her eyes and completed the work God had for her on this earth. The nurse checked her vitals one last time and then turned with tears in her eyes. She told us she had witnessed many deaths but none so "good" as this one.

Yes, Carter…God *is* good.

Psalm 139

Emma Walker, January 30, 1926—March 22, 2005

Epilogue

Seems I've been sitting here for days trying to figure out where to write "the end." To be honest, the adventure continues and I'm not real sure or even all that worried about where it leads. At this point I'm all in. I suppose it's just one of the many perks of age and experience.

I ask myself what I want you, the reader, to walk away with once you've read the last word. Did I talk enough about hope and the power that comes from getting back up after falling down? Do I now quote scripture and favorite philosophers who have helped me along the way? I wonder if I've made you laugh and perhaps pushed you a little closer to opening the door to embrace and learn from your own story.

The words still feel a little clumsy to me and my head hurts from straining to say just the right thing. So, I'm going to leave you with the lyrics of a song I wrote a while back and trust that it will be the best summation…for now.

God of Providence

Hold me in your arms, Lord
And hide me in your heart
Oh the world outside is so cold
And all its arrows sharp
Disillusioned by the heartbreak
And the stain of failure passed
I come stumbling into your presence
Where I find peace at last

Teach me to forgive, Lord,
Even when revenge seems fair
Help me take it to your cross

And leave it there
May the tears that you've cried
Heal the wounds I hide behind
Laying all of my excuses
At the feet of the Crucified

God of Providence
You hold the weight of every weakness
You come to my defense
Take my place before the throne
You say the "debt's been paid"
And you eyes are full of mercy
As I look into your glory
I am staggered by your grace
You're the author of my story
You've been with me
All the way

Thank You!

A: **Alpha and Omega, the Beginning and the End.** There will never be enough words but You know my heart. I love You! **Anyone and Everyone** who has been a part of this story! **Ann Isaacs,** I did it!!

B: **Barny,** my one true love. Thanks for jumping off the cliff with me so many years ago. I love you and I always will.

C: **Chris Carson,** for the paper!

D: **Daddy,** for teaching me how to laugh and, oddly, all about redemption. I love and miss you. **Dave Laster, Tank, Da-Watt,** jus cuz. **Diana aka "Danna-Carter"** for letting me tell *our* story and for being such a careful proofreader. My partner in crime! Love you Sissy! **Denise,** for being brave enough to marry into our crazy and wonderful family. **David Whyte,** poet and philosopher, your words have been a lifeline.

E: **Edd Donald,** for your faithful encouragement, deep convictions and powerful passion for all of us.

F: **Family,** love you more than all the Tule fog in the San Joaquin Valley!

G: **Girlfriends, Tess, Diana, Meg, Kim, Sherry, Nikki, Linda, Jenny, Heidi, Martha, Cheryl,** your friendship is an anchor that holds me steady.

H: **Hard times,** I don't like you but I'm grateful for the lessons.

I: **Incredible Tuesday morning Bible study friends!** My cup runneth over!

J: **Jessi Colter,** for inviting me into your world to dance and sing to your music. I cherish the fact that we share such a precious faith and I'm thankful He gifted me with your friendship so we could ride the rails together. There's a lot more track to go!

K: **Kim Messer,** for holding my hand and giving great weight and value to my voice. Not easy for an editor but you were my champion through this process and I will always be grateful.

L: **Leisha Walker Robertson Cuzin' and 3ʳᵈ Sistuh,** for a life lived that reminds me of the strong and beautiful Walker women, and I'm proud to say, "I'm one of them!"

M: **Mama,** for teaching me about life, love and survival through your struggles and hard fought triumphs. Because of you my faith has deep roots, along with a genuine love for my Heavenly Father. **Monte King,** counselor, coach, confidante, friend, I would never have been strong enough to finish this work without your invaluable contribution to my sanity. Thank you for gently shining a light on the dark places and patiently teaching me that the reign of fear and control are not just manageable but can be turned to good. I will forever be grateful. **Midge Buchert,** my Santa Maria Research Angel with much appreciated bulldog qualities. You are a gift!

N: **Norman,** "Jem" to my "Scout," for watching my back when we were little. I won't forget. Love you, big brother. All my **nieces and nephews,** hope you'll laugh and learn from your rich family heritage. Never forget, God is faithful to redeem and His love will never let you go! Be true for the next generation.

O: **Old friends,** you know who you are.

P: **Perkins family,** looking forward to the next story. **Pastor Ernie Kumpe** and **Pastor Glen Cole** for not only preaching with true integrity but living it as well. You set my heart on a search that I will always be thankful for. Proofreader extraordinaire **Dana Macheli.**

Q: **Quiet time** in the morning.

R: **Redemption!** The three R's: **Robbie, Rosina, and Raedena.** I love being a **Robertson!**

S: **Sharon,** my sister who loved me, taught me, took care of me and convinced me once that I was pretty. Danna and I will *never* forget all you did for us...never! Love you like crazy. **Scotty Smith,** founding pastor of Christ Community Church in Franklin, TN. for being faithful to teach the truth about God's indescribable grace. You just never know who's listening, do ya? **Sons-in-law, Mark, Marc and Jeremiah,** love you and how strongly you love my precious daughters. My girls have chosen well!

T: **The Girls: Becky, Emily and Joanna,** for showing me what *really* matters when the stage is quiet and the people have all gone home. The woman I see looking back at me in the mirror is one proud and happy Mama, and I'm not just a "hey, neighborin'", either! You make me laugh till I wheeze. I love you! **Terrie Lawrence** for never letting me give up and always sharing a powerful word to keep me going.

U: **Unlimited Grace,** thank you **Jesus**!

V: **Visalia, CA.** for loving me well, forgiving me quickly and cheering me on.

W: **Waylon and my Waylon Family**, for the unforgettable adventure that continues to this day. It ain't over yet! Love You'ins!

X: **X-Chromosones and Xylophones,** because together they are unstoppable.

Y: **You'ins,** nuf said.

Z: **Zarling, Megan & John,** for the faith we share, your friendship and the encouragement to write about the Waylon years. My family loves your family!

It takes an alphabet!

Acknowledgements

David Whyte quote printed with permission from ©Many Rivers Press, Langley, Washington. *www.davidwhyte.com*.

When We All Get To Heaven
Eliza E. Hewitt Copyright 1898, Public Domain

Jesus Loves the Little Children
Clare H. Wollston & George F. Root 1921, Public Domain

Hiawatha's Childhood
Henry Wadsworth Longfellow, Public Domain

Little Orphant Annie
James Whitcomb Riley, Public Domain

Safe Am I
Mildred Leightner, Dillon 1938

SMOKE! SMOKE! SMOKE! (THAT CIGARETTE)
Words and Music by MERLE TRAVIS and TEX WILLIAMS © 1947 (Renewed) UNICHAPPELL MUSIC INC., ELVIS PRESLEY MUSIC, INC. and MERLE'S GIRLS MUSIC All Rights on behalf of itself and ELVIS PRESLEY MUSIC, INC.
Administered by UNICHAPPELL MUSIC, INC. All Rights for of MERLE'S GIRLS MUSIC
Administered by WARNER-TAMERLANE PUBLISHING CORP.
All Rights Reserved. Used by permission.

Amazing Grace
John Newton, Public Domain
Photos:

Front cover and author photo by Abby Mitchell, used by permission
Leather and Lace photo used by permission
Carter's Chord photo by Russ Harrington
All other photographs by whomever held the camera...

15857204R00168

Made in the USA
Charleston, SC
24 November 2012